(2001)

D0601362

6142

*Cultural Logics and Global Economies*

# Cultural Logics and
# Global Economies

## MAYA IDENTITY IN
## THOUGHT AND PRACTICE

*University of Texas Press, Austin*

*Cover*
The embroidered hieroglyphic design used on the cover and
throughout is a detail of a *huipil* made by Izmukane' in Tecpán in
1997; photograph by Jamie C. Adams.

The cover photo by Thomas Hoepker shows Kaqchikel linguist
Lolmay visiting the archaeological site of Copán in Honduras.

Copyright © 2001 by the University of Texas Press
All rights reserved
Printed in the United States of America
First edition, 2001

Requests for permission to reproduce material from this work should
be sent to Permissions, University of Texas Press, P.O. Box 7819,
Austin, TX 78713-7819.

∞ The paper used in this book meets the minimum requirements of
ANSI/NISO Z39.48-1992 (R1997) (Permanence of Paper).

*Library of Congress Cataloging-in-Publication Data*

Fischer, Edward F., 1966–
    Cultural logics and global economics : Maya identity in thought and
practice / Edward F. Fischer — 1st ed.
        p.     cm.
    Includes bibliographical references and index.
    ISBN 0-292-72530-2 (cloth : alk. paper) — ISBN 0-292-72534-5
(pbk : alk. paper)
    1. Mayas — Guatemala — Ethnic identity.   2. Mayas —
Guatemala — Politics and government.   3. Cakchikel Indians —
Ethnic identity.   4. Cakchikel Indians — Politics and government.
5. Guatemala — Politics and government — 1985–   6. Guatemala —
Economic conditions — 1985–   I. Title.
F1435.3.E72 F57   2002
305.897′415207281 — dc21
                                                          2001023500

# Contents

Acknowledgments  ix

PART I *Contexts of Study 1*

1  Maya Culture and Identity Politics  3

2  Tecpán and Patzún  31

PART II *Global Processes and Pan-Maya Identity Politics 63*

3  Guatemalan Political Economies and the World System  65

4  The Rise of Pan-Maya Activism  83

5  Constructing a Pan-Maya Identity in a Postmodern World  115

PART III *Maya Identity as Lived Experience in Tecpán and Patzún 139*

6  Souls, Socialization, and the Kaqchikel Self  141

7  Hearth, Kin, and Communities  167

8  Local Forms of Ethnic Resistance  190

9  Economic Change and Cultural Continuity  215

PART IV *Conclusion 241*

10  Convergent Strategies and Cultural Logics  243

Notes  253

Glossary  259

Bibliography  261

Index  281

# List of Figures

1.1  Guatemala  2

1.2  The Twenty-one Mayan Languages of Guatemala  5

2.1  Tecpán, Patzún, and the Surrounding Area  32

2.2  The Department of Chimaltenango and Its *Municipios*  34

2.3  Ethnic Demography of Urban Tecpán and Patzún  35

2.4  Tecpán after the 1976 Earthquake  37

2.5  The Columns in Tecpán's Catholic Church  38

2.6  Brick Stove  41

2.7  Adobe Houses in Patzún  42

2.8  A Traditional Adobe *Tuj*  43

2.9  Playing Tops in Tecpán  47

2.10  The Tlaxcalans at Iximche'  49

2.11  Map of Land Returned in the Xpantzay Lawsuit  53

2.12  Clandestine Graves in Tecpán  60

3.1  Coffee and Cochineal Exports, 1867–1871  72

3.2  Guatemala's Principal Exports  73

3.3  Guatemala's Principal Imports  74

3.4  Total Official Direct Assistance and U.S. Military Aid to Guatemala  80

3.5  Total Official Direct Assistance  82

4.1 Chávez's Supplemental Alphabet for Quí-chè Maya 88

4.2 Flyer Produced by the Sociedad Ixim for the 1994 Elections 95

5.1 Kaqchikel Neologisms and Their Sources 121

5.2 Accepted Kaqchikel Neologisms and Their Metaphorical Bases 122

5.3 Cover of COMG's *Rujunamil Ri Mayab' Amaq'* 126

5.4 "Peoples of Guatemala," a Map Produced by Cholsamaj 129

5.5 "Peoples of Guatemala," a Map Produced by Cholsamaj 130

5.6 "Territory of the Maya People before 1492," a Map Produced by Cholsamaj 132

5.7 Promotional Jingoes from the *Mayab' Winäq* Radio Program 134

6.1 Cave at Pulchich 156

7.1 Kaqchikel Kinship Terminology, Male Ego 171

7.2 Tecpán Household Compound 173

7.3 Barrios of Tecpán 175

7.4 *Cantones* of Patzún 177

7.5 Religion and Ethnicity in Tecpán and Patzún 181

7.6 Procession of Saint Francis of Assisi, Tecpán, 1994 184

7.7 *Cofradía* Drum and Flute Players 186

8.1 Vilma I, the Tecpán Military Base's Candidate for Indian Queen in 1994 197

8.2 Princesa Ixmukane, the Weaving Cooperative's Candidate for Indian Queen in 1994 199

8.3 Kaqchikel Language Proficiency among Indians in Tecpán and Patzún 203

8.4 Patzún *Huipil* with Embroidered Maya Day Names 212

9.1 Primary Economic Activity of Male Heads of Household in Tecpán and Patzún, 1994 218

9.2 Milpa after the *Tercer Trabajo* 221

9.3 Fields of Nontraditional Crops around Tecpán 234

# *Acknowledgments*

My scholarly debts are immense, and this attempt to thank by name those who have helped make this book possible will be incomplete. To those whom I have neglected in my haste, please accept my apologies and gratitude.

This book has emerged from numerous dialogues with Maya collaborators and academic colleagues, and in many ways my own contribution has been in synthesizing and committing these dialogues to paper. My understanding of *la realidad maya* comes largely from informants, friends, and colleagues in Tecpán and Patzún. In particular, the Lux Sacbajá, Tecún Cuxil, Guorón Rodríguez, and Rodríguez Guaján families have made my family feel at home and opened their lives to us in a way that we can never adequately repay. In Tecpán, we were especially fortunate to have befriended Pakal B'alam, whose interminable energy pushed us to take a more active role in community activities and whose sharp intellect continues to unsettle our attempts at neat classification and the construction of parsimonious models. There are many others I should thank in Tecpán and Patzún, but I refrain from mentioning them by name to protect their privacy. The generosity of these individuals, however, lives on in my memory, and I shall forever be in their debt.

Alberto Esquit, Raxche', Demetrio Cojtí, the members of OKMA (particularly Lolmay and Waykan), and other Maya scholars and activists likewise gave generously of their time, sharing with me stories from their life histories, supplying points of fact, and debating subtleties of theory. The work of these individuals, politically as well as scholarly, is exemplary, and it has fundamentally redefined the terms of ethnographic engagement with the field in Guatemalan studies. My own perspective is clearly shaped by my interactions with and admiration for the work of these Maya colleagues.

I could not have written this book or conducted the fieldwork on which it is based without the unfaltering support of my wife, Mareike Sattler. She has been an active participant in my field research and an invaluable intellectual and emotional companion, and she is a largely unacknowledged collaborator throughout the work. During the writing of this book, in its various lengthy stages, Mareike also provided essential practical support: feeding me, putting up with my odd working schedules and sometimes moody behavior, taking care of our children, and countless other small and large kindnesses.

I began to study Guatemala as an undergraduate at the University of Alabama at Birmingham, where Professors Kathleen Martínez (née Logan), John Hamer, and Roger Nance cultivated my interest. I continued my studies in the Department of Anthropology at Tulane University, and the support of that department was central to the completion of this work. My dissertation advisor, Victoria Bricker, offered a fine-tuned mix of encouragement and criticism that has pushed me toward greater precision in my thought and writing. While at Tulane, I conducted my first fieldwork in Guatemala under the tutelage of Judith Maxwell, and she continues to set an example of ethically driven fieldwork that I can only hope to approximate. Judie has variously been professor, confidant, and colleague, offering valuable support in each of these roles; she also generously hosted several of my writing retreats to New Orleans in 1999–2000 while I completed this book. Also at Tulane, Bob Hill provided judicious and helpful criticism of both the content and the style of my work, and collaborative fieldwork conducted with him in 1997 led me to formulate the argument presented in Chapter 6. Both Judie and Bob have shared generously with me their extensive knowledge of the Kaqchikel region, and I still frequently call upon them to clarify points of fact.

Since 1996, Vanderbilt University has provided crucial support for my research and writing and an environment conducive to intellectual debate. Beth Conklin, Tom Gregor, John Monaghan, Arthur Joyce, Annabeth Headrick, and my other colleagues in the Department of Anthropology and the Center for Latin American and Iberian Studies have engaged me in substantive discussions of anthropological theory and practice that helped shape (and hopefully sharpen) the arguments presented here. Also at Vanderbilt, the support staff in the Department of

Acknowledgments ✳ xi

Anthropology, the Microcomputing Laboratory, the Heard Library, and the Medical Arts Group have provided logistical and technical assistance during research and writing.

It was my good fortune that during fieldwork in 1993–1994 Nora England was also conducting research in Guatemala. During my regular visits to her office and home in Antigua, she generously shared with me her perspectives on Guatemala and Mayan linguistics. Her sharp insights and straightforward style directly influenced my research and subsequent writing, and her ethical stance has guided my own political positioning. Both in the field and at meetings in the United States, Kay Warren's incisive critiques have also pressed me to further clarify my own positions.

Invaluable practical support for my fieldwork in Guatemala came from Stephen Elliott, Margarita Asensio de Méndez, and Guisela Asensio Lueg, and the rest of the staff of the Centro de Investigaciones Regionales de Mesoamérica (CIRMA); their cheerful efficiency provided a needed antidote to our frustrations arising from dealing with the labyrinth of Guatemalan bureaucracies. Additional logistic support was generously provided by Daniel Ramírez Ríos, who has long provided me with a home away from home in Antigua. For supplying much-needed moral support in the field I also thank Hal and Jane Starratt, Bill and Noor Harrison, Circe Sturm and Randy Lewis, John Hillhouse, Tommy Tonsmeire, Helen Rivas, and Todd and Christa Little-Seibold. A special thanks also goes to McKenna Brown for his companionship in the field, for introducing me to countless contacts, and for his ongoing support of my research.

A number of colleagues have read parts of previous versions of this book, and I have benefited greatly from their comments. Portions of Chapter 1 and Chapter 6 were previously published in *Current Anthropology* (reproduced with permission of the Wenner-Gren Foundation for Anthropological Research), and the "CA treatment" by Quetzil Castañeda, Johannes Fabian, Charles Hale, Jonathan Friedman, Richard Handler, Bruce Kapferer, and Richard Fox led me to rework my arguments as presented here. John Watanabe offered characteristically useful and insightful critiques of portions of the book, and I have tried throughout to incorporate his concerns with clarity and directness. Gary Gossen, Brian Stross, and an anonymous reviewer read previous versions of the entire manuscript; their comments inspired several rounds of major revisions and provided the encouragement needed to face this work. In addition, David Stoll provided useful advice on representational approaches that have made the work flow more smoothly. Theresa May at the University of Texas Press suggested helpful strategies for these revisions, and her support was crucial in bringing this book to press.

Carol Hendrickson read a previous version of this book in its entirety, and her copious comments (on points of fact as well as logical consistency and style) were invaluable, pushing me to further represent the diversity of lived experience in Tecpán. Carol first introduced me to Tecpán in 1990, and she has encouraged me in my studies ever since. There is a widespread proprietorial tendency among ethnographers toward the people and locations they study. Not true for Carol. With a contagious spirit of intellectual curiosity and openness, Carol facilitated my entrée into the community, introduced me to her friends, shared data freely, and pointed me in the direction of interesting topics to study. I carried a copy of her dissertation with me into the field and consulted it often, and her insights subtly pervade much of my own work.

Mareike Sattler, Guisela Asensio, Arik Ohnstad, and Tim Gilfilen aided in the production of maps and illustrations for this book. In addition, I include several examples of graphic-design work by the Maya publishing house Cholsamaj; these are reproduced here with the kind permission of the Centro Educativo y Cultural Maya Cholsamaj.

Funding for preliminary research conducted in 1990, 1991, and 1992 was provided by the Roger Thayer Stone Center for Latin American Studies at Tulane University. Fieldwork in 1993–1994 was financed by the Inter-American Foundation. Billie Jean Isbell, Beatriz Manz, Robert Sogge, and the other members of the Inter-American Foundation's Doctoral Fellow Committee went far beyond the normal role of a grant-giving body to offer useful theoretical and methodological advice both before and after fieldwork commenced. Funding for follow-up field research in 1997, 1999, and 2000 was provided by the Vanderbilt University Research Council, the National Endowment for the Humanities, and the John D. and Catherine T. MacArthur Foundation. Crucial support for writing was provided by a sabbatical leave from Vanderbilt's College of Arts and Sciences and funded by the Wenner-Gren Foundation for Anthropological Research and the John D. and Catherine T. MacArthur Foundation. This work would not have been possible without the material support of each of these institutions.

*Cultural Logics and Global Economies*

PART

I

*Contexts of Study*

FIGURE 1.1. Guatemala. Map by the author.

# Maya Culture and Identity Politics

Maya culture has been shaped by the favorable and unfavorable circumstances under which it has existed, and yet it remains the same culture developed by our ancestors over thousands of years of history in what is today Guatemala. The form of our culture has changed, but not its essence.

RAXCHE' (1992)

No tradition is constructed or invented and discontinuous with history . . . [traditions] are chosen because of what they distill onto-logically; that is, they make sense and condense a logic of ideas which may also be integrated to the people who make the selection although hidden from their reflective consciousness.

BRUCE KAPFERER (1988)

Early one Sunday afternoon in late October 1981, Doña Ramona Peres Tuj,[1] while working at her market stall in Tecpán, Guatemala, received word that the army was looking for two of her sons. Not knowing if the news should be believed—it could have been a cruel practical joke—she rushed home to alert the family, who decided that the threat was real enough: the Peres Tuj boys had been involved in several Kaqchikel Maya cultural organizations that the army now viewed as subversive, and one of their uncles had been disappeared by unknown men earlier that same week. The fate of those arrested was no secret: everyone had heard the late-night cries of people taken for questioning to the army compound in the middle of town, many of whom never returned; and so the Peres Tuj family decided to take no chances. They hurriedly bundled up a few belongings and were on a bus headed for the relative anonymity of Guatemala City within three hours of receiving the initial threat. In the capital they found a small apartment in a neighborhood filled with some of the tens of thousands of other families likewise flee-ing violence in their home communities. The Peres Tuj family lived in their new urban home for almost eight years, and while the children adapted to their new surroundings with youthful enthusiasm, the par-ents mostly whiled away their time indoors. Don Carlos longed to get back to his fields, which he had hastily entrusted to relatives, and Doña Ramona missed the bustle of the Tecpán market where she had sold sweaters. Their children finished their studies, worked odd jobs along the way to help the family survive, and all went on to attend the univer-sity, at least intermittently.

At the university, the Peres Tuj youths encountered other young Maya students from across Guatemala, most of whom had come to the capital under similar circumstances, and they became involved in a loosely organized network of Maya student groups concerned with pro-moting peace and protecting their cultural heritage. Given the political climate (50–200 people a month were being kidnapped in Guatemala City during the early 1980s, mostly student and labor activists), the groups met in secret. They also took pains to distance themselves from popular leftist groups that supported armed rebellion, focusing instead on less threatening issues of cultural conservation. Since the violence in Guatemala began to subside in the mid-1980s, the number of groups promoting Maya pride and cultural rights has dramatically expanded, part of what I term the pan-Maya movement. With their growing ranks, these groups have taken on higher public profiles (tellingly, their activi-ties now receive routine coverage in the country's major newspapers), which they are effectively able to leverage for greater influence in na-tional political debates.

In 1989, Don Carlos and Doña Ramona returned to Tecpán and be-gan to rebuild the life they had enjoyed there before the violence. It was never quite the same, as suspicion had poisoned so many social relation-ships, but it was certainly preferable to living in the capital. The older Peres Tuj boys stayed on in Guatemala City, continuing their studies and becoming ever more involved in Maya cultural activism; they have since married, had children, and are raising them in Guatemala City. Yet they have not forsaken their ties to Tecpán. All maintain plots of land there to supply part of their family's maize needs, and they fre-quently come home to visit and to participate in special celebrations and ceremonies. This is a pattern typical of the new generation of young, urban-based Maya leaders, and it points to the continued importance of cultural forms developed and played out in myriad small communities within the urban-centered development of a broad pan-Maya identity.

Leaders of Guatemala's pan-Maya movement seek to unite the country's Indian groups, which have long been divided by language, rugged terrain, and local custom. The Maya make up 40–60 percent of Guatemala's 11 million inhabitants (estimates range from the government's official 1994 figure of 41.9 percent to Maya estimates of greater than 60 percent), and most speak one of the country's twenty-one distinct Mayan languages (see Figure 1.2). The Guatemalan Maya thus form

FIGURE 1.2. The twenty-one Mayan languages of Guatemala. Map by the author.

one of the largest concentrations of indigenous people in the Americas, but they are also one of the poorest and most divided. More than 80 percent live in rural areas inadequately served by public services, and almost 60 percent live in conditions of extreme poverty (UNDP 1999). State-level political and economic systems are dominated by a relatively small Spanish-speaking ladino elite, but Maya leaders hope that cultural unification will provide a peaceful path to garner greater Maya political voice in Guatemala's fledgling democracy. Yet Indian leaders are constrained in their creation of a pan-Maya identity, for they must remain true in spirit, if not in form, to the cultural norms that emerge through quotidian lived experience in the rural communities where most Maya live.

This book examines the tensions and synergies that arise from the conjuncture of national pan-Maya identity politics and lived experience in Tecpán and Patzún, two predominately Kaqchikel Maya towns. It brings together data gathered from multiple interdependent locales and levels of abstraction (the town, the state, the "world system"), attempting to trace linkages in the dynamic process of identity formation. My goal is not to privilege one level of analysis over another, but rather to highlight the mutually constitutive relations between local and pan-Maya cultural identities, between territorially grounded identity politics and transnational processes.

The relationship of local cultures to national and international systems has long been problematic for anthropologists (Marcus and Fischer 1986:91–92; Knorr-Cetina 1981:28). On the one hand, there is a long-standing tendency in ethnography to view local systems as discrete clusters of structures that constitute a unique whole. Such perspectives need not negate outside influences on local culture, but in practice they often relegate external influences to a secondary status. At the other extreme, world-system theorists often treat peripheral formations as mere reactants to change emanating from the core of the world system. This book seeks a middle ground, representing Maya individuals as actively seeking their self-conceived best interests while working within larger systems not entirely of their own making.

In the chapters that follow I examine various forms of Maya cultural identity, individual as well as collective, local as well as global. I argue that Maya identities as lived experiences and self-interested presentations share certain discernible patterns linked both to an underlying cultural substrate (internalized through cognitive models) and to a dynamic articulation with increasingly global relations of political economy. After briefly introducing the sites of ethnographic research, I turn to an analysis of Maya identity politics (particularly the rise of the pan-Maya movement) in the context of ladino (non-Indian)-dominated Guatemalan state politics. I show that certain urban Maya intellectuals and leaders have tactically engaged emergent structures of global political and economic relations to advance their own ends and those of their peoples. Anthropologists today are well aware of the constructed nature of identity (more pastiche and contingent manipulation than inescapable heritage), and in many ways the pan-Maya movement is a textbook example of an imaged community. Yet, Maya identity politics are actively shaped by both the larger context in which they exist and the lived experience of individuals living in rural Maya communities.

## *Metaphors and Models of Culture*

Famously paraphrasing Max Weber, Clifford Geertz writes "that man is an animal suspended in webs of significance he himself has spun, [and] I take culture to be those webs, and the analysis of it to be therefore not an experimental science in search of law but an interpretive one in search of meaning" (1973:5). This popular and enduring metaphor neatly captures the cultural properties of creativity as well as of observable structure. Yet, often overlooked in the comparison is that man weaves culture with largely borrowed strands, and the product is but a unique recombination of elements (and even swatches of structure) of other patterns. This is to say that humans exercise individual creativity only within the limits imposed by available (i.e., culturally recognized) material and ideational resources, a point that Geertz himself acknowledges in another of his memorable metaphors: "The culture of a people is an ensemble of texts, themselves ensembles, which the anthropologist strains to read over the shoulder of those to whom they properly belong" (ibid.:452). Cultural actors create their own unique cognitive worlds out of already cultured ideas. The nature of cultural creativity itself thus binds individuals together through points of common reference, reinforcing and creating cultural communities that may or may not correspond to a particular geographic territory.

Like those of spiders, webs of cultural meaning are sticky. Through cultural production in general—and not just fabricating lies—humans weave webs from which they cannot escape, at least not quickly, easily, or painlessly. At the level of internalized culture—individual cognitive patterns uniquely derived from available cultural resources—previous choices set one down a path that delimits the range of one's current opportunities. To many, this process gives rise to a belief in destiny, even if the pattern of causation is apparent only post hoc. At the level of culture in general, such individual "destinies" result in a degree of social stickiness that can be both beneficial (as in a sense of relatedness and purpose, of sharing common elements of cultural reference, and of maintaining a degree of security in a rapidly changing world) and potentially detrimental (as expressed through the zealous maintenance of boundaries, a cultivated ethnocentrism, and so on).

In this book I focus on such cultural stickiness, looking at how webs of meaning are woven between structural elements supplied by the material and social environment. As much recent anthropological theory has made clear, individuals actively construct their own cognitive and cultural worlds, and yet all these idiosyncratic constructions dynamically articulate with certain structural givens. And herein lie the limits of methodological individualism: individuals exercise creativity, but only within certain cultural constraints that are intimately related to the larger processes (often conceived of as "structures," yet themselves inherently dynamic) of national political structure, the world system, and globalization.

## *Essentialism and Anti-essentialism*

Geertz's memorable metaphors and advocacy of interpretive anthropology did much to solidify a movement in the discipline that questions the static and homogeneous image of culture—presumably put forth by earlier ethnographers—to focus on the weaving of webs and not just their solidified structure. As part of this trend, anthropologists have increasingly concerned themselves over the last thirty years with understanding and representing microlevel change and diversity, giving the discipline a heightened sensitivity to individual variation and agency, particularly of the subaltern variety. This endeavor is as much political as intellectual, and it is seen by many as precisely the sort of praxis in which academics should engage—all research, including that which claims neutrality and objectivity, has political implications, and to ignore those implications is naive.

To the end of producing intellectually and politically liberating analyses, a number of anthropologists have adopted a stance of anti-essentialism. Essentialism here refers to the sort of analysis (both folk and academic) that makes "simplistic or universalizing assumptions about domination and uncritically assumes the possibilities or impossibilities of resistance based on a particular form of collective identity" (Knauft 1996:255; see also Obeyesekere 1997). To essentialize, in its pejorative sense, is to reduce the rich diversity of lived experience to social categories that are manageable both intellectually and politically. Essentialism thus reinforces the romantic themes of much ethnography and promotes the delusion of holism expressed in phrases such as "The Maya believe that . . ."

Yet, it should be noted that "essentialism" is itself an essentializing construct, and good ethnographers have long resisted essentializing tendencies in their representations, even before the term became common currency. The nuanced ethnographic observations of Sol Tax, Robert Redfield, Charles Wagley, and other putatively essentialist Maya ethnographers belie simple categorizations of their work as "essentialist." Perhaps the clearest example of scholarship in the tradition of essentialism is Paul Kirchoff's (1943) trait list of uniquely Mesoamerican cultural elements. Kirchoff's list focused on precolumbian traits (hieroglyphic writing, human sacrifice, maize-and-bean agriculture, a sacred 260-day calendar, and so forth), but it became a handy baseline against which to measure the persistence of autochthonous culture and the pace of acculturation. Such a trait-list approach to documenting cultural change, and the underlying notion of the inevitability of Westernization, was widely accepted by even the best ethnographers working in the first part of the twentieth century. At the time, acculturation was seen as largely inevitable: the homogenizing march of progress would continue the world over just as it had in the West, with native peoples unable to resist its imposition and seduction. Progressively modernist ethnographers were thus committed to the Boasian project of documenting lost and soon-to-be-lost elements of traditional cultures, and to this end they frequently resorted to trait lists of traditional and modern elements. Despite such good intentions on the part of their users, trait lists also served as essentializing constructs, both in academic representations (offering clearly defined categories for analytic modeling, as in Robert Redfield's [1941] folk-urban continuum) and in political policies (reducing the essence of a Maya Other in pursuit of social, political, and economic containment strategies). Such approaches have long been employed by the Guatemalan state to justify social engineering programs aimed at directing culture change by manipulating trait-list variables, often with dismal consequences.

Anti-essentialist approaches point out that what we know about the

Maya, or any other group, is ultimately distilled from what we know about particular individuals, a knowledge that is at best incomplete (Said 1978; Clifford 1988). The most successful anti-essentialist approaches wed Geertzian phenomenology to self-referential textual criticism in a way that illuminates the rich complexity of forms and polyvalence of symbols from which social categories and trait lists are distilled (Spivak 1987, 1994; Bhabha 1990, 1994; Abu-Lughod 1991; Gupta and Ferguson 1992; García Canclini 1995; Appadurai 1996). In Maya scholarship, anti-essentialist analyses have effectively critiqued a long-standing perspective that assumed a clear linkage between contemporary Maya culture and ancient Maya forms, showing this as a form of archaeo-romanticism that in many ways supports neocolonial relations of dominance (Hervik 1992; Castañeda 1996; Montejo 1999).

In studies of identity politics, anti-essentialism is closely linked to theories of cultural construction that focus on how individuals and groups actively create their own psychological and cultural realities — weaving the webs of significance in which they live. One particularly fruitful branch of constructivist theory builds on the work (and terminology) of Benedict Anderson (1983) and Eric Hobsbawm (1983) to show how "invented traditions" are strategically deployed in the creation of "imagined communities" (e.g., see Handler [1988] on the Canadian Québecois, Linnekin [1983, 1991] on Polynesian cultural invention, and Chatterjee [1993] on Indian postcolonial nationalism). That traditions and whole cultures are invented is at first blush a radically egalitarian notion, and as carried out, such analyses dramatically unveil the "Wizard of Oz" quality to hegemonic imposition by Western states-turned-nations. Yet the relativism implied by constructivist theory is morally ambiguous, and it has more recently been employed to undermine indigenous claims of authenticity. As a result, the theoretical position of "strong constructivism" (i.e., "one that views the individual as fully plastic, and . . . one that, as a result, cannot provide grounds for a political critique of any given construction" [Reddy 1997 : 329]) has itself become the target of recent subaltern critiques coming both from within the academy and from the subjects of anthropological inquiry. As Nelson observes, "making arguments for hybrid identities, no matter how well supported by the U.S. academy's current hip theory, may feed right in to anti-indigenous arguments that it is all made-up, inauthentic hogwash" (1999 : 133).

While benefiting from its general valuation of subaltern agency, Maya scholars and peasants are suspicious of strong constructivism, seeing in it the same sort of hidden racism that Slavoj Žižek attributes to multiculturalism. Characteristically provocative, Žižek writes that

> multiculturalism involves patronizing Eurocentrist distance and/or re-
> spect for local customs without roots in one's own particular culture. In
> other words, multiculturalism is a disavowed, inverted, self-referential
> form of racism, a "racism with a distance" — it "respects" the Other's
> identity, conceiving the Other as a self-enclosed "authentic" com-
> munity towards which he, the multiculturalist, maintains a distance
> rendered possible by his privileged universal position (1997:44)

Thus, the apparent irony is that Maya scholars turn to discourses of modernist essentialism rather than to multiculturally sensitive construc-tivism to justify their reconstructions of ethnic identity. The scientific exactitude of modernist discourse helps Maya activists legitimate claims on the Guatemalan state, claims largely based on positions of cultural authority and authenticity rendered through cultural continuity. In-deed, such essentialist views of culture underwrite many contemporary ethnic movements the world over. As the former subjects of colonial and neocolonial governments seek to recover and assert their ethnic distinctiveness, they quite naturally turn to those elements that are per-ceived as being most authentic, the apparent essences of their culture. Anthropologists steeped in anti-essentialist theory often take an am-bivalent stance toward this sort of essentialism, and most appear to sup-port the philosophy of indigenous self-determination while proffering constructivist critiques that undermine their subjects' notions of cul-tural authenticity (Watanabe 1995; Fischer and Brown 1996; cf. Allen 1992 and Tedlock 1993:156).

### In Defense of Culture

In its most radical form, anti-essentialism attempts to undermine the concept of culture itself.[2] Yet, as Christoph Brumann (1999) points out, there exists a widespread, although largely implicit and differently rep-resented, similarity in the concept of culture as invoked by contempo-rary anthropologists from all theoretical perspectives. Perhaps, then, we should acknowledge and examine these similarities, not in an effort to impose a hegemonic position but to complement our heightened aware-ness of the differences that separate our positions. Brumann (1999:S1) states that "the root of the confusion is the distribution of learned rou-tines across individuals: while these routines are never perfectly shared, they are not randomly distributed. Therefore 'culture' should be retained as a convenient term for designating the clusters of common concepts, emotions, and practices that arise when people interact regularly." This is a pragmatic approach to the representation of realities that can be observed and recorded. As Ulf Hannerz (1992:109) remarks, culture is "the most useful key word we have to summarize that peculiar capacity of human beings for creating and maintaining their own lives together, and to suggest the usefulness of a fairly free-ranging kind of inquiry into the ways people assemble their lives" (cf. Rodseth 1998).

Culture is symbolic, which does not imply a negation of its material aspects, for just as the material world is symbolically organized by culture, so too is the symbolic organization of culture realized through the lived dialectic between ideational constructs and "real world" circumstance. Culture is, to varying degrees, shared, as both a condition and a consequence of its social transmission. Yet there is no homogeneous ideal model of culture embedded in the minds of cultural actors and no disembodied and uncontested Durkheimian ideal encoded in social structure. The boundaries of cultures are not so clear-cut as ethnographic maps suggest, and these boundaries are ever more blurred in the postmodern age of telescoping time-space differences.

Cultural actors are differentially implicated in larger systems of relations and they develop divergent and idiosyncratic views of themselves and their cultures. And yet there exists an ever changing field of social discourse that they appear (to themselves and to others) to share, a field only partly accessible to cultural outsiders. At one level, this field is clearly delimited by language, dress, and other markers of group affiliation. In turn, such surface markers reflect underlying cognitive schemas that facilitate intersubjective understanding, what Michael Herzfeld (1997) calls "cultural intimacy." These cultured patterns of thought are idiosyncratically internalized by individuals while maintaining a dialogic sharedness that demarcates fields of cultural identity.

Identity—ethnic or otherwise—is always a particularly motivated representation of cultural difference—in short, culture in social action. As Carol Hendrickson notes, ethnicity "provides a rationale for action, at least in the case of the Maya population [of Tecpán]. An indigenous person might consciously and explicitly speak out, act a particular way, or criticize another human being in accordance with his or her perceived ideal of what it is to be an Indian and how this ideal should find expression in the world" (1995:31). For some, it has become acceptable to treat culture and identity as interchangeable, a view that neatly dovetails with instrumentalist conceptions of cultural construction. Cultural elements can be and are self-consciously deployed and manipulated by individual actors in the course of events both grand and small; but culture itself (conceived of more as gestalt than trait list) acts on these individuals and delimits their options in very subtle — often subconscious — ways. This leads us to the irony that culture is dynamic while remaining continuous. Cultural symbols are continually construed and reconstrued through practice, and social fields of common identity are redefined through changing categorizations of ethnicity. Yet, the wonder of culture is that, through symbolic transposition and internally logical transformation, continuity is maintained by giving old forms new meaning and giving new forms old meaning.

Lila Abu-Lughod (1991) exhorts anthropologists to begin "writing against culture," meaning to focus on change and idiosyncratic variation in ethnographic accounts in a way that explicitly critiques the sense of homogeneity implied by the term *culture* (cf. Clifford 1988). Like many anti-essentialists, Abu-Lughod is more strident in her position statement than in her specific methodological suggestions. She herself chooses to focus on particular individuals and circumstances, minutely contextualized in space and time. Her aim is to confront the reader with the vivid and undeniable heterogeneity of actions motivated by competing (cognitively and socially) intentions, and thus to break down the illusion of homogeneity often attached to synthetic cultural description. But Abu-Lughod's tactical approach need not preclude making broader conclusions from our field data. The importance of her book *Veiled Sentiments* (1986) rests partly, but not solely, on her empathetic descriptions of Bedouin women's inner lives; it is widely used in undergraduate courses because of the larger *cultural* significance of her data and what these can tell us not only about a few particular women but also about other women *like* them. We need not say all Bedouin women are the same to accept that there are important commonalities in their socialization, structural position in society, and even the nature of their agency and intentionality.

The issue of individual diversity versus cultural commonality brings us to the heart of much recent debate in anthropology. As Abu-Lughod and others point out, ethnography that ignores individual variation cannot adequately represent actual lived experience. And yet, at the same time there exist patterns of thought and behavior commonly held among individuals — in short, culture. These patterns are most evident in salient cultural metaphors and cognitive models, both of which act as fluid templates against which particular actions (and innovations) take place. The "science" of cultural anthropology is concerned with modeling these patterns and their dynamic interrelationship; the art of ethnography lies in sensitive humanistic representations of the same patterns and in the acknowledgment of diversity.

In contrast to Abu-Lughod's exhortation to write against culture, I argue in this book for the utility of culture in analyzing the complex circumstances in which Maya self-identity and worldview have been maintained and (re)interpreted (both externally and internally) through interindividual and intercollectivity interactions. Such an argument does not necessitate a naive return to the static essentialism of an earlier era or to the reductionism of vulgar cultural evolutionism. At the same time, it is important to recognize and account for the importance of continuity as well as change in cultural systems; of cultural commonalities as well as idiosyncratic variation; and of intersubjectively perceived (if not wholly objective) structural relations (or relations of structuration) in regional, state, and global systems as well as individual agency and local manifestations of collective intentionality. I adopt what Paul Gilroy (1993) has called an "anti-anti-essentialist" stance, arguing that we need not reject the commonality and continuity indexed by the culture concept in order to acknowledge and theoretically account for individual variation and change.[3]

Students of the Maya have long attempted the sort of balance that Gilroy advocates. Victoria Bricker (1981), for example, argues for the existence of a culturally continuous mythical substrate reproduced through Maya historical representations of ethnic conflict. Bricker does not attempt to reduce behavior to a slavish commitment to tradition. Rather, she shows how existing symbolic structures are actively deployed in the process of giving meaning to contemporary events, and how these structures are both replicated and transformed through practical action and material and social contingencies.[4] She acknowledges the weight of tradition, but sees it not as determinant in and of itself but as a resource (in Giddens's sense of the word) that plays into the ongoing construction of agency and structure. Gary Gossen (1974), Eva Hunt (1977), John Watanabe (1983), and Robert Carlsen (1997) similarly document mythic and ideological substrates of Maya culture, relating similarities to shared cultural patterns and environmental contexts. In Gossen's words, such studies "reveal deep, generative roots for derivative phenomena that occur in both time and space," forming part of a "regional ideational logic that follows its own rules" (1986:4–5).

## *Cultures and Their Logics*

Different cultures (conceived of, following Brumann 1999 and Rodseth 1998, as overlapping distributions of cognitive and behavioral patterns) are marked by different logics of internal organization. This is not to deny that cultures are dynamic and porous or to claim that other cultures are incapable of the sort of formal logical reasoning characteristic of the Western tradition (cf. Lévy-Bruhl 1926; Lévi-Strauss 1966). Rather, the concept of cultural logics reaffirms the importance of cultural relativity (à la Boas 1938) and of anthropology's contribution to the critique of Western reason (Marcus and Fischer 1986). The notion of cultural logics builds on constructivist theories in seeking to elucidate cognitive mechanisms of improvisation and proactive cultural construction. Cultural logics are not hard-and-fast rules (although they may appear solidified in particular schemas that lend themselves to formal modeling), but dynamic, shared predispositions that inform behavior and thought. Cultural logics cannot predict particular actions, but they do lend a sense of regularity and continuity to behavior though post hoc analysis.

Change is an integral part of culture, but such change must be reconciled with preexisting cognitive schemas in a manner that allows for an intersubjective sense of cultural continuity, even — perhaps especially — in the face of dramatic externally induced modification. In this regard, Bruce Kapferer rightly stresses the simultaneity and inseparability of sociological and psychological factors. Comparing nationalist mythologies in Sri Lanka and Australia, he observes that "these ideologies contain logical elements relevant to the way human beings within their historical worlds are existentially constituted" (1988:19). In this view, idiosyncratic variation, the ultimate basis of cultural change, is reflexively linked to underlying structural paradigms: "no tradition is constructed or invented and discontinuous with history . . . [they] are chosen because of what they distill ontologically; that is, they make sense and condense a logic of ideas which may also be integrated to the people who make the selection although hidden from their reflective consciousness" (ibid.:211).

Benjamin and Lore Colby (1981) provide an explicit description of the workings of Maya cultural logics as expressed in the thought and behavior of individuals. Focusing on the life of a single Ixil day-keeper, they are able to reconstruct detailed cognitive schemas and decision-making models, which they link to larger organizing metaphors and cultural grammars. As the Colbys make clear, the processes of cultural logics are simultaneously generative and constrained, idiosyncratic and context-dependent, while predicated on a shared understanding of acceptability.

Patterns of cultural logics (expressed in metaphors, historical narratives, religious beliefs, social sanctions, observed behavior, and in myriad other ways) are received by individuals through the processes of socialization and ongoing social interaction, and yet they are also redefined through these very processes. Cultural logics are realized (and thus, for the observer, can only be meaningfully analyzed) through practice. And this practice has a marked constructive quality, with new symbolic forms and meanings emerging from the dynamic interaction of individual intention (itself culturally conditioned but not predetermined), cultural norms (variably enforced through reflexive social interaction), and material contingencies (encompassing not only local ecologies but also structural position in global systems of political economic relations). As Hendrickson points out in her study of Tecpán, "persistence and change are integrally related" (1995:197). She continues:

> What endures needs to be recreated daily, in different ways, for people to be aware of it as "always there." Indigenous activists who urge people to be conscious of their Maya heritage, to wear *traje* [traditional dress], to speak *lengua* [a native language], and to practice *costumbre* [local customs] recognize this if only implicitly. The persistent is also hard to shake, as it keeps reappearing — sometimes in very changed and "invisible" forms — even if people desperately want it to change. . . . What endures, however, is not necessarily static: change itself can be a predictable, enduring quality of life. . . . Thus, the past is seen as "the past" only insofar as it lives at the moment, and the new makes sense only insofar as it relates to, builds on, or contrasts with the old or traditional. (ibid.)

As Hendrickson suggests, cultural actors' self-interests and the ways they see fit to pursue them are variably conceived in relation to received cultural forms and normative patterns. It is useful here to recall Pierre Bourdieu's discussion of the containing nature of the *doxa*, which he defines as "the aggregate of the 'choices' whose subject is everyone and no one because the questions they answer cannot be explicitly asked" (1977:168). This is to say that the realm of what is taken for granted is continually delimited through the practice of social interaction, which, expressed through both orthodox and heterodox positions, reinforces the undiscussed foundations of the restricted field of cognitive and cultural possibilities.

Cultural logics (and the *doxa* they produce) change and expand through interaction with other, differently conceived fields of reference, which is to say that the realm of the thinkable does not exist in cultural isolation (an implicit premise of the containment strategy of cultural essentialism). Individuals and cultural groups often termed "marginalized" are deeply implicated in the world system, today more than ever, and fields of meaning and identity space (such as those denoted by the core-periphery distinction) are decreasingly confined by time and space distances. As the bounds of *doxa* expand, there is certainly a blurring of boundaries in regard to specific elements. Yet, though Appadurai (1988), Gupta and Ferguson (1992), and Hannerz (1996) rightly note that cultural communities need not correspond to a readily delimited geographic location, on the far margins of hyperspace and postmodern mobility — such as in rural Guatemala — physical proximity remains the single most influential determinant of both cultural and self-identity.

Meaningful cultural boundaries appear if we look not at specific elements but at the relationships between them. Watanabe (1990a, 1992) points out that the very act of sharing the same physical space leads to the formation of a shared sense of community and sensibility concerning appropriate behavior (see also Wilson 1993; Hervik 1994, 1999). This holds true in the cases of Tecpán and Patzún: reflexive lived experiences in particular social contexts produce a powerful sense of community-based identity, a field of cultural discourse from which outsiders are excluded. This discursive field is delimited not only by overt markers (language and dress, for example) but also by the shared sensibilities of which Watanabe writes, the fluid consensus about what constitutes acceptable behavior. This cultural sensibility, in turn, rests on shared generative cultural logics.

Maya cultural logics provide only a broad underlying foundation for comprehending and producing thought and behavior; they are productive and generative while ensuring continuity; and though by nature idiosyncratically internalized, their specific social instantiations may be deemed rational or irrational by others based on consensual norms, indicating their shared, normative quality. Such cultural logics, because they are cognitively deep, change at a much slower pace than surface elements. Partha Chatterjee (1993) makes an analogous point in his study of anticolonial nationalist movements. Chatterjee distinguishes two cultural domains, the material and the spiritual. He defines the spiritual as "an 'inner' domain bearing the 'essential' marks of cultural identity" and notes that "the greater one's success in imitating Western skills in the material domain . . . the greater the need to preserve the distinctiveness of one's spiritual culture" (ibid.:6). Change occurs in both of these domains, united by a complex system of feedback mechanisms, but change at the surface level of material culture occurs most rapidly. Change in underlying cultural logics (Chatterjee's spiritual domain) moves at a slower pace because of the intimate interdependency of their elements.

The approach I take in this book builds on Bourdieu's (1977) model of the habitus and Anthony Giddens's (1984) description of the "modalities of structuration." Bourdieu defines the habitus as "systems of durable transposable dispositions, structured structures predisposed to act as structuring structures, that is, as principles of the generation and structuring of practice and representations which can be objectively 'regular' and 'regulated' without in any way being the product of obedience to rules" (1977:22). He explains that the principles of the habitus are so fundamental that they are taken for granted: "what is essential *goes without saying because it comes without saying:* the tradition is silent, not least about itself as a tradition" (ibid.:167; cf. Tyler 1978; Shore 1996:54). Through an "economy of logic," the set of relations of the habitus is applied to many different domains, and in this manner invention conforms (although in unpredictable ways) to subjective limits on thought imposed by the habitus. Bourdieu appears to argue that individuals are constantly improvising their culture, yet these improvisations can only be made on the basis of past cultural experiences that are conditioned by the internalized cultural logics of the habitus. Nonetheless, Bourdieu fails to extend his argument to account for the processes of cognition through which the habitus is manifest, and he ultimately undercuts the power of cultural agency by resorting to a form of material determinism ("practice never ceases to conform to economic calculation even when it gives every appearance of disinterestedness" [1977:177]). In this book, I extend Bourdieu's analysis by examining the dynamic interplay between individually internalized cognitive models, culturally shared structuring structures of the habitus, and broad political economic processes.

Giddens's (1984) work on structuration offers a partial corrective to Bourdieu's reductionist view of agency. Giddens focuses on the interactive dynamics of the duality of structure: structures exist only as they are "instantiated in action" by knowledgeable human agents, and yet these very instantiations are based on "rules and resources, recursively implicated in the reproduction of social systems" (ibid.:377). Giddens breaks free of the implied tautology (agents enact structure while structure conditions agents' actions) by focusing on the knowledgeability of agents and their access to resources (as broadly conceived); by positing the generalizability of rules; and by acknowledging that structure is ultimately embedded in cognition (existing as "memory traces, the organic basis of human knowledgeability" [ibid.]). Thus, structuration (the dynamic process involved in the historically specific conjunctures of structural duality) involves knowledgeable (in the sense of enculturated) actors reflexively indexing cognitive schemas (themselves built upon the knowledge and availability of cultural and material resources) in innovative ways through social practice. Yet Giddens errs in focusing on the aggregate application rather than on the individual internalization of social rules. To avoid a deterministic view of agency one must account for the idiosyncratic internalization of cultural schemas (cf. Sewell 1992). As I argue below, it is the idiosyncratic internalization of received cultural schemas that composes the cognitive bases of cultural logics and thus of agency. Such a view of cultural logics allows one to theorize the role of agency without reducing it to mechanical structural enactment or atomistic self-interested individualism.

### *Idiosyncrasies and Socialization*

Culture is that which is shared and relationally construed while at the same time ultimately existing only in myriad idiosyncratically internalized forms. Idiosyncrasies are centrally important to the process of cultural maintenance and formation (Crapanzano 1980; Obeyesekere 1981; Abu-Lughod 1986): seemingly novel cultural forms emerge and flourish while others fade into disuse (Anderson 1983, Hobsbawm 1983, Chatterjee 1993), and yet cultural boundaries remain and cultural groups are identifiable based on objective (albeit changing) criteria. Thus, the essence of culture remains its sharedness; even the most unique and outrageous thoughts and actions of an individual are formulated, enacted, and interpreted in reference to shared (to varying degrees) cultural constructs.

Idiosyncratic variants of shared cultural logics are encoded in cognitive schemas during the course of socialization. Socialization here refers to the unique conjuncture of social and cultural information dynamically articulated over time with individual life histories. From these received data are gleaned patterns of cultural meanings and social relations that must be reflexively reconciled with biogenetic predispositions and existing cognitive models, and from this ongoing reconciliation emerge internalized cultural logics indexed to the external social and material world. An individual's socialization is unique because of the particular configuration of social forms to which one is exposed; the precise conjunction of these forms in time and space are never the same for any two individuals. Yet, this idiosyncrasy is built upon the conjuncture of shared elements, both synchronically (the temporal and spatial context of socializing events, of which there are an innumerable quantity) and diachronically (as received information is reconciled with previously received information). The compound effect of consistently reinforced received cultural information is the formation of an idiosyncratic variant of a common cultural logic. Change in one's internalized cultural logics can and does occur in later life as a function of interaction with the material and social world, and catastrophic (environmentally, socially, personally) events can dramatically change one's worldview.

The foundation provided by cognitively encoded cultural logics gives rise to surface structures such as mental models and cognitive schemas. The development and maintenance of a cultural logic involves a reflexive indexation of cognitive preconceptions and predispositions to social and material relations. Through such practical activity, derivative cognitive schemas and their underlying cultural logics are reinforced (when the social and material world conform to the expectations of an internalized cognitive model) and are changed (when expectations are not fulfilled and a working hypothesis of a cultural logic must be modified). An internalized cultural logic is thus partly a function of life histories intersecting with social relations. Yet, in studying the practical basis of cultural logics, we must move beyond extreme methodological individualism to situate the field of culture not only within the minds of individuals but also in the position of individuals and populations in global processes of political economy. The broad structural framework of the global system is historically received, and yet one's structural position does not merely follow from circumstances of birth, but emerges from the active engagement of individuals with received norms and systemic processes.

### Cognitive Models

Cultural logics condition the improvisation of cognitive models as they are called upon in specific social contexts. In part, this book is concerned with understanding the individualized cognitive bases of shared Maya cultural patterns. All cultural models are by their nature internalized, and thus integrated into an idiosyncratically unique gestalt: culture does not exist independent of the mind (see Gentner and Stevens 1983; Shore 1996; Strauss and Quinn 1997). At the same time, in examining the lives of a number of Maya individuals, I show how idiosyncratic mental models are built out of both received knowledge and ongoing interaction with the social and material world—in short, out of available cultural resources. In domains as varied as spirituality, agriculture, and sports, the specific conjuncture of events acting on an individual throughout his or her life uniquely affects how that person views and acts in the world. Yet, although the specific conjuncture of events is individually unique, the elements themselves are by and large shared, understood in relation to social conventions even if they are not themselves conventional. Take, for example, the case of a middle-aged Kaqchikel woman in Tecpán who explained to me her visceral dislike for soccer matches and their associated revelry. She remembers as a young girl watching her father drink heavily, and subsequently become abusive, when he went to soccer games on the weekends. These early childhood experiences conditioned what has proven to be a resilient cognitive link (both natural and logical), tainting the pleasure of soccer as sport with the memory of domestic violence. She understands her own sons' passion for the game, recognizes its potential health and social benefits, and has resigned herself to living in a house full of soccer fanatics, but it still pains her to attend games or even watch them on television. This woman's view of soccer is certainly idiosyncratic, the result of cognitive patterns built up through her unique life history. At the same time, her internalized cultural logic is built upon a more broadly shared model of soccer in society (even as construed in partial opposition to that cultural model).

Practical experience forces one to constantly modify and improvise one's cognitive models and cultural logics, thus inextricably linking the social and material world to the cognitive realm. In converting cognitive models into practical activity, individuals enter into structural relations with others. These structures cease to be purely idiosyncratic, placed as they are in relation to myriad other externalized structures, and thus can no longer be controlled solely by an individual's intentions. As Marshall Sahlins (1985:149) notes,

> in action, people put their concepts and categories into ostensive relations to the world. Such referential uses bring into play other determinations of the signs, besides received sense, namely the actual world and the people concerned. *Praxis* is, then, a risk to the sense of signs in the culture-as-constituted, precisely as the sense is arbitrary in its capacity as reference. Having its own properties, the world may then prove intractable. It can well defy the concepts that are indexed to it. Man's symbolic hubris becomes a great gamble played with the empirical realities.

Conjunctures of externalized cognitive models both perpetuate and modify the preexisting cognitive schemas of social interlocutors who are actively engaged in a consensual discursive community (Habermas 1990). If perceived relations conform to held models, those models are reified, but if actions produce unintended results, the models must be modified.

## *World-System Models*

Each mind may indeed be a world unto itself, and yet there also exists a world external to the individual, one filled with practical experience, unseen material constraints, and shared circumstances. Although this larger world may at times seem far removed from the minutia of quotidian cognitive modeling, global processes exert a strong influence on the ways in which individuals conceive of and live in their worlds.

World-system theorists focus attention on the historical development of global capitalism and its effects on the political and economic structures of marginalized societies (Baran 1957; Frank 1967; Wallerstein 1974; Cardoso and Faletto 1979 [1967]). Dividing the world into a core of advanced capitalist countries and a periphery of underdeveloped countries, such approaches show that capital and capital-intensive manufacturing have long been concentrated in the core countries of Western Europe and North America, part of a global economic system that renders peripheral economies dependent on the core. World-system theorists have used this basic model to analyze how the historical development of capital-intensive manufacturing in the West combined with colonial and neocolonial expansion in southern countries to create global economic structures that concentrate capital accumulation and development in core areas. The structural logic of capitalism thus revealed is simultaneously based on expansion (of labor, capital, and consumer markets) and on concentration (of wealth in the hands of the most efficient producers); on a global scale, as markets for raw materials from the tropics expanded from the sixteenth century onward, capital accumulation was concentrated in the manufacturing and industrial economies of core countries, fueling their continued expansion. After manufacturing innovations in textile production provided the initial impetus, feedback mechanisms built into the capitalist system acted to restrict capital accumulation to the core while "developing underdevelopment" in the periphery to ensure a continued cheap supply of goods and labor (Luxemburg 1913; Cardoso and Faletto 1979 [1967]). This has led to the situation today in which the whims of core markets largely dictate production of primary export products in peripheral areas, and these large core markets encourage global competition between peripheral regions to keep prices low for raw materials. Large core corporations are able to leverage their access to capital-intensive means of production to charge high prices for the manufactured goods that they export to the periphery, thus maintaining the cycle of capital concentration in core areas.

Early formulations often erred in portraying the world system as a monolithic behemoth, unilaterally imposing its hegemonic structure on local systems and individuals. The system itself seemed to take on a life independent of individual action and intention while largely determining the rules of engagement between global forces and local producers. Immanuel Wallerstein (1979) goes so far as to claim that the world system is singularly capitalist, and that surviving "pre-capitalist" forms of production are not actually pre-capitalist, enmeshed as they are in global capitalist relations of production. In this view, the system is greater than the sum of its parts, led by an internal logic of its own creation—indeed, a true system in the sense that no one actor can unilaterally determine the effects of his market actions. In many ways, however, such a perspective mystifies the very object of analysis, for, ultimately, the system is built out of the varied specific actions of individual actors (see Godelier 1972; Terray 1972; Laclau 1977; Meillassoux 1981).

A useful corrective to overly deterministic world-system models is found in the work of Richard Fox (1985), who takes as his starting point dramatic instances of culture change precipitated by new terms of engagement with global political-economic structures. His study of

Punjab anticolonial resistance uncovers the ways in which individuals appropriate and manipulate cultural symbols as well as material objects for situationally contingent ends. Fox goes on, however, to point out that "as people build their current culture out of pieces of the old and live out their material conditions in new ways, so their social world takes on new configurations" (1985:197). Thus Fox acknowledges that cultures—not just individuals—manifest the properties of change through referential practice, but his focus on dominance and resistance leads him to stress the instrumentality of such change: "contemporary individuals and groups take pieces, not the pattern, of the past and form them into new social arrangements" (ibid.; see also Friedman 1994: 136). Yet, as Fox himself shows in his ethnographic analysis, patterns (albeit extrapolated post hoc) can and do persist through time as an intersubjectively perceived cultural continuity.

Late-twentieth-century capitalism (marked by post-industrialization in core countries and offshore production and assembly in the periphery) has opened new arenas of resistance and new venues for development for marginalized peoples around the world. Today the world system is less monolithic than ever because of its increasing points of direct articulation with local systems and individual actors. The power of core countries, then, to dictate the direction of the world system is much diminished, although hierarchical structures remain (Kapferer 1988). The emergence of new forms of economic structures is closely correlated in time and space to the rise of identity politics and various forms of hyphenated nationalism in peripheral areas. Indeed, it appears that ethnicity has eclipsed the importance of class identity in stimulating struggles of resistance.

This postmodern identity space has been colonized by the pan-Maya movement and other ethnic movements around the world, and these movements have actively engaged in a dialectic negotiation of boundaries within the postdependency framework. In so doing, pan-Mayanist leaders and rural Maya peasants alike have co-opted new forms of communication and production and deployed them in ways that make sense in terms of Maya culture. Contextualizing local forms of identity politics within Guatemala's changing position in the post–Cold War global political economy and the increasingly transnational links between international and local organizations, I attempt in this book to elucidate the mutually constitutive nature of identity politics played out in local contexts but thoroughly informed by national and international systemic relations.

## Engaging the Field

Anthropology is forging a new type of engagement with the field. Long distinguished by a passion for fieldwork and a reliance on participant observation, anthropologists are now more sensitive than ever to the potential political implications of their work and its impact on the lives of those they study, part of what Les Field calls a "political sea change toward advocacy" (1994:238). In turn, anthropologists are increasingly likely to be challenged about the political implications of their method-ologies and findings, if not from traditional colleagues then from former subjects turned colleagues. Martin Diskin (1995:175) predicts that a

> greater awareness of the field might well become the task of anthro-
> pologists because it will soon be raised by those we study as they
> develop the capacity to read and criticize our work. Their criticism
> will often express the accusation that anthropologists' allegiances and
> interests lie elsewhere than with those being studied. And texts will be
> produced that flatly contradict anthropological judgement and writing
> based on the impossibility of outsiders' understanding native culture.

Diskin's predictions have already come to pass in the politicized con-text of Maya studies, with an increasingly vocal group of young Maya scholars — Guatemala's first generation of Maya Mayanists — develop-ing a persuasive and critical postcolonial stance in their works. This stance is predictably problematic for foreign anthropologists, as most Maya intellectuals "see social science as profoundly political by defini-tion and consequently doubt the motives and intentions of foreign re-searchers who act as if their verbal support for indigenous issues should be accepted at face value" (Warren 1998:79).[5]

Indeed, nothing quite tests the limits of a commitment to cultural relativism and multivocality as does a native's critique of one's work (Warren 1992; Watanabe 1995). This was brought home to me a few years ago when a book that I co-edited, *Maya Cultural Activism in Gua-temala* (1996), was the subject of a critical review by Enrique Sam Colop, a prominent Maya lawyer, scholar, and contributing author to the volume in question (Sam Colop 1997). In his critique, Sam Colop accuses North American scholars of essentializing Maya culture — of trying to reduce its rich diversity into a manageable, homogeneous cate-gory of the sort that has long served as a weapon of political contain-ment and as a tool of misguided social engineering programs. Although this was not the first time I had been challenged about my intentions and research agenda (in the course of fieldwork, I was frequently asked to defend my position and explain exactly what I was doing *for* the Maya people), Sam Colop's critique was especially troubling. My knee-jerk reaction was anger at having my self-perceived good intentions ig-nored and at being lumped together with a line of thought I see myself as resisting. More troubling still was Sam Colop's implication that any argument I might make would be tainted by my structural position in the global system of neocolonial relations.

Such critiques should not, however, force us to the shelter of aca-demic jargon and cynical irony. As Michael Herzfeld observes, "distinc-tions between fact and judgment may not be universally clear and may themselves be culturally determined, but . . . inserting our own claims to factual precision into that perspective strengthens rather than weak-ens them because it broadens the empirical basis of assessment" (1998: 69). Ideally, then, the dialogue engendered by native critiques of our work should encourage a new type of engagement with the field in which we understand "ourselves" to be them as well as us (Fabian 1991:264), and that engagement should have as its goal the creation of "dialogues through texts, not just within them" (Watanabe 1995:41; see also Hervik 1994; Hastrup 1995).

The present work has grown out of an ongoing dialogue (an "imper-fect rapport" in Nelson's [1999] words) with urban Maya scholars and rural Maya people about their cultural identity. For the most part, it has been an amicable discourse, although, as Sam Colop's critique shows, the potential for contention and dispute always exists as deepening dia-logues uncover potentially divergent agendas and allegiances. I suspect that the Maya reactions to this book will be varied: some will find value in it, others will have reservations, seeing it as potentially detrimental to their precarious political position or as another not-so-subtle act of academic imperialism. Many will have neither the time nor the interest to read it (although, as I write, it is always in my mind that some of the individuals I write about will read my perspective on their lives). Yet we cannot determine the lives of our formulations after we have pub-licly spoken them or written them down, which is not to say that we should stop trying—or that we should stop making generalizations.

As Diane Nelson (1999) notes, the fieldworker's best-intended soli-darity quickly turns in practice to "fluidarity," a dynamic condition marked by murky, contingent, and ever-fluctuating moral relations. Success in fieldwork—socially, politically, and scholarly—depends on negotiating, and thus understanding, these fluid relations. Immersing

oneself in local relations through intensive participant observation allows one to be trained in the logic of situationally contingent responses
and socially acceptable fluidarity. As others have noted, this process is
akin to the socialization of children, with all the trials and errors entailed. Sensitive ethnography (self-aware yet actively engaged in other
peoples' lives) is more than literary construction because its protago-
nists are not fictional characters but real individuals, and the empathy
and understanding they elicit are with other human beings engaged in
the same system as ourselves.

I first began to study the pan-Maya movement in the summer of
1990, at the end of my first year of graduate studies, while participating
in Tulane's Intensive Summer Course in Kaqchikel Mayan Language
and Culture led by Judith Maxwell and McKenna Brown. Through
talks and field trips, the course provided an opportunity to meet many
of the movement's leaders, and I was quickly captivated by their blend
of scholarship and political activism. At that time there was little interest in the movement as an object of study—the foreign scholars involved in pan-Mayanist activities were more active participants than
detached scholars—and I settled on it as the topic of my dissertation
research.[6] Because of my training in political economy, I started by
documenting the broad, national-level manifestations of pan-Mayanism
and exploring the movement's significance for the Guatemalan economy and political structure. As my studies progressed, I became interested in the relationship of national Maya leaders to their assumed base
of support: the inhabitants of the thousands of Maya towns, villages,
and hamlets that cover Guatemala more thoroughly than the country's
road system. Leaders of the Maya movement were inevitably relatively
affluent, lived mostly in Guatemala City, and were well educated. What,
then, did the general populace think of their new philosophy? Had most
Maya even heard of it? And if they had, could Maya subsistence farmers allow themselves the luxury to worry about such seemingly esoteric
problems? This book is my attempt to answer these questions through
an analysis of the relationship between the national pan-Maya movement and local expressions of Maya cultural activism in Tecpán and
Patzún.

My field research (carried out over twenty-eight months between
1990 and 2000, the bulk of it in 1993–1994) has been almost evenly
divided between working with urban-based Maya scholars and activists
and working with residents of the Kaqchikel towns of Tecpán and Patzún. When not working in Guatemala City, I have most often set up my

home in the field in Tecpán, and this prolonged proximity has allowed me to collect much more detailed and nuanced data from that town than from Patzún. Thus, this is not a balanced and controlled ethnographic comparison. Nonetheless, I frequently refer to Patzún in the pages that follow to both provide support for and represent exceptions to the patterns I describe for Tecpán.

Data were gathered through hundreds of hours of formal and informal interviews. These interviews were held in smoky kitchens over countless cups of sweet, watery coffee; in the market as vendors peddled their wares; in fields as I helped plant or harvest; in sweat baths; on the street; and at countless other mundane locales. Over fifty hours of these interviews were tape-recorded, but more commonly I took notes that were later transcribed in my fieldnotes. Additional data come from extensive surveys (covering 10% of each town's households) administered with the help of four local assistants in 1994.

The role of the anthropological fieldworker in the community he or she studies is a tenuous one. On the one hand, s/he seeks to be an impartial observer of the actions of others. Observation, however, always involves participation, and in participation, one's impartiality becomes compromised. In Tecpán, my wife and I went to great pains to remain neutral in the context of divisive local political and social relations.

Before moving to Tecpán in 1993 we had already made several contacts there. Carol Hendrickson, who has worked in Tecpán for over twenty years, generously introduced me to a number of her friends and acquaintances during the summer of 1991, and she herself has continued to be an important source of inspiration and information on the community. Through Judith Maxwell and several Tecpaneco teachers in Tulane's summer course in Kaqchikel language and culture, other contacts were made as well. As a result of these contacts, my wife and I were recruited to teach classes in English and German at a local Maya-run school; our classes in these prestige languages were offered free to students enrolled in a Mayan language course in order to attract participation. The volunteer teaching positions opened many doors for us. Our students often invited us into their homes and willingly gave interviews; others in town heard that we were teaching English classes at the town hall and accepted this as a legitimate raison d'être for a couple of foreigners who were not Peace Corps volunteers or missionaries. (The Peace Corps did not send anyone to the area between 1981 and 1993, so having foreigners live in town was something of a novelty.)

To the extent possible, my wife and I adapted ourselves to the daily rhythms of life in Tecpán. We lived much as our neighbors did. Our home was a two-room former schoolhouse. We slept, cooked, and ate in one room and devoted the other to a large study and workroom. If anything, we lacked many of the amenities found in most Tecpán houses: there was no shower (we bathed in the outdoor sink (*pila*) before eventually building a sweatbath on the patio), and our few pieces of crudely constructed furniture were often inadequate to accommodate guests. Nonetheless, we were content and were able to participate in most aspects of local life. We shopped in the market and patronized local stores, shared meals with friends and neighbors, periodically attended church, and heard and were the subject of countless stories. We had a car, and often we were enlisted to transport people and things; we lent our large study to local groups who needed a meeting place; and the fact that we were foreigners automatically gave us a certain stature in the community, among ladinos and Indians alike. As foreigners, we were allowed a great deal of leeway in our associations and were exempt to a large degree from the barriers that separate social groups in Tecpán.

## Summary

The first section of the book provides both the broad and the particular contexts of the study. The present chapter presents the theoretical background of my argument, and Chapter 2 proceeds by introducing the Guatemalan case and the specific contexts of daily life in Tecpán and Patzún, the two Kaqchikel Maya towns in which I have worked. Part 2 ("Global Processes and Pan-Maya Identity Politics") provides the macroframework for the detailed ethnographic data that follow by examining Guatemalan political economies and the rise of national pan-Mayanist identity politics. Chapter 3 looks at Guatemala's changing position in global structures of political economy, and Chapter 4 shows how Maya leaders have taken advantage of post–Cold War ideological shifts to colonize new political space for themselves in state and global systems. I argue that Maya identity politics are actively shaped by the larger context in which they exist, and that Maya leaders have actively and tactically leveraged emerging patterns of global political and economic relations to their own ends. In Chapter 5, I look at how these processes are played out in pan-Mayanist (re)constructions of salient cultural symbols such as dress and language. In Part 3 ("Maya Identity as Lived Experience in Tecpán and Patzún"), I relate the macrocontext of the world system and pan-Maya identity politics to the lived experience of culture in Tecpán and Patzún, showing how the "invention of tradition" is constrained by cultural forms maintained and adapted through concrete social actions. In examining cultural models of the heart and soul, I find salient principles of metaphysical balance (Chapter 6). In Chapter 7, I document the diversity of local and individual identities encompassed by "Maya-ness," focusing on kinship relations, hearth groups, and barrio affiliations. In Chapter 8, I return to the issue of cultural construction raised in Chapter 5, but look at local forms of cultural creativity, self-expression, and ethnic resistance. Part 3 ends in Chapter 9 by relating the idea of cultural logics to new forms of local production strategies intimately tied to political economic systems. I conclude with Chapter 10 by bringing these data to bear on my argument that Maya forms of identity politics are based on forms of Maya culture whose range of expression is delimited by both global and local structures of political economy.

# 2　Tecpán and Patzún

The essence of the Maya movement in Guatemala is the *pueblo maya*.

DEMETRIO COJTÍ CUXIL (1997)

There is nothing really to Tecpán, except that it is next to the Iximché ruins. It is also the closest place to Antigua where you can buy lamb's meat.

*HENRY'S HINTS ON GUATEMALA* (1993)

The colorful Sunday market [in Patzún] is well worth a visit . . . , with the majority of women dressed in the brilliant reds of the local costume.

*THE REAL GUIDE TO GUATEMALA AND BELIZE* (1990)

Despite guidebook assessments, Tecpán and Patzún are special places for reasons that go beyond lamb's meat and colorful costume, and traveling to them evokes fond memories for me. Coming over the steep and winding Pan-American Highway from Guatemala City, having ascended about 5,000 feet in 75 kilometers, one encounters the turnoff to Patzún across the street from a busy Texaco gas station. From there, a bumpy 13-kilometer stretch of road (at first paved, then gravel, and finally dirt) continues southeast through Patzicía and on to Patzún (see Figure 2.1). Patzún is located on the far edge of a vast plain, and coming from Patzicía it looks oddly scrunched on the high ground, its perilously steep streets contrasting with the flat expanse of cultivated plain that stretches out below. Local history tells that Patzún was once located in

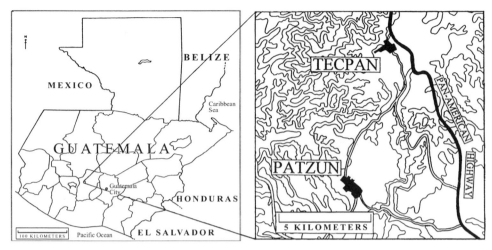

FIGURE 2.1. Tecpán, Patzún, and the surrounding area. Map by the author.

the middle of the plain, but that repeated flooding forced the town to move to higher ground. Today, the contrasting colors of maize, broccoli, and cauliflower break up the plain's expanse into a patchwork of separate plots, vividly announcing the fecundity of the land.

Tecpán rests on the flat lands of a narrow valley, just over a mountain and across a river from Patzún, a distance of about 8 kilometers as the crow flies and of about 13 kilometers (and 45 minutes in a car) via the winding road. Tecpán's main artery is not the rugged dirt road that connects it to Patzún, but the Pan-American Highway, the country's primary roadway, which skirts the town's urban center at kilometer 89. The Tecpán Valley, traversed by the Río Molino, is fertile agricultural land, but the fields around town are more uniformly planted with maize or wheat, leaving a less memorable impression than the approach to Patzún.

Tecpán, partly due to its closer proximity to the Pan-American Highway, is generally considered by Patzuneros and residents of surrounding towns as one of the most affluent Maya communities, and it is home to a large regional market on Thursdays. From the earliest days of Spanish contact, Tecpán has been more fully integrated into colonial and then Guatemalan state political and economic structures than has Patzún. Yet the history of Tecpán is not one of passive assimilation. Indians from Tecpán have long co-opted strategic aspects of national systems and used them as tools of resistance, contributing to the disproportionate representation of Tecpanecos among national Maya leaders and the town's reputation as a *"municipio vanguardista"* (Hendrickson 1995:25). This makes Tecpán an especially appropriate place to compare local forms of cultural identity to those promulgated at the national level by pan-Mayanist leaders (many of whom are Tecpanecos living in Guatemala City).

Because of its relative geographic and economic isolation, Patzún is widely considered to be a more culturally conservative town than Tecpán. Indeed, based on certain commonly used markers of Maya cultural identity (language, dress, and reliance on milpa agriculture), Maya Patzuneros are less acculturated (and thus seen as more authentically "Indian") than Tecpaneco Kaqchikeles. But Patzuneros are no slaves to tradition, and they are frequently more progressive in local civic awareness than Tecpanecos. There exists in Patzún a vibrant local tradition of Maya activism, a community-focused activism that contrasts with the national-level efforts of most Tecpaneco Indian leaders. Like their counterparts in Tecpán, upwardly mobile Patzunero Indians highly value education as a means for self-advancement, but after obtaining a university degree, more Maya from Patzún than from Tecpán return to their home communities to live and work. This pull back to Patzún has led to a relatively large and well organized local cadre of educated, politically active Maya leaders and to the formation of a number of cultural organizations that sponsor projects as varied as running a private school, promoting participation in *cofradía* rituals, and recording oral histories. Despite the differences between the two towns, cultural identity politics in them are broadly convergent in both ideology and practice. This convergence points to commonly held Kaqchikel (and Maya) cultural norms of behavior and innovation that provide the foundation for the sort of ideology abstraction central to the pan-Mayanist agenda.

### *Changing Social Landscapes*

Tecpán and Patzún are both *municipios* (townships) located in the administrative department of Chimaltenango. Within each *municipio* there are a number of different types of settlements. In Tecpán, which covers 201 square kilometers, there are thirty-four *aldeas* (villages), six *caseríos* (hamlets), six *fincas* (large farms), and the urban *cabecera municipal* (town center) of Tecpán Guatemala. The *municipio* of Patzún covers

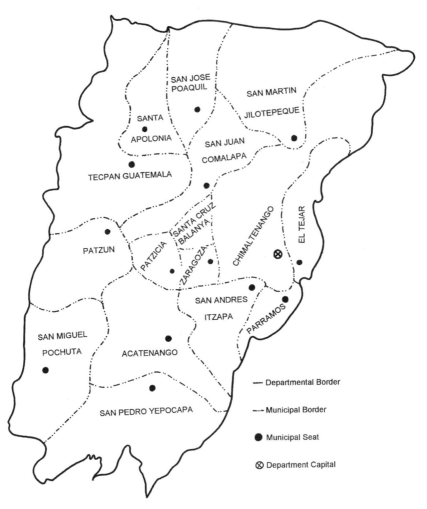

FIGURE 2.2. The Department of Chimaltenango and its *municipios*. Map by the author.

124 square kilometers and contains ten *aldeas,* twenty-five *caseríos,* and twenty-nine *fincas* in addition to the *cabecera municipal* of Patzún (see Figure 2.2).

   In Guatemala's national hierarchy of towns, Patzún is a *pueblo* (town) of the second order, whereas Tecpán enjoys the honorary status of *ciudad* (city). Tecpán's ranking reflects its historical importance as the country's first Spanish capital, and a plaque in the *municipalidad* (town hall) states that the status of *ciudad* was formally bestowed upon the town on July 25, 1924, in honor of the four-hundredth anniversary of the founding of "the first city of Guatemala founded in Ixinche [*sic*]." Guatemala's Instituto Nacional de Estadística (INE) calculates the 1994 population of the entire municipality of Tecpán at 41,152 and that of Patzún at 32,563, both representing substantial yet unexplained drops from INE's own 1990 estimates (INE 1991, 1996). Figure 2.3 shows 1994 INE census results reporting the population of Tecpán's urban center as 9,121 (72.71% Indian) and that of Patzún as 13,760 (88.9% Indian). Also in Figure 2.3 are my own surveys, covering 10 percent of the households in the two town centers and carried out two months before the 1994 INE census, which found that 93.1 percent of Patzuneros sampled identified themselves as Indians, while only 67.3 percent of Tecpanecos claimed Indian identity. This variation may be partly explained by the permeability of the categories "Indian" and "ladino"; so fluid are the categories that certain individuals are able to "pass" in either one, depending on social circumstances and contextually defined self-interest (cf. Hendrickson 1995:32–33). Most significant for present purposes, however, is that in both towns self-identified Indians compose a large majority of the local population, even if the

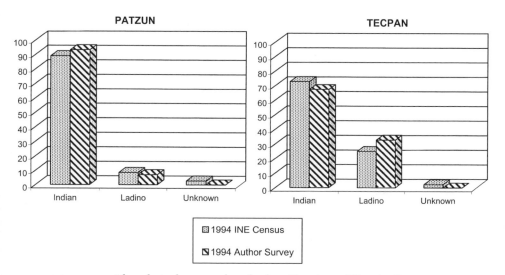

FIGURE 2.3. The ethnic demography of urban Tecpán and Patzún. Source: 1994 Official Census (INE 1996) and the author's 1994 surveys.

relative percentage of self-identified Indians in Patzún is significantly greater than in Tecpán.

Tecpán and Patzún are bounded to the north by the Continental Divide and to the south by a chain of active volcanoes that separates the hot and humid Pacific coastal plain from the more temperate highland areas. Located on the edge of the Ring of Fire surrounding the entire Pacific Ocean, it is a geologically active region, which works to both its benefit and detriment. The rich volcanic soils have blessed the area with fertile lands, and the high altitude (between 6,000 and 7,000 feet) contributes to a climate adaptable to two, and sometimes even three, harvests per year. Outcroppings of lime in the surrounding mountains is used in construction mortar and for processing dried maize; and the area's dense forests, albeit rapidly being replaced by farmlands, have supplied the country with exotic woods since the earliest days of colonialism. The volcanoes are far enough away so as not to pose a threat from lava flow, but earthquakes are common.

In the predawn hours of February 4, 1976, a series of devastating earthquakes shook the Guatemalan highlands. The largest, with its epicenter along the Motagua-Polochic Fault that runs just north of the Tecpán/Patzún area, registered 7.5 on the Richter Scale. (For comparison, it is estimated that the 1906 San Francisco earthquake was of a 7.7 or 7.9 magnitude.) An estimated 23,000 people were killed and another 76,000 were severely injured throughout the central highland region, with property damage exceeding $1 billion. Patzún was hard hit. It is estimated that 85 percent of the town's structures were damaged and over three hundred residents killed. Yet the devastation in Tecpán was worse still: official estimates report that 100 percent of the town's buildings were destroyed, killing some three thousand people, most crushed by their falling houses as they slept.[1] Remembrances of the earthquake in Tecpán vividly recount that not a single house or business was left standing, a memory largely supported by photographs of the period (see Figure 2.4). It is said that the facade and outer walls of the church alone survived, rising up from among the rubble to provide a landmark from which to gain one's bearings.

Some explain the resilience of the church building by recounting a story of its construction. It is said that when the church was first built, one Maya artisan was buried alive in each of its four corners. Akin to the Classic Maya earth gods who hold up the four corners of the earth, the unfortunate workers interred in the church support the structure

FIGURE 2.4. Tecpán after the 1976 earthquake. Photo courtesy of the U.S. Geological Survey.

during earthquakes. Additional earthquake protection comes from the columns in the interior of the church, which are reported to have been carved from living trees whose roots are still firmly planted in the ground (see Figure 2.5).

Tecpán's priest at the time, now an elderly man whiling away his days in the parsonage of a small church in Parramos, vividly recounts the memory of administering last rights to masses of bodies waiting to be buried with bulldozers sent by the government. Many recall the pain of having to dig out the bodies of relatives who were buried as they lay sleeping, and, worse, hearing the cries of victims whom they could not reach.

International aid from both governments and private groups was swift to arrive, if incomplete. In Tecpán, the earthquake relief effort is remembered as the start of rapid Protestant expansion in the community, with foreign churches and groups such as the Salvation Army coordinating much local aid distribution while using the opportunity to

FIGURE 2.5. The columns in
Tecpán's Catholic church.
Author photo.

seek converts as well. Tecpanecos recall the impression made by the
huge loads of clothing, food, and building materials brought by helicopters that landed regularly on the soccer field just outside of town in
the weeks and months after the earthquake. Distribution of goods was
at first haphazard, and the helicopters are said to have been swamped
by local citizens as soon as they landed. In her rush to get the last
of a batch of brightly colored housedresses, one Maya women is reported to have dropped her shoe while scrambling out of a departing
helicopter—winding up with a nice dress but with only one shoe to
walk in.

Among Patzuneros and Tecpanecos, an unusual lust for material objects (and envy in general) is considered socially dangerous and engen-
ders suspicion among one's friends and neighbors. In many areas of
highland Guatemala, as elsewhere in Latin America (see, for example,
Taussig 1980), commodity fetishism is conceptually linked to metaphysical imbalance, evil, and, through Christian imagery, to the devil.
Faustian barters are not uncommon, and many of the town's wealthiest
individuals (both Indian and ladino) are said to have sold their souls to
either the devil or local earth lords in exchange for worldly possessions
(cf. Wilson 1995). One story I heard repeatedly (and in several varia-

tions as told about different individuals) claimed that a successful but greedy local businessman possessed a strongbox full of gold that, no matter how much was spent, always remained full; anyone other than its owner who looked inside, however, would see only a tangled mass of black snakes, a clear sign of its nefarious origins. In addition, Tecpán, Patzún, and other Maya towns have a number of local traditions that serve to alleviate tensions built up through unequal class relations, including reciprocal exchanges, shamanistic rituals, and *cofradías* (religious brotherhoods). But with the rapid influx of foreign aid after the earthquake, local production and distribution channels and the norms that governed them quickly broke down. In the reconstruction efforts the families of local aid representatives almost inevitably had their homes rebuilt first, a fact frequently commented on to this day. Though tragedy often brings out the best in people, it can also bring to the surface latent tensions.

In Patzún, conditions were not so dire as in Tecpán. Fewer (although still a substantial number of) buildings were destroyed; official estimates report that 85 percent of buildings were damaged, although oral histories recall that fewer homes were completely destroyed. Patzún also suffered substantially fewer deaths and injuries. Local accounts attribute this good fortune to the durability of local adobe construction, although most of Tecpán's pre-earthquake buildings were also built of adobe. Local organizations also seem to have been more successful in working out equitable channels of distributing foreign aid, and an especially close relation was cultivated with the development arm of the Norwegian Lutheran Church. Collaboration between local leaders and the Norwegian group led to a broadly conceived program of both reconstruction and development, involving not only the rebuilding of houses but the construction of a material and organizational infrastructure to facilitate communitywide economic growth and diversification. Partly as a result of these efforts, Patzún has a number of active cooperative organizations that provide production and marketing assistance as well as a wide range of social services to members and the community as a whole. The largest cooperatives, CECOPA (which receives funding from Norway) and Dos Pinos (formed as part of a government initiative), offer subsidized pesticide and seed sales, access to telephone and fax services, and small farm loans. Their success has stimulated the formation of a number of other local cooperatives. Tecpán has many fewer and less successful cooperatives, and its leaders have a reputation for pursuing their interests at the state rather than at the local level.

Indeed, Maya Tecpanecos often hold up Patzún as an example of the sort of local activism their own town is lacking.

### An Opportunity to Modernize

Development workers and town officials in Tecpán decided that the earthquake damage provided an opportunity to modernize the town's urban layout. To this end, during the reconstruction Tecpán's quaint and narrow colonial streets were substantially widened and flanked by drainage ditches. A few houses were rebuilt in the adobe-block style of the past, but, encouraged by aid agencies, most were constructed out of cinder block reinforced with rebar, a precaution against future quakes. Most of Tecpán's cinder-block houses include an off-the-ground stove built into a kitchen wall, a fact often lamented by older residents as inhibiting family gatherings around the hearth (Figure 2.6). Patzún looks very different from Tecpán partly because it suffered less damage in the 1976 earthquake; additionally, many more of Patzún's houses were repaired or rebuilt with adobe or wattle-and-daub constructions (see Figure 2.7).

As one comes into Tecpán on the main road, the several-story-high roof of the large colonial church peeks over the tops of house walls. In front of the church is a small tree-shaded park with a concrete fountain, styled after a Maya pyramid, and the *concha,* or shell-shaped amphitheater. The church and park face the northeast side of the town hall, which itself faces a larger park and the national police station on the far north side. Before the earthquake, the town hall was a grand two-story colonial structure housing government offices as well as a public school, but the new municipal buildings reflect a drab attempt to copy colonial styles. On the west side of the park is the public health office, where there are usually groups of people from the outlying *aldeas* waiting to see a doctor. Just off the square to the east rises the three-story Gran Hotel Iximche, built on the site that was occupied by an army compound during most of the 1980s. The view to the north of the plaza is dominated by a line of mountains; on one peak a cross was erected to look down over the town. The tops of these mountains surely offer a spectacular view of the whole Tecpán valley, though in the early 1990s local residents cautioned against going there because of the danger of running into guerrillas or army patrols.

The post-earthquake buildings that line the streets of Tecpán reflect

FIGURE 2.6. Brick stove. Author photo.

FIGURE 2.7. Adobe houses in Patzún. Author photo.

the uniformity of hasty reconstructions and the gradual addition of piecemeal extensions to accommodate growing families. The cinderblock walls of house compounds line the streets and present a common defense against inquisitive eyes, making it difficult to determine just where one family's property ends and another's begins. Behind their walls, house compounds vary around a common theme. Almost all comprise rooms arranged around a central courtyard. Some rooms are connected by a doorway, while others are independent, even structurally separate, from the main building. Most houses have a *troje* (room or building where maize is stored) and a *pila* (an outdoor sink where clothes and dishes are washed and water is kept) in the main courtyard. About 25 percent of the houses in Tecpán have a *tuj*, a type of sweat bath long used by the Maya for bathing as well as for ritual purposes.

Traditionally, *tujs* are conical in shape and made of adobe (see Figure 2.8). Today, most *tujs* are cinder-block constructions, six to eight feet square, with a roof that reaches four to five feet at its apex, although one successful family in Tecpán has a *tuj* that seats up to eight

FIGURE 2.8. A traditional adobe *tuj*. Author photo.

people, is large enough to comfortably stand in, and has a built-in shower for washing off before leaving. The main door of the *tuj* is usually about three feet high, requiring one to crawl in on hands and knees; while the *tuj* is in use this door is covered by a thick wool blanket. A much smaller opening allows access to a dirt fireplace surrounded by volcanic stones. In preparing a *tuj* for use, a metal bucket of water is placed inside next to the hearth, and a fire is built. The fire is then allowed to burn down to coals, which takes two to three hours, and the *tuj* door is left open to let out most of the smoke. The *tuj* will now stay warm for several hours, allowing the whole family to bathe. Same-sex relatives often bathe together two or three at a time; less frequently, couples bathe together, taking advantage of their only opportunity for complete privacy in the house. One enters the *tuj* with a candle and two buckets, one empty and one filled with cold water. The cold and hot water are mixed together in the empty bucket, and one first bathes and then enjoys the heat, lying on the wooden plank bench and occasionally sprinkling the rocks with water to produce more steam. Inside the *tuj*, one is naked, completely exposed physically, and it is often a time of intense intimacy and personal reflection, with conversations touching on the most personal of concerns.

Despite the fact that Guatemala bills itself as the land of eternal spring, Tecpán is considered a cold place. It is said to be far too cold to raise turkeys, for example, so when they are needed for a large fiesta, they must be bought at markets in Antigua, Sololá, or even Patzún, all considered to be substantially warmer. The cold never reaches levels of physical danger (snow, for example, is unheard of, and the average temperature is 17° C), but most Maya Tecpanecos also believe that the cold can be metaphysically harmful. Important aspects of local Maya cosmology rest on axiomatic principles of balance and equilibrium, and this balance is often expressed through categorizations of metaphysical temperature. To be chronically cold — in one's physical person as well as in one's personality — can sap the will to live and the force that animates life. To be cold, then, is a dangerous condition, and *tujs* thus serve both hygienic and spiritual functions, cleansing the body while warming the soul. *Tujs* are often called "little volcanoes" because of the resemblance of their traditional design to mountains and volcanoes, and volcanoes and caves in mountains are both considered to be geographic locations where metaphysical heat and power are concentrated (discussed further in Chapter 6; cf. Wilson 1995).

Patzún is considered to be a much warmer place than Tecpán, and thus to enjoy a healthier climate. Patzún's warmth, however, is partly a function of its proximity to the hot lowland areas to its west, home to Guatemala's sugar and cotton plantations. Patzuneros have long engaged in seasonal labor on these plantations, a mixed blessing at best. Employing mostly migratory laborers who also maintain subsistence plots in their home communities, plantation owners are able to pay below-subsistence-level wages. In effect, household food production subsidizes the labor costs of sugar, cotton, and other such commodities on the world market, providing Guatemala with a slight competitive edge. The plantation business is also notorious for its coercive labor recruitment and retention practices, including offering high-interest loans well in advance of the harvest season and indebting workers through inflated charges for room, board, and company-store purchases. Although plantation labor provides an important source of income for many poor households, Patzuneros most often view this as coming at the expense of personal health, social relations, and the maintenance of family lands. At the same time, as Kearney (1996) points out for Mixtec households, the income derived from such seasonal labor often provides the cash Patzún households require to pay taxes and utility bills and to buy seed, fertilizer, and pesticides for milpa production.

As in all tropical regions, the area around Tecpán and Patzún has two seasons, one wet and one dry. Sporadic rains begin in late April and early May, rapidly increasing to an intensity and frequency maintained from late May until mid-October, when they begin to subside, stopping completely sometime in November. Late November until the following May is marked by an almost complete absence of rain. A migratory white bird, the *azacuán,* is said to fly ahead of the rains, announcing their imminent arrival every year. These birds are considered messengers of the gods, and, as such, they not only announce the rains but also bear witness to the continued favor of the gods. Yet the rains often bring their own particular problems.

FIELDNOTES — TECPÁN, APRIL 11, 1994

Today the rain came. Since the construction workers had yet to begin laying the asphalt for the *calle principal* that leads to Iximche', it will now be another year before the road is paved. This is the second consecutive year that the same thing has happened, and I imagine that this road will turn out to be one of the most costly in the country. When we moved to Tecpán in November of 1993, the roadbed was at least three feet below driveways and front doors. In January, crews began hauling loads of dirt, sand, and gravel to build it up over three feet high, a process that took over three months. And now, it will all wash away, just as it did last year.

A broader range of social seasons is reflected in the surprisingly strict sequence of games the children in Tecpán and Patzún play. Throughout the year one finds groups of boys and young men congregated at street corners wagering on games of chance, or rather games of fate, as a winner's luck is attributed to its cosmic source. Bets range from a few centavos for adolescents to hundreds of quetzales at high-stakes games. Starting at Carnival season, *taba* is the game of choice. The *taba* is an animal's knee-cap, and prestige is attached to the largest *tabas*, those of bulls being the best. Players toss the *taba*, betting on whether it will fall convex-side up or down. By default, the thrower bets that it will fall convex-side up, his opponents bet the opposite, and their money is laid down on the playing area. Spectators may then bet among themselves. *Taba* is played throughout Carnival, Lent, and Holy Week. By the start of the rainy season, marbles have replaced *taba* as the preferred game. Players explain that the rain settles the dust of the town's dirt streets, creating hard, flat playing fields. The boys, and less often girls, try to hit the marbles of their opponents, thus removing them from the game; the owner of the last marble left wins. By August, tops have replaced marbles as the main game occupying children's time. Among the many ways to compete with tops are "Kill the Pig" (in which players try to overturn opponents' tops) and playing with marbles (pushing marbles with a top across a finish line drawn in the dirt). Acorns are also used as tops, and they seem to work quite well, although most children now play with store-bought wooden models (see Figure 2.9). In the fall, interest turns to yo-yos, with players racing to complete ten or one hundred up-down cycles or engaging in various games with more complex rules, such as mandating the hand motions one must make when setting the yo-yo off on a cycle. In late October and November, kites replace yo-yos as the diversion of choice, and the Day of the Dead (November 1) always promises a colorful display of elaborate homemade kites flown in the cemetery, with messages to dead ancestors attached to the tails. As Christmas approaches, cards occupy the attention of youths,

FIGURE 2.9. Playing tops in Tecpán. Author photo.

who play various poker and hearts-derived games. And so the cycle continues.

### Places and Names

Just as Guatemalans frequently point out that the United States is not by itself America, Tecpanecos often note that the name of their town is Tecpán Guatemala, not just Tecpán. Indeed it appears that the country itself was named for the Nahuatl toponym for the precolonial Kaqchikel polity of Iximche', located at what is today Tecpán. Edmonson (1971: 3) speculates that the word "Guatemala" derives from the Nahuatl *quauhtlamallan* (place of many trees), a literal translation of the ethnonym "K'iche'" (many trees). However, in a letter from Iximche' dated July 27, 1524, Pedro de Alvarado writes, "I left the city of Uclatan [Utatlán, the K'iche' capital] and arrived in two days to this city of Guatemala where I was very well received" (1972:46), clearly using "Guatemala" to refer to Kaqchikel territory, specifically to its capital at Iximche', and not to the K'iche' polity. Further evidence to support this interpretation comes from a drawing executed by an unknown Tlaxcalan artist from Central Mexico who accompanied Alvarado on his conquests (see Chavero 1979:79). Shown in Figure 2.10, the scene, titled *Quauhtemallá,* depicts Alvarado and his Tlaxcalan troops attacking the Kaqchikeles. Above the heads of the combatants, the artist includes a stylized drawing of an eagle (a *quauhtli* in Nahuatl). It thus seems most likely that the Kaqchikel area was known to Nahuatl-speaking Central Mexicans as "the place of the eagles." "Tecpán" likewise derives from a Nahuatl word often glossed as "palace" or "capital," thus "Tecpán" and "Guatemala" would have been used together to refer to Iximche' as the capital of the Kaqchikel polity.

Writing at the end of the seventeenth century, Fuentes y Guzmán (1933:387) reports that Tecpán was locally known as Patinamit and the archaeological site of Iximche' as Ohertinamit (see also Gall 1983). The Kaqchikel word *tinamit,* derived from the Nahuatl *tinamitl* (Edmonson 1971:3), may be glossed in English as "town," and *pa* serves as a directional prefix meaning "in," with the connotation of "place of"; thus Patinamit translates as "in [the] town." *Ojer* (or *oher*) means "old," and so Ojertinamit is "[the] old town." One might assume from this that Fuentes y Guzmán fell into the trap of one of the oldest of linguistic misunderstandings: when asked "where do you live?" his native informants replied "in the town," or, when referring to the site of the former

FIGURE 2.10. The Tlaxcalans at Iximche'. Drawing by Mareike Sattler based on reproductions in Chavero 1979.

Kaqchikel capital, "the old town." However, Tecpanecos and Patzuneros alike often refer today to Tecpán as Patinamit, suggesting that perhaps Fuentes y Guzmán's recording was accurate. Tecpán, having first been home to the Kaqchikel capital and then for a brief period to the Spanish capital and the center for the region of the new political-economic order, was *the* town in the area. Just as people often refer to Guatemala City today as "the city" and suburbanites refer to New York as "the city," Tecpán was "the town."

The name "Patzún" has several possible etymologies. As mentioned, the Kaqchikel *pa* means "in." The last part of the name may come from *su'n,* a type of sunflower found in the area today, and this is the interpretation promoted by the Rubios brand cigarette billboards located at the entrances to the town. A more likely etymology derives the word from *pa* and *tz'un* (leather). Several Patzuneros tell of the town having once been a dependent *aldea* under the political control of Tecpán.

When *aldea* residents decided to form a separate town, they bought their land from Tecpán, with part of the payment being one of the bells now in Tecpán's church. The land sold was measured and marked with a rope made of leather (which Robert Hill informs me was not an unusual practice), and the new town was named "the place of leather," or Patzún in its hispanicized form. Historical records fail to confirm this account, although Patzún was certainly in the immediate sphere of influence of first Iximche' and then Tecpán, and oral histories in Tecpán corroborate the story of the church bell.

Given the importance of historical representation to national pan-Mayanist agendas, one might expect that a significant percentage of Indians in Tecpán and Patzún would espouse revisionist views of local history, emphasizing the grandeur of precontact Kaqchikel society and the active role their ancestors played in the colonial development of their towns. In fact, when asked when and how Tecpán was founded, all those who responded to my survey said simply, "July 25th, 1524," the date Pedro de Alvarado is said to have established a Spanish capital at Iximche'. Only 4 of 168 respondents (2.4% of the sample) went on to explain the importance of Iximche' as a powerful precolonial center. (I should note that David Carey collected oral histories of Tecpán from a number of local Kaqchikel speakers in 1997 and 1998. Though his sample was biased toward local cultural activists, it is significant that he found that a heightened awareness of Iximche's importance provides people from Tecpán with "a keen sense that their ancestors predated the Spanish arrival" [n.d.:85].) In Patzún, only 5 respondents to my survey (2.7% of the sample) claimed knowledge about how and when their town was founded, and each reported that Patzún was formerly an *aldea* of Tecpán.

The local view of history as reported in Tecpán largely conforms to state-sanctioned historical representations, with Spanish contact being the starting point. This folk historiography provides a common foundation for the construction of local identity by transcending ethnic boundaries. Tecpán is often described by individuals from neighboring areas as a progressive, rich Indian town, and there is widespread pride among Maya and ladino Tecpanecos alike about the town's illustrious history as the first capital of Guatemala and, to a lesser extent, as the site of the Kaqchikel capital. Tecpanecos are proud of the size of their market, the wealth of local businessmen, and the cosmopolitan nature of local society as seen in the offerings of international programming on the local bootleg cable television system, the availability of AT&T's USADirect international telephone service from the pay phone at the town hall, and the occasional presence of foreign anthropologists and linguists.

Patzuneros, although they share less of a common memory of their history, also take pride in their community. The belief that Patzún was once an *aldea* of Tecpán that gained independence highlights the importance of geographic commonality in the construction of local identity and the value placed on self-determination and social cohesiveness. The Patzún version of history situates the town's origin in a regional context, tying it to Tecpán, whereas the Tecpán version ties that town's history to the global process of Spanish colonization. Thus, the more parochial view of history found in Patzún is closely tied to Kaqchikel history (through its relationship with Tecpán), whereas the view from Tecpán is more closely tied to the history of Spanish expansion. In a sense, the Tecpanecos' views of the world and their place in it are less myopic than those commonly found in Patzún, even if both are recognizable variations on a common theme.

### Histories of Assimilation and Resistance

Spanish chroniclers, Fuentes y Guzmán (1933), Vázquez (1937), and Cortés y Larraz (1958), as well as the North American adventurer Stephens (1949), all mention Tecpán and Patzún in their writings. Tecpán consistently merits greater consideration, but one gains the impression that both towns were seen as generally unremarkable. David McCreery (1994:40) writes that in colonial and postcolonial times, "from the edges of the plains of Chimaltenango through the Sierra de los Cuchumatánes the western *altiplano* was above all the domain of the Indian." From this perspective, both Tecpán and Patzún lay on the border between the Indian and Spanish worlds of colonial Guatemala. The towns maintained ties to colonial Spanish society, and the royal road (*camino real*), which connected Mexico City to its subsidiary seats of government to the south, ran through both towns. Yet both were overwhelmingly inhabited by Indians and were closely tied to indigenous regional markets to the west. Tecpán and Patzún were of comparable size in the late seventeenth century: Hill (1992:28) reports that Patzún's population was approximately 2,400 and Tecpán's population was about 2,800. By 1770, Tecpán's population had grown to 5,708 while Patzún's had increased to only 3,600, reflecting a greater integration of Tecpán into the Spanish political economy.

Among the documents in the cramped and musty stacks of the Archivo General de Centro América (AGCA) in Guatemala City are the proceedings of a lawsuit filed in 1658 by Indians from Tecpán against two prominent local creole landowners.[2] Folios 30r through 44r of the document are three separate texts written in Kaqchikel (a court-ordered Spanish translation follows), commonly known as the Títulos Xpantzay (see Berlin 1950; Carmack 1973; Recinos 1984; Hill 1992). Carmack (1973:50) believes that the Kaqchikel portions were written in the 1550s, though they were not submitted to the court until 1658. The first document is titled "Título Original 1524 años" and is signed "Don Pedro de Alvarado"; it can be assumed that this date is not accurate and was included only to add authenticity to Indian claims to their ancestral lands. The other two documents provide a history of the Xpantzay family, who were nobles before Spanish contact and who remained important leaders in the Tecpán community throughout the colonial period. Most scholarly attention has focused on these pages of indigenous text, though the lawsuit as a whole paints an interesting picture of indigenous resistance to Spanish rule. The story begins in 1569 when the Spanish Crown granted a large plot of land to Alonso Gutiérrez de Monzón. The only condition of the grant was that large herds of cows, bulls, and horses (*ganado mayor*) were not to be raised on the land, as they would threaten adjacent Indian crops. By the mid–seventeenth century the land in question had been passed down over several generations and had been transferred between families at least once. Eventually the land was inherited by Francisco de Argueta, who proceeded to place several large herds of cattle on the land. Thus it was that in 1658 Pedro López Expanxay (Xpantzay) led a group of kinsmen and other Indians from Tecpán in suing Argueta for return of the land, based on Argueta's violation of the terms of the grant. Legal proceeding lasted for five years until, in 1663, Xpantzay and the other plaintiffs won their suit against Argueta; Figure 2.11 shows the area that the court mandated be returned to the Indians. That the Indian plaintiffs won counters simplistic representations of colonial oppression and shows the willingness and capability of Tecpaneco Indians to work within the Spanish legal tradition to fight for their own self-advancement (see also Hill 1989:179–187).

Despite such sporadic gains, the extent of Indian-held plots and

FIGURE 2.11. Map of land returned to Tecpán Indians in the Xpantzay lawsuit. Tecpán in upper left; Patzún in lower right. Photo by Robert Hill; with permission from the Archivo General de Centro América.

communal lands was greatly eroded during the colonial period. This process was further accelerated after Guatemala's independence from Spain, propelled by the increasing acceptance of liberal economic tenets. In 1836, the liberal government passed legislation that mandated that all communal lands be converted to private property, and though the implementation of the law suffered setbacks from conservative and Indian resistance, the legislation was frequently used by ambitious ladino landowners seeking to expand their holdings. David McCreery writes that ladinos took advantage of the law to obtain Indian communal lands in Tecpán, and that by the 1860s it was apparent that "ladinos had been 'buying' small plots in Tecpán's ejidos since the early colonial period, 'and from these many small pieces they formed large plantations and pastures, considering themselves owners and lords of this land and controlling the ejidos'" (McCreery 1994:82, quoting from a document in the Sección de Tierras of the AGCA). Today, a few small plots of community forest are all that remain of Tecpán's once extensive communal lands, and these are threatened not so much by ruthless ladino plantation owners as by greedy elected officials.

## Local Government

Local politics in both Tecpán and Patzún are based on a fluid and complex system of partisanship that involves kinship ties, barrio associations, class allegiances, and ethnic positions. One gains the impression that there is much backroom maneuvering among local ladino elites, although I was never privy to such discussions. When talking about local political leaders, residents of both Tecpán and Patzún often speak of other nonelected individuals — sometimes named, more often not — who hold the "real" power and call the shots for those in public office. Somewhat cynically, it is assumed that many, if not most, political decisions reflect such partisanship, and thus local politics are often fraught with personal animosities.

During the colonial period, Tecpán and Patzún were classified as *pueblos indios* and at that time formal positions of local authority were mandatorily occupied by Indians, most of whom claimed precontact noble ties. As the political insulation surrounding Indian towns was gradually reduced, and ladino populations increased in size and importance, parallel structures of governance emerged. One, led by Indians, represented indigenous concerns and managed local Maya festivals and communal lands. The other, led by ladinos, governed most other town affairs and implemented state-mandated policies. This dual structure broke down under attack from the nation-building legal reforms promoted by the Guatemalan state in the 1940s and 1950s. Under these reforms, the state recognized only a single system of municipal governance, a move that effectively allowed ladinos to monopolize local government posts.

This monopoly changed in the late 1960s, as Indians in Tecpán, Patzún, and other Maya communities began to better coordinate their participation in local elections. As a result, since 1970 Patzún's government has been dominated by Indians. In elections in 1970, 1972, 1974, and 1976, Indians from the moderate Christian Democratic Party won the post of alcalde (mayor). In the 1978 election, held as General Romeo Lucas García emerged as the winner of fraudulent national elections for president, an Indian from the Partido Revolucionario (Lucas García's party) was elected alcalde, but he declined to take office because of the dangers associated with escalating war in the country. A ladino businessman stepped in to assume the post, but he was soon assassinated (reportedly by the guerrillas). The governor of the Department of Chimaltenango then installed a well-respected Indian man as alcalde, and Indians have held the post ever since. Politics in Patzún are marked by the participation of a number of active and powerful *comités cívicos*, which are de facto local political parties that, provided the *comités* are recognized by the state's Supreme Electoral Tribunal, can nominate candidates for local offices. Although rarely posing a substantial threat to more established parties, *comités cívicos* almost always support Maya candidates, and they are rapidly becoming an important vehicle for Maya political activism (de Paz 1993:60–75). In Patzún, the *comités cívicos* provide an important means through which Indians are able to pursue their political interests while avoiding the associations with national party politics that are often viewed locally with suspicion. As a sign of their importance, in November 1995 an Indian candidate from the Comité Cívico de Patzún (COPA, whose symbol is the sun rising over a milpa) was elected alcalde.[3]

Elections in Patzún are held every two years, but Tecpán, because of its official status as a *ciudad*, elects an alcalde every four years. As in Patzún, an Indian was elected alcalde in Tecpán in 1970, marking a significant shift in local political structures. The 1970 election was important first because of the mobilization of Indian voters who voted en masse for the first time. Throughout the 1950s and 1960s education levels of Indians in Tecpán (as well as in other parts of the country) had steadily increased, due in large part to the efforts of the state's bilingual education program. The resulting better-educated and more politically savvy Indian electorate chose the 1970 election to nominate Vascilio Cua, a traditional though politically moderate Indian, as candidate for mayor in a test of the integrity of the democratic process. Winning over a number of ladino landowners with a platform of maintaining the status quo, Cua was supported by the Christian Democratic Party and, surprisingly, swept the elections. He is remembered by local Indians as an honest and humble man who always wore traditional dress (*traje*), even at political functions, and preferred to speak in Kaqchikel.

The subsequent 1974 elections brought to office Santiago Colom, another Indian candidate put forth by the Christian Democrats, who, like Cua, always wore *traje* and spoke in Kaqchikel. Both these Indian mayors are remembered as honest but not highly effective. One man recalls that "though they did not rob from the city coffers, . . . they did not do a lot for the development of Tecpán." Colom, for example, is said to have refused to let GUATEL (the state telephone company) install lines in Tecpán because the telephone would bring in corrupting outside influences. Colom is also reported to have said, "I was poor when I went into office, I was poor when I came out, and still people call me a thief: it would have been better to steal something while I was mayor since everyone believes that I did anyway." (Colom's *primer consejal*, his top aide, later became one of the first persons "disappeared" from Tecpán in 1980.)

Just as in Patzún, a ladino won Tecpán's controversial 1978 election, a result widely explained as a backlash to the slow pace of change preferred by his Maya predecessors. The new ladino alcalde, Caterino Galiendo, served only until 1981, when he was killed ( *justificado*) by the guerrillas in an attack on the town hall. In the aftermath of the attack, the military occupied Tecpán and gathered together all the male residents in a public meeting to elect a new alcalde. Under the watchful eyes of the army, residents elected Pedro Tocoro, an Indian man who was to serve his full term, from 1981 to 1985. It is unclear whether Tocoro previously had ties to the army, but after his election, he quickly allied himself with this obviously greater power. Around the same time, the army installed Margarito Costop, a friend of Tocoro's, as the local civilian military commissioner. From 1981 to 1985, Tocoro and Costop largely acted under the direction of army officials, while managing to pursue long-standing personal vendettas and to enrich themselves through various forms of extortion. (In 1993, Costop was arrested after extorting Q50,000 [approximately US$9,000 at the time] from a former friend in Tecpán by threatening to kill the man's four children.)

In 1985 Felipe Sapor Chalí was elected as Tecpán's alcalde, and he was the first to serve the five-year term mandated by the 1985 constitution. Sapor is widely believed to have made a small fortune by selling wood from the communal forest. After he left office, a biethnic commission was formed to look into his financial activities and possibly pursue prosecution. The committee mysteriously dissolved after a private meeting with Sapor, and most of my informants believe that the committee members were bribed. It is said that during Sapor's term a number of ladinos tried to take over control of the local armed civil patrols. One Indian man told me that the ladinos hoped "this would be a chance to finally kill some Indians." This same man went on to explain why the ladino plot failed: "it was us, the Indians, who first made contact with the military—look at Tocoro and Costop—and it was us who formed the civil patrols, and so the army did not turn against us."

In 1990 Sarapio Xuya Ajcet, a Christian Democrat and a soft-spoken Kaqchikel man who always formally dressed in a coat and hat, was elected alcalde. Xuya initiated a number of large public works projects, including expanding the town's indoor market and restoring the town hall to its colonial glory. Nonetheless, he, like so many of Tecpán's alcaldes in the past, has been accused of stealing wood from community lands. By 1994 he was looking forward to leaving public office.

In anticipation of the 1995 elections, a number of Indians formed a *comité cívico* to nominate a candidate for alcalde. Members of the committee complained that while Xuya may not be corrupt, he is neither dynamic nor aggressive enough to fight for the town's development.

FIELDNOTES — TECPÁN, APRIL 30, 1994

At a party for his daughter's quinceaños, Víctor and I got a chance to talk for a while and I asked him about the *comité cívico* he was forming. He said that the problem here in Tecpán was that nobody wants to participate, that they were still timid from the violence, and that they had held a preliminary reunion and only one person came out of the twenty invited. Everyone said that it was a good idea and told him "do it," but nobody wants to be in at first. He said that here people were too extreme, either leftists or rightists, "to the point that they promote violence," and that there was very little middle ground.

Although the *comité cívico* did eventually coalesce and nominate a candidate for alcalde, the group divided over kinship and barrio ties before the election, paving the way for an uncontroversial ladino bureaucrat to be elected.

## Military Presence

The local governments of both Tecpán and Patzún occupy a tenuous position between constituent mandates and state authority. During the early 1980s in particular, the power of local government was largely usurped by the military. In Patzún, the army first established a presence in the town following the 1976 earthquake but then greatly increased local forces in the early 1980s. On December 20, 1982, guerrillas bombed Patzún's police station, a favored target in attacks throughout the highlands, and held off local army troops for two days. Military reinforcements arrived in town four days later, surrounding the town center and declaring martial law. The army maintained a strong presence in town for the next several years, although they never built a formal garrison. From 1981 to 1987 all local adult males were required to participate in the notorious Patrullas de Acción Cívico (PACs; Civic Action Patrols). The PACs were organized by the national police and the army; although armed with only sticks, machetes, and the occasional antique rifle, the patrols were charged with protecting the town against guerrillas from 8 P.M. to 8 A.M., seven days a week. Ostensibly voluntary (but in practice mandatory), participation in the PACs placed an onerous burden on local Maya men, taking time away from their farming and other productive activities (see Krueger and Enge 1985). During this time the local military commissioner required everyone in town with a vehicle to pay a Q300 (at the time, equivalent to US$300) war tax, money used to buy a pickup truck later employed in kidnapping several suspected guerrilla sympathizers. In 1989 the military abruptly left Patzún. Many claim that town residents kicked the army out; others state that several Patzuneros hold high positions in the military and that they ordered the evacuation to protect their community. Whatever the cause, Patzuneros are proud of their independence from the military and see it as a sign of community cohesiveness and self-determination.

In Tecpán, an army presence has been felt more directly. For almost ten years, starting in the early 1980s, the army occupied one square block off the town square. Neighbors recall the screams that would come from the compound at night, and almost everyone in town had a relative or close friend called to the barracks for questioning, never to be seen again. Tecpanecos remember 1981 as the year in which the violence took hold in their town. In May of 1981, Tecpán's Catholic priest was shot down by masked men outside the parish house on a busy market day. Although he was no radical, he did promote ethnic reconciliation and even attempted to learn the Kaqchikel language. His assassins are described by eyewitnesses as two men, riding a large motorcycle, dressed in dark fatigues and wearing black masks. Recollections of a rapid burst of shots suggest that the gunman had an automatic weapon. The assassins drove straight through town, despite the streets being closed for market day and filled with vendors, and escaped immediately down the Pan-American Highway. The local office of the national police force refused to conduct more than a cursory investigation of the murder.

In late November of the same year, guerrillas, perhaps in reaction to the murder of the priest, occupied the town for one day, holding all the municipal officials in the town hall before blowing up it, the police station, and the jail with dynamite. One man recalls being on his way to catch a bus into the city, around midday. As he approached the town square he heard much commotion, followed by a number of gunshots. Seeing people begin to flee, he crawled underneath a nearby bus and soon heard two massive explosions that shook the ground. Shortly after this attack, the military set up their feared garrison just off the town square.

During this time, life was greatly disrupted, and it was no longer even safe to cultivate fields located in outlying hamlets, as these could be used to provision guerrilla troops. An unknown number of individuals were kidnapped, tortured, and killed. Twenty clandestine graves have been discovered in the area around Tecpán, and it is likely that the actual number is much higher (see Figure 2.12).

Similar to the situation Paul and Demarest (1988) recount for San Pedro La Laguna, local officials in Tecpán with actual or presumed military ties often used their positions for self-enrichment or to carry out revenge for past grievances. One elderly woman recalls having to regularly pay a military commissioner from the proceeds of her market stall in order to keep her children's names off the military hit list.

Indians in Tecpán often speak of the early 1980s as the time when the monkeys came out of the hills. It is said that one could hear their cries as they ran through the streets at night. People tried to stay inside their homes to avoid meeting the monkeys, for it is believed that when a person is caught by a monkey, he or she becomes one as well. Local Maya believe that monkey people appear human much of the time, only taking on the physical appearance of monkeys on certain nights, but that they are at all times a conduit for evil forces. Carol Hendrickson (personal communication 1999) reports stories of such individuals taking the form of monkeys at their death as well. Clearly the prohibition on night excursions, based on a fear of monkeys, was utilitarian: if not monkeys, then certainly guerrillas and soldiers were a dangerous presence. Interestingly, Bricker (1973:91) reports that during Carnival festivities in Chamula, a group of courtiers called the Monkeys, who wear uniforms reminiscent of French grenadiers, are sometimes addressed with military titles. She further notes that "in Chamula mythology the monkey is symbolically equivalent to the *pukuh* (evil spirit)" (Bricker 1973:93; see also Gossen 1999). Though monkey stories in Tecpán do not reflect the comical aspect of monkeys seen in Chamula, there seems to be a certain link between these cultural representations of monkeys,

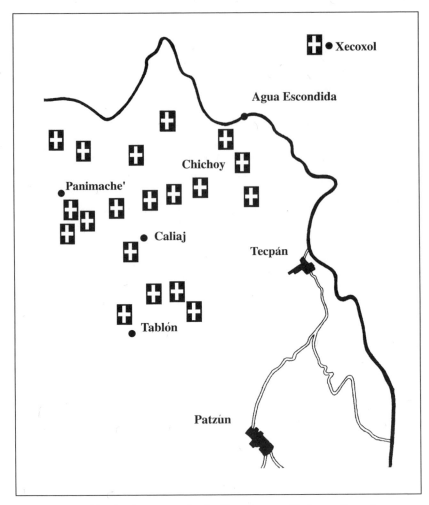

FIGURE 2.12. Clandestine graves in the Tecpán area. Redrawn from the Grupo de Apoyo Mutuo and *Prensa Libre*.

perhaps indicating ancient Maya beliefs. Accusations of being a monkey, which are not distinguished from those of being an *aj itz* (evil sorcerer), are also used to sanction social deviance; the two individuals that I know and heard accused of being monkeys are both antisocial, unmarried, and stingy, and they rarely bathed. Monkey people are also said to possess mysterious books that hold the secrets of evil sorcery and are often filled with illustrations of fantastic and grotesque creatures. At one level these books and their illustrations symbolize the powerful and potentially dangerous chaos of the wild (as opposed to the orderliness of social community) to which monkey people have succumbed. In the context of the violence of the early 1980s, they also represented the danger of the written word and of possessing literature that could be interpreted as subversive by the military.

In 1989 the army garrison was moved to the former Casa de Cultura (Culture Center) next to the municipal soccer field on the edge of town, and in 1995 it was moved still farther away, to a location alongside the Pan-American Highway. By the mid-1990s the violence had died down, and kidnappings and disappearances had become more rare. In fact, the one kidnapping in town that occurred in 1993–1994 was attributed to ex-soldiers, using the skills they learned when working for the army. In this case, a ransom was demanded and paid, and the person was released unharmed. Local residents found this less frightening and more comprehensible than the seemingly random kidnappings of the 1980s. Nonetheless, the army's presence is still felt in everyday life: army patrols still march through town at strategic times meant to intimidate the local population. For example, in 1993 a ritual feast honoring a local saint, Maxutio, was resurrected for the first time in twelve years. Before the violence, the image of Maxutio would be paraded through town as his caretakers recited embarrassing rumors about prominent townspeople and read lists of grievances against local officials (see Warren 1978 for an account of this figure in the nearby community of San Andrés Semetabaj). The organizer of the Tecpán Maxutio feast was murdered in 1981, and the celebration was abandoned until 1993. During the 1993 parade, soldiers followed along the edge of the crowd of spectators, making derisive comments to one another, and not surprisingly, no gossip or grievances were publicized. On another occasion, in 1994, a group of Maya priests gathered at the site of Iximche' for a ceremony, during which the army chose to schedule machine-gun practice in the forest surrounding the site.

Although the period of *la violencia* is formally over, its effects shape the culture of both towns, and many fear its recurrence. It is thus only with great trepidation that local residents have been willing to participate in the sorts of cultural activities promoted by the pan-Maya movement.

PART

II

*Global Processes*

*and Pan-Maya*

*Identity Politics*

# 3

# Guatemalan Political Economies and the World System

Capitalist modernization, particularly in the case of a dependent capitalism with strong Indian roots, does not always destroy traditional cultures as it moves forward; it can also appropriate them, restructure them, reorganize the meaning and function of their objects, beliefs, and practices. . . . In order to integrate the popular classes into the process of capitalist development, the dominant classes destructure ethnic, class, and national cultures—all of them, though, subject to a common logic—and reorganize them into a unified system of symbolic production.

NÉSTOR GARCÍA CANCLINI (1993)

To understand daily life in places like Tecpán and Patzún it is necessary to look beyond town boundaries to the larger systems that affect local conditions. In this chapter and the next, I turn attention away from the particulars of lived social experience in Tecpán and Patzún to examine the restraints imposed by national and international contexts of political economic relations. In particular, I focus on Guatemala's changing position in the world system and how this has affected Maya culture and identity politics at the national level. These data will then provide the macro framework for increasingly specific descriptions of Maya culture in Tecpán and Patzún in the chapters that follow.

## The Changing World System

The changes in and dramatic restructuring of the global economic system over the last two decades have forced us to reconsider many of the assumptions of classic world-system theories. There is no broad agreement on what to call this new phase of globalization: Fredric Jameson (1991) terms it "late capitalism," Lash and Urry (1987) prefer to call it the "end of organized capitalism," and Jonathan Friedman (1994) sees it as a "post-dependency phase" of world capitalism. All agree that it is a fundamentally new stage of capitalist development related to post-industrialization and post-Fordism (marked by a shift of investment and consumption toward information and service sectors) in core countries and processes of transnationalization (especially drastic reductions in transportation and communication costs and the lowering of tariff barriers) affecting peripheral areas. As the virtual collapsing of time-space distances allows for the creation of ever larger markets, the boundaries between core and peripheral areas become increasingly blurred. Today, industrial production—formerly the hallmark of developed economies—is rapidly being moved from core areas to peripheral regions, reversing the classic pattern of modern global commodity flows (periphery → core → periphery). No longer are raw materials simply imported from peripheral countries and processed in core areas, where exchange value accumulates. Increasingly, assembly, if not complete production, of consumer goods destined for sale in both core and peripheral countries is carried out in peripheral regions. This shift in production implies a decentralization of capital accumulation patterns between the core and periphery at both the global and local levels.

Transnationalism encourages direct articulation between peripheral economic formations and global markets, unmediated by state-level, elite-dominated market structures. This increases efficiency, as resources that were formerly allocated toward directly unproductive profit seeking (maintaining the legal distortions in market structures that act to funnel capital flows to the core) are invested in production (Bhagwati 1982; de Soto 1986). Such a reallocation of capital resources (cutting out the middlemen) has had a significant impact on social relations. It would seem, as Friedman (1994) suggests, that a decentralization of capital accumulation at the global scale (post-dependency world capitalism) is closely correlated with the revival of ethnic interests. The decentralization of capital accumulation has greatly benefited many marginalized ethnic groups, who begin to see (whether for socio-biological [van den Berghe 1981] or political-economic [Smith 1984a] reasons) that their best interests are represented not by a state, but by a nation or ethnic group. Thus the irony of transnationalization is that it leads to heightened nationalism, or as Lash and Urry (1994:17) put it, "globalized localization."

Friedman (1994) argues that the world system is characterized by alternating periods of hegemonic expansion from a few powerful centers and subsequent periods of fragmentation and hegemonic contraction. During "stable hegemonic phases," the global political economy largely conforms to the predictions of world-system theory. In contrast, during periods of core hegemonic contraction, "new small and rapidly expanding centers emerge, outcompeting central production, leading eventually to a situation in which the center becomes increasingly the consumer of the products of its own exported capital" (1994:169). The post–Cold War era of late-twentieth-century global capitalism presents a new case of simultaneous expansion and contraction in core hegemonic structures. On the one hand, a pronounced expansion of certain dominant Western political ideologies has occurred (as seen in discourses of "liberal democracy," "free markets," "neoliberalism," "transparency," and so on). At the same time, there has been a dramatic increase of investment in core areas in fictive (i.e., nonproductive) capital that has led to decentralized patterns of global capital accumulation benefiting formerly peripheral areas (cf. Jameson 1991).

This decentralization of global patterns of capital accumulation has ideologically stimulated and materially underwritten movements to revive ethnic traditions long submerged by Western expansion, as is the case of Maya identity politics in Guatemala. Nelson notes that post-Fordist processes "help form the conditions of possibility for Maya-hackers [read: cultural activists], state support for Mayan cultural rights, and Guatemala's peace process" (1999:355). She goes on to observe that "just as Mayan culture played a role in liberal and dependency models of national development (explaining backwardness and the failure of revolution), it also helps structure Guatemala's participation in global post-Fordism" (ibid.). Below I detail the changing role of Maya culture in state development programs and world-system models, leading to an analysis of how macrolevel political economic processes have shaped contemporary Maya strategies of identity politics.

### *Essentialism as Theory and as Realpolitik*

Essentialist perspectives of culture have long underwritten modernist state policies in Guatemala. In this view, Indians have been perceived by the Guatemalan state as a hindrance to the form of modern government they aspire to, namely the nation-state model stemming from the Western tradition (Fischer 1996; cf. Bonfil Batalla 1981 on this process in Mexico). The seeds of this thought may be traced to the enlightened liberal politics that emerged in Guatemala in the late eighteenth century and flourished intermittently after independence in 1821. The liberals envisioned a state based on the model of Europe nation-statehood, which involved integrating the Indians into Western society. An educated yet homogeneous population was seen as key to political stability and economic prosperity. The liberal agenda was, superficially at least, less racist than the conservative ideology, for it portrayed Indians not as innately inferior beings but as potentially productive members of society. Nonetheless, in practice — precisely because it was more culturally relativist than conservative thought — the liberal philosophy undermined the material and social bases of Maya culture because it proposed that to realize the political-economic potential of Indians, the Indians must be coerced into abandoning their primitive culture. Indians, or more accurately, Indian cultural forms, were seen as barriers to the creation of a unified nation and thus to progress.

John Browning's (1996) review of state policy toward Indians in the eighteenth and nineteenth centuries documents the changing ideals of that era. He cites a speech by Jacobo de Villaurrutia, secretary of the liberal Sociedad Económica, in which Villaurrutia predicts a prosperous economic future based on cultural assimilation: an initial boom in the manufacture and sale of Spanish clothes and shoes to the Indians, followed by another boom as Indians began to buy European furniture for their houses, and so on, ad infinitum. After independence in 1821, the liberals were finally able to put their ideals into practice, and they worked for fifteen years breaking down the political and economic (and less successfully, social) barriers between Spaniards and Indians and pushing toward modern nation-statehood.

The liberal agenda suffered a great setback in 1839 when the conservative Rafael Carrera came to power and promptly began to dismantle the liberal reforms. Woodward (1993) notes that, initially at least, Carrera's policies acted in the interest of conserving Maya communities, protecting them in colonial fashion from the corrupting influence of non-Indian society. Carrera, a peasant himself, established an alliance of conservative traditionalists to maintain colonial structures based on agriculture and coercive tribute: just the sort of structural irony that Marx (1963 [1852]) outlined in *The Eighteenth Brumaire of Louis Bonaparte* concerning contemporaneous events in France. In 1871, liberals once again came to power under the leadership of Justo Rufino Barrios. Barrios effectively dismantled many of the conservative counter-reforms and initiated a grand scheme of privatization and titling of land-holdings. In the process, many of the indigenous social structures built around communal property were abolished and many Indians lost control over land that their families had cultivated for generations (Mc-Creery 1994). A double blow was dealt to the Indians through the implementation of forced-labor laws, whereby Indians were required to work for the state or for private landowners designated by the state. Under Barrios, a state strategy underwritten by coffee and other large plantation interests took hold that continues to this day, with leaders basing their nation-building project on the model of Western European nation-states. This strategy, however, was not readily embraced by the Indians, as Indian culture forms inhibited Indians from giving up their land and entering into the "free" labor market of plantation workers (see Smith 1984a and 1988 for a provocative analysis of the history of labor and capital interests in Guatemala).

Such modernist, essentialist perspectives underwrote the *indigenista* philosophy that emerged throughout Latin America in the late nineteenth century that was "designed to obtain the conformance of Indians to labor controls through 'civilizing' and 'educating' them" (Adams 1991:181). *Indigenista* policies took on greater importance in the nationalist plans of Latin American leaders in the 1940s, especially after the formation of the Instituto Indigenista Interamericano; Guatemala opened its own Instituto Indigenista Nacional (IIN) in 1945. The *indigenistas* (who were by and large not Indians) espoused their policies in a rhetoric of cultural sensitivity and probably believed in their good intentions, but their ultimate goal was to integrate Indians into homogeneous, non-Indian national societies (see Barre 1982). Following the tenets of essentialist ethnography, the Maya were seen as those people who spoke a Mayan language, wore traditional dress, and practiced precolumbian rites. If they could be made to speak only Spanish, stop wearing traditional dress, and wholeheartedly adopt Christianity, then they would cease to exist as Maya, and the Guatemala state could then claim the status of nationhood so appealing to progressive ladino elites and politicians. This was social engineering at its best and worst—a technocratic elite using state-of-the-art (for the time) social science to formulate policies that sought political and economic development through cultural assimilation (e.g., see Ewald 1967). Nelson (1999:90) quotes an especially straightforward policy statement from a 1956 IIN document: "The Indian with more buying power and with national culture will be a better producer and consumer and a more active citizen.

To achieve this we must adapt him scientifically through our acculturation program." The fact is, of course, that despite the hopes of non-
Indian government officials and the predictions made by essentialist
analyses, the Maya have not disappeared. Indeed, by all accounts there
are more Maya today than at the time of Spanish contact (see Lovell
and Lutz 1995).

## Guatemala: Profile of a Dependent Region

Throughout most of its modern history Guatemala has been a classic
model of Latin American export dependency, the material reality from
which world-system theory was extracted. Actually, Guatemala, like all
countries, has what is best characterized as a mixed economy — mixed
in the sense of both production diversity and ideological consistency.
With a long history of cumbersome bureaucratic control and oligarchi-
cal inside dealings countered in recent years by a push for free-market
reforms and liberal democracy, Guatemala exhibits a particular form of
uneven development that fits neatly into neither classic world-system
theory nor neoclassical assumptions of rationality. At first glance, the
Guatemalan case may appear to be a textbook study in the structures
of political economic dependency that evolved from the colonial en-
counter, and much evidence supports such a view. Guatemala's economy is heavily dependent on the export of a few primary products to
the core markets of North America and Western Europe. The country
is in a structurally weak bargaining position in global commodity markets due to the inelasticity of demand for products such as coffee and
the intense competition from other peripheral tropical regions. An almost insignificant portion of Guatemala's GDP comes from capital-
intensive production, and the country's relative economic advantage
on the world market is low wages for labor-intensive production. A parallel domestic economy of subsistence production subsidizes the seasonal wage labor of plantations. It would seem that to remain linked to
the world economy Guatemala is relegated to a role of dependency in
which it must continue to develop underdevelopment in order to leverage the competitive advantage of poverty (i.e., low wages) in global
markets.

Cambranes (1985) outlines the cycle of economic dependency that
developed in Guatemala during the colonial and early independence
periods. In the mid–eighteenth century, Guatemalan exports consisted

largely of indigo, highly valued in Europe for its deep blue dye. Between 1772 and 1781, Guatemala produced an average yearly yield of 697,200 pounds, virtually all of which was exported. As European markets in luxury goods became more democratic (with money and not social class setting consumption barriers), exports rose to an annual average of 972,189 pounds between 1783 and 1892. By the 1820s, however, indigo markets had become stagnant, prices were falling, and production of the more lucrative cochineal dye had begun to replace indigo in economic importance. Cochineal is a vivid red dye extracted from the cochineal insects that feed on the nepal cactus; the nepal cactus is, conveniently, amenable to plantation life, and large cochineal "farms" expanded rapidly in the areas around Antigua and Atitlán in the early 1800s. By 1824 cochineal had replaced indigo as Guatemala's primary export in terms of earnings, although trade in both dyes continued at a great volume throughout the nineteenth century (Cambranes 1985:23; McCreery 1994:117–122). McCreery argues that cochineal production, based on a few large plantations, "had little direct effect on land tenure or use in most of rural Guatemala" (1994:122). Significantly, McCreery also notes that there were a few small producers of cochineal, especially in the early boom days of the trade, and that traders would make loans to producers payable in dried cochineal after harvest, a pattern that legally replicated the coercive labor practices of colonial plantations, but with an economically liberal justification. By 1870, coffee had replaced dyes as Guatemala's single most important export, a position that it retains to this day (see Figure 3.1).

Though coffee has remained Guatemala's principal export since the late 1860s, other crops have come to supplement these export earnings, primarily bananas, sugar, cardamom, and cotton. All of these exports share the characteristics of being labor (rather than capital) intensive in their production and needing sufficiently large and efficient plantations to enable them to compete on the basis of price with other producers around the world (and, in the case of dyes and sugars, with cheaply produced synthetic alternatives coming out of the Western industrial complex). The high market-entry barriers to such production (namely the need to buy a lot of land, and, especially in the case of coffee, to support production for several years before realizing the first returns on one's investment) keep both economic and political capital restricted to a small class of wealthy, well-connected, and inevitably ladino landowners. This political-economic structure replicates the global pattern

FIGURE 3.1. Coffee and cochineal
exports, 1867–1871, in pesos.

| Year | Coffee | Cochineal |
|------|--------|-----------|
| 1867 | 415,878 | 1,068,047 |
| 1868 | 788,035 | 891,513 |
| 1869 | 790,227 | 1,266,613 |
| 1870 | 1,132,298 | 865,414 |
| 1871 | 1,312,129 | 876,025 |

*Source:* McCreery 1994:126.

of core and periphery relations within the periphery itself, with the geo-graphic references of metropole and hinterland (see Lutz and Lovell 1990).

Although the relative proportions of Guatemala's exports have fluc-tuated over the years, the basic structure of reliance on primary prod-uct exports has remained in place. This agro-export structure was laid down during the colonial period, and its subsequent permutations have not yielded it indistinguishable from its early form. Products have changed and so has the distribution of wealth, although access to the large-scale capital required for entry into plantation agriculture re-mains largely restricted to a small class of ladino elites. Figure 3.2 shows Guatemala's principal exports for given years between 1871 and 1996.

As we see, Guatemala has successfully diversified its principal ex-ports, although the top earners are still all agricultural crops. With the exception of some nontraditional production (discussed more fully be-low), and to a lesser extent cardamom, these crops are grown on plan-tations that depend on seasonal labor, the cost of which is subsidized by household subsistence production. De Janvry (1981) and Moberg (1992) view such economic structures as disarticulated: since the most productive sector of the economy is based on export production, pro-ducers are not dependent on local consumer demand and wages are thus allowed to be kept at a bare minimum, even below minimal subsis-tence levels.

Figure 3.3 shows Guatemala's imports from 1973 to 1996, broken into the broad categories of raw materials, consumer goods, and capital

FIGURE 3.2. Guatemala's principal exports, in millions of U.S. dollars.

| Year | Coffee | Sugar | Bananas | Cotton | Cardamom | Ntax[a] |
|------|--------|-------|---------|--------|----------|---------|
| 1871 | 1.47   |       |         |        |          |         |
| 1913 | 12.25  | 0.35  | 0.83    |        |          |         |
| 1955 | 75.50  | 5.20  | 17.00   | 60.00  | 30.58    |         |
| 1973 | 151.00 | 22.20 | 27.20   | 48.00  |          |         |
| 1982 | 358.90 | 26.50 | 110.60  | 141.70 |          |         |
| 1986 | 522.30 | 51.70 | 73.40   | 28.00  | 27.50    | 98.90   |
| 1989 | 380.00 | 72.10 | 87.10   | 27.70  |          |         |
| 1993 | 276.00 | 153.00| 106.20  | 12.60  | 38.00    | 203.80  |
| 1996 | 472.00 | 202.00| 155.00  | 17.80  | 39.00    | 312.50  |

[a] Nontraditional agricultural exports, including broccoli, cauliflower, fresh fruit, and cut flowers, among other recently commercialized crops.

*Source:* Bulmer-Thomas 1987 and *The Quarterly Economic Report: Guatemala, El Salvador and Honduras* and *Country Profile: Guatemala, El Salvador, Honduras,* published by *The Economist* Intelligence Unit.

goods. We see that roughly half of all imports are raw materials, a large percentage of which consists of fuels; remaining imports are almost evenly split between consumer and capital goods.

The structure of Guatemalan exports and imports shown in Figures 3.2 and 3.3 is broadly consistent with world-system explanations. Guatemala mostly exports raw materials (and of these, most are agricultural products that have highly developed global commodity markets) to "core" countries, primarily the United States, while it imports finished manufactured goods and even staple agricultural supplies (products of the highly mechanized agro-industries of North America). Competition between Guatemala and other coffee-producing countries (all also "peripheral," such as Brazil, Mexico, and Kenya) in markets that show little elasticity of demand keeps prices low. In order to make what is considered an adequate profit, producers have consolidated holdings while keeping labor costs low through coercive (at best) labor policies. Guatemalan plantations are infamous for employee-recruitment practices in which local labor subcontractors offer modest advances months before the harvest season in return for low-wage contracts.

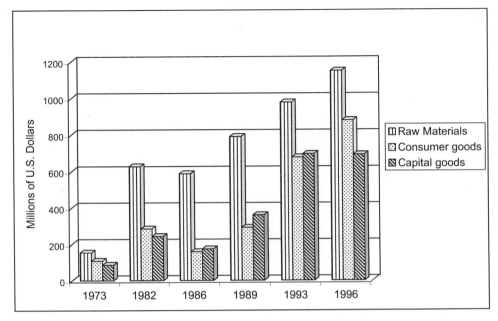

FIGURE 3.3. Guatemala's principal imports, in millions of dollars. Source: *The Quarterly Economic Report: Guatemala, El Salvador and Honduras* and *Country Profile: Guatemala, El Salvador, Honduras,* published by *The Economist* Intelligence Unit.

## *The Politics of Dependency*

In 1944, a coup led by high-ranking liberal military officers brought to an end a series of brutal dictatorships that had plagued the country for over half a century. The following year Juan José Arévalo was elected president. Under the leadership of Arévalo and his successor Jacobo Arbenz, and inspired by a post–World War exuberance over the progress of nations, Guatemala embarked on an ambitious project of change. Following a European model of societal progress (progress measured in social as well as economic terms), the revolutionary governments of Arévalo and Arbenz sought to modernize the country's political and social infrastructure and thereby bring about a more equitable distribution of wealth. Despite some perception at the time to the contrary, their policies were based on free-market capitalism as much as on socialist theory. As Jim Handy (1984:103) writes, Arévalo and Arbenz "were determined to create within Guatemala a modern capitalist economy, breaking down what they perceived to be the lingering remnants of feudalism."

Their efforts, however, frequently clashed with the interests of foreign corporations operating in Guatemala. The largest and most powerful of these was the United Fruit Company (UFCO), with controlling interests in the country's railroad, communications, and banking sectors. In retaliation for Guatemala's state attempts to appropriate large unused parcels of its land, UFCO manipulated its considerable political and media connections in the United States to mobilize popular opposition to Guatemala's revolutionary government, ultimately leading to its overthrow by CIA-backed forces in 1954 (Schlesinger and Kinser 1982).

In this context, Jonathan Friedman's typology of alternating periods of hegemonic expansion and contraction is illuminating. During the 1945–1954 revolutionary period, postwar international balances of power and relations were being negotiated and redefined. Powerful Western states were undergoing internal crises, resulting in a temporary contraction of their hegemonic expansion into areas of the world "peripheral" to the core Euro–North American constellation. The socially liberal yet thoroughly modernist regimes of 1945–1954 took advantage of this contraction to push for a reconfiguration of Guatemalan political-economic structures to facilitate a form of development not dependent on the whims of the West. As the Cold War configuration of global political economic relations began to solidify into the poles of liberal democracy/capitalism and socialism/communism in the early 1950s (seen in the rise of McCarthyism in the U.S., for example), Western hegemonic expansion began again in earnest, now marked by a competitive edge with moral, ideological, political, and economic stakes. Powerful foreign interests, particularly that of the UFCO, and Guatemala's conservative economic elite leveraged the anticommunist sentiments of the U.S. government to put an end to what is euphemistically referred to as the ten years of spring in Guatemalan history.

The 1954 counterrevolutionary coup brought exiled Colonel Castillo Armas to power, setting a precedent for the string of right-wing military leaders sympathetic to U.S. anticommunist campaigns who would rule Guatemala for the next thirty years. In 1963 (the date commonly ascribed as the beginning of Guatemala's civil war), an incipient revolutionary movement, supported by Cuba, emerged in the eastern Guatemalan highlands. This civil war clearly shows how global hegemonic interests and local intentions can be simultaneously played out on the same battlefield. Marxist revolutionaries in eastern Guatemala, disenfranchised middle- and upper-class intellectuals, and officers who received funding and ideological support from the Eastern Bloc via Cuba sought to adapt Castro's adaptation of Lenin's interpretation of Marx's thesis to the particulars of the Guatemalan situation. Local animosity as well as ideological conviction fueled revolutionary fighting, although the military, backed by an overwhelming access to technologies and arms supplies, prevailed by the late 1960s. Strong military ties between Guatemala and the United States had developed in the wake of the 1954 coup and the mounting friction of the Cold War. This, of course, was a time of great modernist optimism in the United States and Western Europe. The great war had been won, and both the victors and the defeated were rapidly rebuilding their economic infrastructures based on enlightened plans that would solve the lingering effects that followed the first great war and had led to the second. To be sure, there were battles still to be fought (although a deep-seated belief in progress made victory appear inevitable), but here the enemy was monolithic — either the communist menace or capitalist imperialism, depending on one's position — and moral choices were clear-cut. For democratic capitalism, the path was to promote development around the world through institutions such as the Inter-American Development Bank and the International Bank for Reconstruction and Development. But by the early 1960s, Latin American middle-class economic aspirations based on national economic growth were not being met. Higher education was viewed as one path to socioeconomic development, but the academic atmosphere worldwide and in Latin America at the time was one of increasing leftism and interest in Marxism, a breeding ground for guerrillas inspired by Fidel Castro and Che Guevara. The fortification of ties between the United States and the Guatemalan military was promoted by the United States to nip the Central American communist menace in the bud so that it did not become another Vietnam; at that time, Latin America was still geopolitically important to the United States in a way that it has ceased to be in recent years.

By the early 1970s, guerrilla groups reemerged in Guatemala, this time in the Indian-dominated western highlands. By 1972 the Ejército Guerrillero de los Pobres (EGP) had organized a column of combatants in the jungles of El Quiché, winning converts by attempting to speak native languages and by assassinating especially cruel plantation owners (Payeras 1983). The state responded by intensifying its antiguerrilla

military campaigns and its support of secretive death squads throughout the 1970s.

In 1978, General Romeo Lucas García took control of the government, and he and his brother, the minister of defense, escalated military
actions against the population at large. Because the guerrilla movement was now based in the Indian highlands, ladino elites' Cold War–
inspired anxiety about Marxist revolutionaries converged with their
long-smoldering fears of an Indian uprising, creating the ideological
justification for the ethnocidal campaigns directed by the military. Ostensibly, the military effort aimed to stamp out guerrillas, but they targeted not only active subversives but also *potential* subversives, a category often understood to include all Indians. This goal was ideologically based on the army's "cosmopolitan worldview" that divided society into a progressive modern ladino urban sector and a primitive, antimodern rural Indian sector (Richards 1985). Fighting a hemispheric
battle against communism provided the Guatemalan state with the
moral justification to attack Maya culture at its roots (if necessary, raz-
ing the towns and villages where it found expression), thus forcing the
Indians' integration once and for all into a ladino-envisioned nation-
state. Ironically, military leaders at this time were fond of paraphrasing
Mao Tse-tung to rationalize their policy of "draining the ocean in which
the fish swim" (see Molina Mejía 1984:38; Falla 1988:235).

A 1982 military coup brought to power General Efraín Ríos Montt,
a fervent born-again evangelical Christian. During his rule, Guatemala
saw both the collapse of its agricultural export market and a rapid ac-
celeration of the war between the military and Marxist insurgents, who
found increasing support in rural areas due to the worsening economy.
Ríos Montt maintained the military philosophy of the Lucas García administration—either the native populace accepted beans and ideological indoctrination or they were subject to extermination as accessories
to the fact—and in 1982 he adopted the National Plan for Security and
Development, which sought political, economic, psychosocial, and military stability (Torres-Rivas 1984; AVANCSO 1988).

Thus, in Guatemala, as in much of the world, native peoples were
unwillingly pulled into an ideological battle between two competing
Western political philosophies. The non-Indian population of Guatemala, who had long feared an Indian uprising, were taking no chances
with the hearts and minds of their Indian subjects, and so supported
the military's counterinsurgency campaign. The Indians, for their part,
were pushed toward involvement with guerrilla groups by the ever-

increasing repression they suffered at the hands of the state. As a result of their swelling base of support, guerrilla groups led a number of successful campaigns in the early 1980s: throughout the highland region city halls and police stations were bombed, local military officials were killed, and the guerrillas took control of a number of townships. Guerrilla organization also improved with the formation in 1982 of the Unidad Revolucionaria Nacional Guatemalteca (URNG), a unified policy-making body composed of various regional rebel forces. Guerrilla victories were, however, quickly countered by military action and widespread repression, and as a result, guerrilla forces were severely crippled by the end of Ríos Montt's rule. During this war, over four hundred villages were destroyed, tens of thousands of people were killed, and hundreds of thousands were displaced (AVANCSO 1992; Falla 1994).

After eighteen long and bloody months, Ríos Montt's reign was ended by another coup, in August of 1983. He was succeeded by General Oscar Mejía Víctores, who presided over the election of a constituent assembly in 1984, the writing of a new constitution in 1985, and the passing of power to the democratically elected Marco Vinicio Cerezo of the Christian Democratic Party in January of 1986. This democratic opening offered hope for Guatemalans that the civil war could be peacefully ended through constitutional and legal reform, and thus further weakened the guerrillas' base of support. The initial optimism following Cerezo's election was quickly dimmed by charges of widespread corruption and cronyism within the Christian Democratic Party. Rumors of massive misuse of government funds from the national to the local level greatly reduced public respect. For example, a new government program distributed millions of dollars for street-paving projects in rural communities, but in many towns the work was never completed, although local Christian Democrat officials became noticeably wealthier.

Cerezo's popularity had fallen drastically by the end of his term, and the 1990 elections brought to power Jorge Serrano Elías, a born-again Christian of MAS (Solidarity Action Movement). In 1993, Serrano conducted an autocoup, dissolving Congress and the Supreme Court while giving himself broad powers under a state-of-emergency order. Serrano had seriously overestimated his support from the military and underestimated the international diplomatic reaction to his coup. Further, his move had the unintended effect of catalyzing opposition not only to his leadership but to the whole structure of backroom military power that he had hoped would support him, thus bringing together an unlikely coalition of progressive business interests, human rights groups, and Maya activists that would play an important role in the 1996 Peace Accord negotiations. As a result, three months after his brazen power grab, Serrano was forced to flee to Panama, where he reportedly leads a life of great luxury after having come to office on the verge of personal bankruptcy.

The early 1990s was a tumultuous time in Guatemala's recent history not just because of the growing pains of a fragile democracy and the internal pressures of sectors vying for political position in the post–civil war structure; it was also a time of dramatic realignments in the global political economy, a period of rapid hegemonic contraction, to use Friedman's terms. With the fall of the Berlin Wall in 1989 and the shifting of global alliances in the post–Cold War era, the world has witnessed a more sustained contraction in the expansiveness of Western hegemony than even that of the immediate post–World War II period. This contraction eroded the material and ideological bases of Guatemalan state hegemony as well as that of both sides of the civil war, as seen in post–Cold War shifts in international funding.

Because of its location in a hot spot of the Cold War, Guatemala adopted a state policy in the late 1970s and early 1980s that was oriented toward securing state territory against the threat of communist expansion, a goal ideologically informed and materially underwritten by the West. Figure 3.4 summarizes official U.S. direct economic assistance and military aid to Guatemala from 1974 to 1990.

These data show a dramatic increase in foreign assistance levels beginning in 1976. The proximate cause of this increase was the funding of reconstruction efforts following the devastating February 1976 earthquake, but the increase was sustained because of both an innate bureaucratic resistance to reducing funding levels — embassies can be counted on to make a strong case for continued funding — and heightened concerns over the spread of communism among impoverished Central Americans. The U.S. policy of development was consistent with the logic of modernity and was, I believe, on the whole well intentioned, even if it does appear misguided in hindsight: it was thought that communism should be fought not only on the battlefield but also at its roots, combating the poverty that fueled its growth through assistance programs. Thus from 1976 to 1985, foreign aid flowed into Guatemala at the heightened level begun with earthquake disaster relief. Following the election of Christian Democrat Vinicio Cerezo in 1985 and the re-

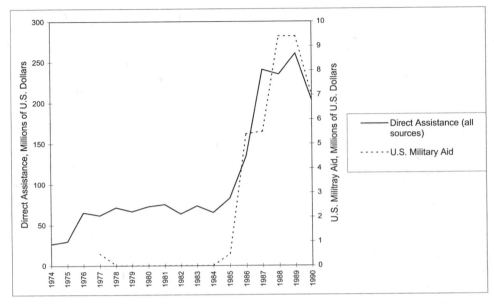

FIGURE 3.4. Total official direct assistance and U.S. military aid to Guatemala, 1974–1990, in millions of dollars. Source: from data compiled by the Organization for Economic Co-Operation and Development, *The Economist* Intelligence Unit, and Barry 1992.

duced levels of fighting in the country's civil war, foreign economic assistance was increased in support of democratization programs and postwar economic restructuring. Foreign aid flows to Guatemala peaked in 1989, and have since continued at slightly reduced levels as international concern has shifted to Eastern Europe.

Figure 3.4 also shows the fluctuations over time in U.S. military aid to Guatemala. During the height of the violence (1978–1984), the U.S. Congress refused to appropriate any military assistance for Guatemala, in protest of widespread and blatant human rights abuses. Nonetheless, Guatemala was still able to obtain military aid from countries such as Germany and Israel (themselves recipients of U.S. military largesse), and the *New York Times* reports that covert CIA funding continued to flow into the country at the rate of about $10 million a year (Weiner and Dillon 1995).

Nonlethal military aid was resumed following the 1985 transition to democracy, rapidly expanding to reach its all-time high of $9.4 million in 1988–1989 and then falling to $7 million in 1990 and to almost negligible levels in subsequent years. Since the fall of the Soviet Union, the United States and its allies are increasingly reluctant to support Guatemalan military action against left-wing insurgents, especially when it involves blatant abuses of human rights, and the U.S. Congress has twice suspended military assistance (in 1991 and 1996) to protest the handling of specific human rights cases. Despite these sustained decreases in foreign aid, the budget of the Guatemalan armed forces has decreased only slightly, from $171 million in 1990 to $102 million in 1997.

The end of the Cold War also brought about a broad shift in the attention of Western powers away from Latin American conflicts and toward the rapidly opening markets of Eastern Europe. Throughout the 1990s, policy changes in the West, along with their impact on development programs, have been informed by neoliberal economic views, and neoliberal political philosophy has emerged as a compelling "third way" that transcends traditional distinctions between Left and Right (see Giddens 1999). Neoliberal policies have supported a reduction in direct foreign assistance to Guatemala and other Latin American countries, as their proponents argue that free markets — more efficiently than governmental meddling — can and should do the work of development. Perhaps there was also a tinge of ethnocentrism involved in shifting levels of international assistance: having poured billions of dollars over three decades into Latin American development plans with little sign of progress, the United States and other Western countries began to cast a favorable eye to those Eastern Europeans who had been yearning for development while fettered by the yoke of communism. As a result of policy shifts in the West and the changing contours of the global political economy, Latin American foreign assistance remained constant in the 1990s while funding for former Eastern Bloc countries grew dramatically. Figure 3.5 compares relative levels of official direct assistance for Guatemala, Latin America, and Eastern Europe for the decade from 1986 to 1996.

These shifts of international power relations have resulted in a contraction of traditional Western hegemonic influence in Guatemala and the rest of Latin America, a pattern that Friedman (1994) calls "postdependency." Western influence has not disappeared, but it is now most commonly exercised through free-market mechanisms, which are more subtle than heavy-handed political impositions. This emerging neo-

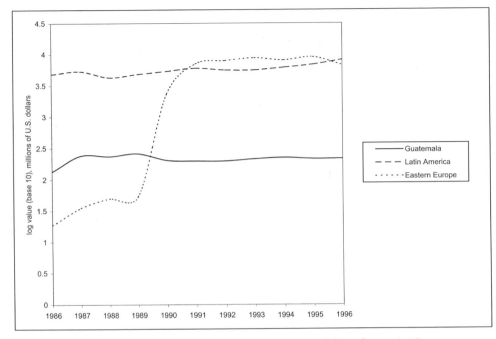

FIGURE 3.5. Total official direct assistance (calculated from figures in *Geographical Distribution of Financial Flows to Developing Countries,* published by the Organization for Economic Co-Operation and Development, Paris); scale shows log (10) value of assistance in millions of dollars. Figures for Latin America include Central and South America and the Caribbean; the 1986–1989 figures for Eastern Europe consist of aid mostly to Albania and Yugoslavia.

liberal world order (Giddens's "third way") has resulted in a period of redefinition for the Guatemalan state: its raison d'être can no longer be to hold the front line in a hemispheric battle against communism. It is being forcibly weaned from foreign aid while trying to redefine the role of the military and the civil sector in a fledgling democracy.

As Nelson (1999) points out, such reorganization carries multiple potentialities for Maya peoples, some beneficial, others detrimental. Though many disparage neoliberal reform as an insidious tool of neocolonialism, I show in the next chapter how Maya activists have been able to take advantage of recent openings in the Guatemalan political arena to pursue their subaltern agendas.

# The Rise of
# Pan-Maya Activism

4

When I hear the word "culture," I reach for my gun.
HERMANN GOERING (BORROWING FROM HANNS JOHST)

When I hear the word "gun," I reach for culture.
POPULAR SLOGAN QUOTED IN ŽIŽEK (1997)

Out of the fires of the Guatemalan holocaust has risen, Phoenix-like, a pan-Maya movement demanding from the state a recognition (and revindication) of Maya linguistic, social, territorial, political, and economic rights (Nelson 1991, 1999; Smith 1991; Fischer 1993, 1996; Cojtí Cuxil 1994; Warren 1998). The strength of the pan-Maya movement (in terms of supporters and political power) has grown exponentially since the late 1980s, and its accomplishments are extraordinary, given Guatemala's recent history of violent repression.[1] The pan-Maya movement has benefited from the postmodern trends of rising globalization, transnationalism, and what Fox (1997) calls the phenomena of "hyperdifference" and "over-likeness" (cf. Wilk 1995). It is the great irony of postmodernity that as time-space distances have undergone "virtual" collapse there has been a proportionate increase in the symbolic expression of ethnic difference, and thus distance.

This chapter turns to the emergence of modern Maya identity politics in Guatemala, correlating events in the history of Maya activism to the changing political economic contexts discussed in Chapter 3. I show that the pan-Maya movement has emerged from the unique temporal conjunctures of Maya and Western, local and global, modern and traditional, and symbolic and material systems of structuration, which themselves are historically informed and conditioned by the ongoing praxis of lived experience. Looking at the pan-Maya movement's organizational strategies as well as the life histories of particular Maya leaders, this chapter brings together the global context and formal structure of the movement with the cultural and idiosyncratic bases of its ideological development. I demonstrate that broad similarities in life histories and circumstances conditioned the development of pan-Mayanism in a select group of activists.

These discussions return us to theoretical concerns with "essentialism" and "constructivism." I argue that the sort of self-conscious constructivism of Maya activists (which explicitly aims to be true to an essentially conceived Maya past) differs from the form postulated in many postmodern accounts of the construction of culture and ethnic identity. Maya activists are constrained not only by their position in global relations of political economy but also by their relation to the Maya populace at large whom they seek to represent. These sometimes competing structural positions are interwoven with individual intentionality and a desire for self-advancement. Yet, underlying the structures of conjuncture that make up the unique history of pan-Maya activism is a common culturally logical thread that provides for intersubjectively perceived cultural continuity.

### Constructing Pan-Mayanism

Building a pan-Maya identity seemingly goes against the grain of centuries of Maya tradition in which the community serves as the primary point of identity reference (see Tax 1937; Wolf 1957; Warren 1978; Watanabe 1992). The movement's leaders promote associations based on linguistic groups, which they hope will then foster broader pan-Maya identification. And herein lies a potential contradiction in the pan-Mayanist project: pan-Mayanists trace the foundations of their identity back to an ethnohistorical construction of pre-Hispanic societies, while the vast majority of Maya peoples root their identity in geographical place and in known genealogical continuities. Most rural Maya can trace genealogical links back four, five, maybe even six generations, but never back to precontact times. In contrast, pan-Mayanists are actively promoting the identification of Indians with a common pre-Hispanic past—one to which a significant number of Maya feel only a remote connection. Thus, for some Westerners, many ladinos, and a few Maya, pan-Maya activism carries the taint of inauthenticity: this is not really

Maya culture—that was lost generations ago—but merely a politically strategic reconstruction.

It is undeniable that the pan-Maya movement is a social construct, built using past symbols and structures to meet current contingencies. And, as with all social constructions, individual self-interest is at work on several different levels. Pan-Maya leaders are generally young and ambitious, and interest in and support for the movement has opened up to them a relatively large number of lucrative positions in NGOs and increasingly in private businesses. These are men and women who want to send their children to good schools, who would like to buy a car or trade up to a better car, and who have many of the other desires that go with living in the modern world. At the same time, they also sincerely want a better future for their peoples. In a sense, this can be interpreted as self-serving as well: if something is good for all Indians, then it will certainly be good for them too. Yet, it would be misleading to reduce their complex individual intentions solely to such self-serving motives. Pan-Maya leaders are not generally cynical bureaucratic types, jockeying for position. Some tensions exist between Maya groups staking out their territories in terms of funding resources and areas of activity, but visiting the offices of Maya organizations and talking to workers there, I was always struck by the zeal with which people discussed the broad goals of the pan-Maya movement, from the leadership to the cleaning help. For the most part, these are very high-minded institutions and even the mundanity of bureaucratic work has not led workers to lose sight of the larger goal of bettering the conditions of the Maya people. Further, the form of constructivism pan-Mayanists practice differs significantly from that of academic theory in its integral engagement with practical issues. Maya scholars are self-consciously constructing new bases for Maya identity, and yet their constructivism is based on an essentialist notion of history and the value of authenticity. They feel that it is imperative that they be true to their Maya past; to do otherwise would indeed leave them adrift in a surreal ocean of ungrounded symbols. Identity must, as Richard Wilson (1993) and Jonathan Friedman (1994) make clear, be anchored in a conception of a continuous history.

In this regard the pan-Maya movement differs little from other ethnic movements that have emerged in the post–Cold War context of global relations. For all such movements, notions of authenticity play a crucial role in the process of cultural invention, something that many anthropologists find disconcerting (see Linnekin 1983, 1991; Handler 1988). Like these other movements, Maya activism is taking advantage of decreased tensions in current world politics to revive and strengthen a cultural heritage that has been submerged by centuries of external and internal, overt and covert, colonialism (Chatterjee 1993). As have these other ethnic activists, pan-Mayanists have also ably leveraged international law and popular opinion toward their own ends, benefiting greatly from the dramatic decreases in communication and transportation costs that go hand in hand with transnationalism and globalization (cf. Danforth 1995; Kearney 1995). The uniqueness of the pan-Maya movement is most apparent in its circumspect political demands, which are much less confrontational than the ethnic politics of Eastern Europe in the 1990s. Guatemala's period of violence was all too effective in instilling a deep-seated fear of confrontational state resistance. Recently I was interviewing a Maya leader who was in the United States for a brief visit, and the subject turned to the violence. Removed by thousands of miles and years of relative peace, he still lowered his voice and checked to make sure no one was listening before he broached the topic. It will be many years before such effects are erased.

## Post–World War II Maya Activism

The history of the pan-Maya movement has been detailed elsewhere (Bastos and Camus 1993, 1995; Fischer 1996; Fischer and Brown 1996; Gálvez and Esquit 1997; Warren 1998; Nelson 1991). Here I will confine myself to a brief discussion of several major periods in the development of Maya activism, showing their relation to contemporaneous global process. I begin with the florescence in Maya identity politics that followed the end of World War II. After the war there was a renewed faith in the power of progress and the inevitable destiny of modernity in the West and around the world. It was as if, having seen the depths of human possibility, Westerners needed the hope of a bright future proffered by an enlightened view of progress. At the same time, during and immediately following the war, Western hegemonic expansion was severely restricted. During the war, spheres of hegemonic influence were fiercely contested and at the same time solidified; Western resources were not devoted to expanding markets in underdeveloped regions but to supporting an ideological variant of the Western tradition. Likewise, in the postwar years, resources were allocated to rebuilding the political economic infrastructure of the West and, to a lesser extent, Japan. It was a war to unite Europe, to unite the West, and postwar efforts were oriented toward solidifying the union. Many saw World War II as the inevitable outcome of the end of World War I, and programs of massive reconstruction assistance, most famously the Marshall Plan, were funded to avert another great war. The practical result, in peripheral areas, was a postwar contraction in Western hegemonic influence; in Guatemala this state of affairs was capitalized upon by the politically and economically liberal governments of 1945–1954.

Postwar Maya identity politics are not explainable without reference to this larger framework of global change, and yet they are not explainable solely through reference to such larger forces. Maya activists of the 1940s and 1950s largely held a modernist vision of ethnic development and progress, yet it was a vision not wholly derivative from the Western tradition (cf. Adams 1991). Notable in this regard is the subaltern approach to scientific linguistics pioneered in the 1940s by Adrián Chávez (1904–1987), a man many contemporary Maya activists refer to as the father of the pan-Maya movement. Chávez, a K'iche' Maya teacher and scholar, is best remembered for his translation and analysis of the sacred Maya text the Popol Wuj (which he spelled Pop Güj, a document often called "the Maya bible") and his orthographic innovations for Mayan languages. Unhappy with the rough approximations required when using Latin characters to represent Maya phonemes, Chávez created alphabets in the late 1940s to write K'iche' (which he first spelled as Quí-chè and later as Kí-chè), Kaqchikel (at first Cakchiquel, later ✧a✧ Qui quil' el), Mam, and Q'eqchi' (Kekchí), which, with minor adaptations, could be used to write all other Mayan languages. These alphabets were largely based on Spanish orthography, but also included new diacritics and symbols inspired by a wide range of native American iconography. The complement of new symbols for K'iche' and their iconographic bases are shown in Figure 4.1.

Introducing orthographic revision is a difficult task even in the best of circumstances. For Chávez, the problem was not so much political (although his plan did meet resistance at many levels, the newly installed Arévalo government was broadly sympathetic to his goal of encouraging development and disseminating scientific knowledge to rural peoples) as technological: in the absence of typewriters and printing dies, his system was relegated to handwritten messages and laboriously revised typescripts, such as that shown in Figure 4.1. Although Chávez introduced his Quí-chè alphabet in 1945, twenty years transpired before he was able to see it in typescript, thanks to the efforts of the German cultural attaché to Guatemala, who commissioned both a custom typewriter and a corresponding set of type from a Costa Rican

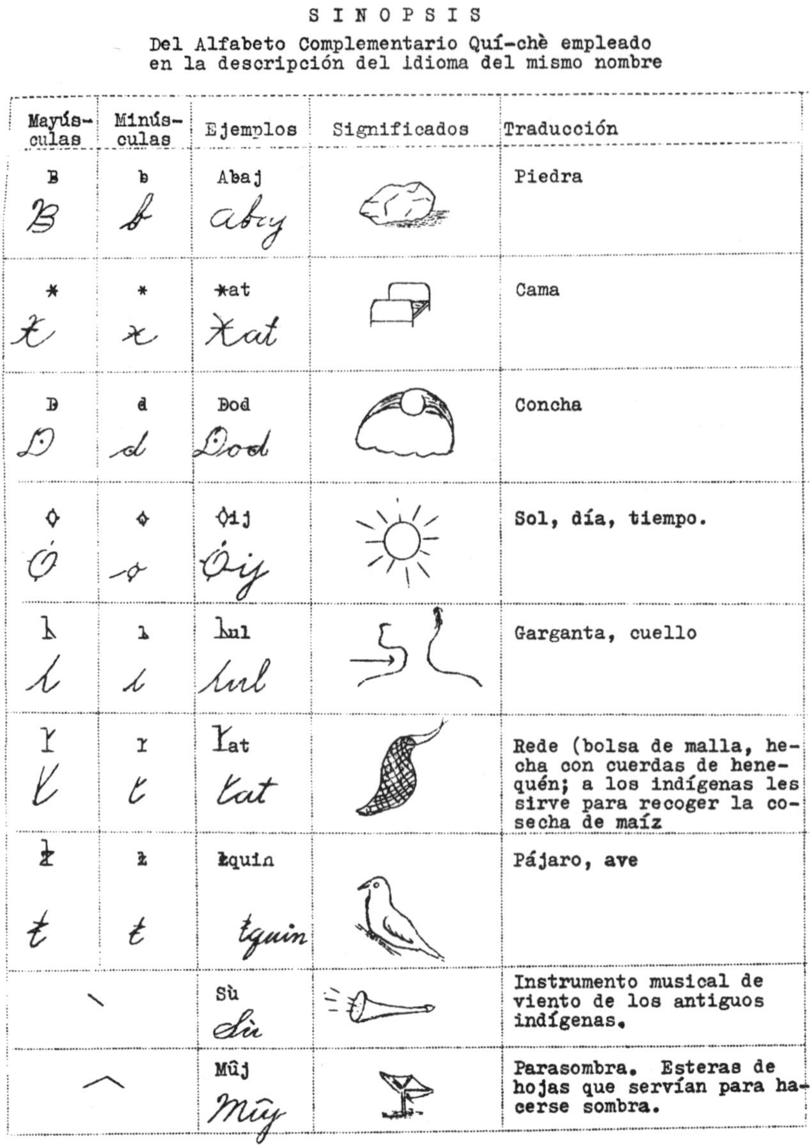

Del Alfabeto Complementario Quí-chè empleado
en la descripción del idioma del mismo nombre

| Mayús-culas | Minús-culas | Ejemplos | Significados | Traducción |
|---|---|---|---|---|
| B | b | Abaj | | Piedra |
| * | * | *at | | Cama |
| Ð | d | Ðod | | Concha |
| ◊ | ◊ | ◊ij | | Sol, día, tiempo. |
| ι | ι | ιul | | Garganta, cuello |
| Υ | ι | Υat | | Rede (bolsa de malla, he-cha con cuerdas de hene-quén; a los indígenas les sirve para recoger la co-secha de maíz |
| ƶ | ƶ | ƶquin | | Pájaro, ave |
| ＼ | | Sù | | Instrumento musical de viento de los antiguos indígenas. |
| ＾ | | Mûj | | Parasombra. Esteras de hojas que servían para ha-cerse sombra. |

FIGURE 4.1. Chávez's supplemental alphabet for Quí-chè Mayan.

university. In 1967, Chávez's *Maya Ɛ̃ib* became the first book to be published using the new type, but the Chávez alphabet continued to flounder in relative obscurity, failing to garner the critical support needed to make it a viable alternative to state-sanctioned Latin scripts. The idea of a unified alphabet, however, was taken up again in the early 1970s by a team of U.S. and Maya linguists, and by the mid-1980s it had become the rallying point for the formation of the pan-Maya movement.

Chávez also envisioned and directed a landmark conference for which he brought together indigenous teachers from across the country to address common concerns about bilingual and bicultural education in Guatemala. Held in June of 1945 in the city of Cobán, the Primera Convención de Maestros Indígenas de Guatemala produced few practical pedagogical innovations; its enduring significance was in demonstrating the potential for ethnically based collective action and providing a pan-Maya organizational model that was later widely copied within the pan-Maya movement. In 1949 Chávez organized a similar pan-Maya conference, Primer Congreso Lingüístico Nacional, which he envisioned as an ongoing forum for indigenous linguistic debates. (The second Congreso, not held until 1984, marked the beginning of the current period of rapidly expanding pan-Maya activism.) The Academia de la Lengua Maya Kí-chè (ALMK), which Chávez co-founded in 1959, continues to be an important national player in the promotion of Maya culture, and Chávez himself remained active in the Maya struggle until his death in 1987. He is the closest thing to a symbolic figurehead to be found in the pan-Maya movement, and his portrait hangs in more than a few offices of Maya organizations.

### *Maya Activism and Outside Influences*

Chávez and his associates were not alone in promoting Maya development in the 1950s. The same modernist confluence of postwar developmentalism, state liberalization, and grassroots activity that set the stage for Chávez's indigenism played into the development of alternate strategies as well. For example, during the 1950s, groups of evangelical missionaries began to expand throughout Guatemala, accelerating a process of Protestant conversion that began in the 1920s (Garrard-Burnett 1998). Primary among these was the Wycliffe Bible Translators/Summer Institute of Linguistics (SIL), founded in Guatemala in 1952. At the time, President Arbenz's liberal government was seeking ways to incorporate rural populations into a unified political and economic bloc, and the SIL was able to sell the government on its plan to encourage inclusive socioeconomic development through literacy programs. Literacy held an important role in the beliefs of SIL missionaries, and their global project of translating the New Testament into all the world's languages was inspired by a biblical passage that implies that the second coming will follow the day that everyone on earth has access to the Word. The Arbenz government was not keen on the SIL's missionizing, but saw the group as a cheap and effective means of modernizing the country's education system. The SIL was thus granted a contract by the Instituto Indigenista Nacional (IIN) to supply schoolbooks and train teachers in Indian areas. The joint IIN/SIL venture was aimed at incorporating Maya children into the national education system, thereby laying the foundation for the cultural integration so important to the Guatemalan state. The SIL's goals, however, did not stop there, for their ultimate aim was and is to erode the strong position of Maya religion and of Catholicism and to promote Protestantism through translations of the Bible (see Stoll 1982). The extensive work of the SIL in Guatemala over the last forty-five years has received mixed reactions from foreign academics and Maya activists alike. On the one hand, SIL missionary linguists have produced the most extensive body of descriptive linguistic data available for Mayan languages, they run the country's most successful literacy program, and they have trained hundreds of native Maya linguists. On the other hand, the SIL has steadfastly refused to embrace the unified alphabet for writing Mayan languages (discussed below), their literacy programs act as vehicles for their particularly strident form of anti-Catholicism, and despite having trained a large cadre of native linguists, their leadership remains exclusively composed of expatriate missionaries (see Cojtí Cuxil 1990: 20–23). As is so often the case in well-meaning development programs initiated from the outside, SIL missionaries have been only partially successful in imposing their vision on the Maya peoples, and the training they have provided has been employed toward unforeseen ends, such as cultural activism. SIL programs helped foster the growing interest among young Maya in their native languages, and provided them with the technical and social resources to pursue this interest. Many contemporary cultural activists trace their involvement in linguistic issues to SIL programs. The SIL also helped to found Guatemala's first organization dedicated to the promotion of indigenous literature, the Asociación de Escritores Mayences de Guatemala (AEMG), a group that has become a key player in pan-Mayanist activities (García Hernández 1986). Though not ungrateful for the unwitting support provided by the SIL to Maya activism, most pan-Maya leaders are highly critical of the SIL and its philosophy. Indeed, resistance to the SIL provided the pan-Maya movement with an important early source of oppositional unity.

Partly in reaction to the inroads being made by Protestant groups such as the SIL in Guatemala and throughout Latin America, and partly in response to internal pressures to focus on the social obligations of Christianity, the Catholic Action movement emerged in the early 1950s as an important force for social change. In their efforts to make the scriptures relevant to the daily lives of rural farmers and peasants, Catholic Action workers explicitly focused on economic and political issues. Ironically, the conservative national hierarchy of the Catholic Church at first hoped that Catholic Action would help combat radical, communist politics on a local level by providing an acceptable outlet for Indian frustration with social inequality in the country (Warren 1978: 88–93; cf. Miller 1990).

The Catholic Action program was built around a system of training native catechists prepared by Maryknoll missionaries of the Catholic Foreign Mission Society of America. In the program, parish priests trained Indian catechists from outlying areas, who then returned to their villages to give classes in contemporary Catholic doctrine and prepare people to take the sacraments. Like the SIL program, Catholic Action efforts sought to expand literacy among Maya Indians while fostering greater religious commitment. Ideologically it was felt that native catechists not only would expand the coverage of missionizing efforts but would actually be the most qualified to adapt scriptural teachings to the realities of their own communities. The catechists would act as points of articulation with the larger society, bringing literacy, political awareness, and God to the backwaters of the Guatemalan countryside. Catholic Action also shared with the Protestant ethic a disdain for syncretistic forms of Catholicism developed in the colonial period, especially the *cofradía* system of religious brotherhoods (Falla 1978a; Berryman 1984). Following the Second Vatican Council (1962–1965) and the Medellín Conference of the Latin American Episcopal Council (1968), there was a marked shift in Catholic Action programs from theological to social issues. Out of these meetings there emerged a consensus among a large number of progressive priests that the Church must concern itself with improving the material conditions of its followers, raising the consciousness of the poor and enabling them to become the authors of their own destiny (Berryman 1984:27–29). This progressive element within the Church became heavily involved with the formation of cooperatives, schools, and health services (Calder 1970; Berryman 1984). Many of the young catechists trained in these programs became community leaders and activists, and propelled what Shelton Davis calls a "'sociological awakening' of the Guatemalan Indian population" (1988:16; cf. Falla 1978b, 1988; Berryman 1984). Though the Church's vision of development was decidedly a modernist and Eurocentric one, its efforts acted to empower a progressive segment of the Maya population to pursue policies of their own design. Notable in this regard were the efforts of numerous parish priests to arrange for educational scholarships either in the capital or abroad for promising young Maya boys and, to a lesser extent, girls. Many contemporary Maya leaders trace their earliest ethnic awakening to the teachings they received in Catholic schools or foreign universities, and these leaders have come to espouse views contrary to those of their sponsors.

From the mid-1950s through the late 1960s, Maya cultural activism went into hiatus. The 1954 coup had installed Colonel Castillo Armas as president, the first in a long string of heavy-handed military leaders. After the success of Castro and Guevara in Cuba, Guatemalan resistance to the military regimes focused on armed revolution. Throughout the 1960s the government was engaged in a fierce battle with guerrillas operating in the country's ladino-populated eastern highlands, and security forces initiated a dirty war against all forms of state resistance that left little room for Maya activists to pursue their demands. By the late 1960s, however, the guerrilla movement had seemingly been defeated, the country's state of siege gradually subsided, and Maya began to pursue political demands more publicly once again.

The early 1970s witnessed a renewed interest in native language study and linguistic rights legislation as put forth by the still active Adrián Chávez. Particularly noteworthy is the role played by the Proyecto Lingüístico Francisco Marroquín (PLFM). The PLFM had been founded by a group of Benedictine monks as a Catholic alternative to the linguistically based missionizing of the SIL, but leadership was taken over in 1971 by a group of secular linguists and development workers with close ties to OXFAM, the Ford Foundation, and the U.S. Peace Corps. Leveraging these international connections for financing, the PLFM hired noted linguist Terrence Kaufman as a technical consultant and embarked on an ambitious program of linguistic research and training. Under Kaufman's direction, teams of U.S. linguists (mostly graduate students) were assigned to field sites across linguistic regions, where they simultaneously collected research data and trained groups of young Maya in the methodology of technical linguistics. The more than eighty Maya associates of the PLFM trained through this program went on to carry out their own linguistic studies, producing numerous dictionaries and grammars, and to take control of the PLFM's governing board. After becoming a self-governing Maya body in 1975, the PLFM began to explore ways to ensure financial self-reliance for the organization. Toward this end, they established what has become a highly successful Spanish-language school catering to foreign tourists (see www.plfm-antigua.org). The school serves a dual developmental purpose, providing an employment outlet for out-of-work Maya teachers while investing the school's profits in native linguistic research on Mayan languages. For a brief period in the 1980s the PLFM Spanish school's immense success threatened to overshadow the group's initial purpose of promoting Mayan language usage, but after several tumultuous changes in leadership, the group reemerged at the vanguard of pan-Maya linguistic activism in the 1990s.

### *The Political Relevance of Cultural Identity*

The early 1970s saw a flurry of cultural as well as linguistic activism centered in the K'iche' region. Between 1970 and 1972 the Asociación Indígena Pro Cultura Maya-Quiché, the Asociación de Forjadores de Ideales Quichelenses, and the Asociación de Escritores Mayences de Guatemala were all established in Quetzaltenango to promote Maya culture (Arias 1990). Most dramatic was the 1972 founding of an indigenous political party led by a group of young K'iche' professionals. The party, Xel-hú, named after the K'iche' toponym for their home city, Quetzaltenango, anticipated many of the demands espoused by Maya leaders in the 1980s and 1990s. Specifically, Xel-hú's leaders stressed the need for national pan-Maya unity and a symbolic revaluation of Maya culture, but they opted for a grassroots approach, focusing their efforts on getting Indians elected to local offices in a few towns in the Quetzaltenango region. Though they failed in their attempt to gain control of Quetzaltenango's city government (in fact, none of their candidates were elected there), they were influential in electing San Juan Ostuncalco's first Indian mayor in 1976 (Ebel 1988:177–178). Xel-hú continues to be an important political force in Quetzaltenango, and in

1997 the party's candidate, Rigoberto Quemé, was elected mayor of the city.

Inspired by the example of Xel-hú, a group of politically active Kaqchikel Maya founded an organization in Tecpán to support Fernando Tezaguic Tohón's 1974 bid for a congressional seat. Acting as a de facto political party, Patimamit was instrumental in Tezaguic's election as a congressional deputy for the Partido Revolucionario. In the same elections, another Kaqchikel man, Pedro Verona Cúmez of Comalapa, was elected to Congress. Although these were not the first Maya congressional deputies, the significance of their election stems from the fact that they were the first to "identify themselves as Indians at this level of power" (Falla 1978b:440; see also de Paz 1993:27–28). Personal feuds between the two deputies, fueled by sensationalized press reporting, hindered their ability to establish any sort of coalition, and neither was able to introduce the pro-Indian reforms called for in their campaign platforms. Nonetheless, the one-term tenures of Tezaguic and Cúmez significantly expanded the political arena open to Maya cultural activism at the state level, showing that, acting as a unified voting bloc, Maya groups could leverage their numerical majority in western Guatemalan townships to garner political power.

Indeed, in 1994 Tezaguic revived his political career along with his idea of forming an indigenous political party. The group he founded, the Comité Proformación del Partido Político Sociedad Ixim, aligned itself with the moderate-left Partido Reformador Guatemalteco (PREG) and presented Tezaguic and Edwin Domingo Roquel Calí as candidates for congressional seats in the 1994 elections. Sociedad Ixim's campaign, whose slogan was "Hombres de Maíz al Rescate del País" (Men of Maize to the Rescue of the Country), updated the pro-indigenous platform Tezaguic had promoted twenty years earlier, and stressed his acceptance of the ideas of pan-Mayanism and the notion of "harmony in diversity" (see Figure 4.2). Though neither candidate won, the fact that they organized a viable campaign based on cultural issues opens the door for future Indian-based political initiatives.

With the hope of gaining Maya legislative power while avoiding the personality cults fostered by Tezaguic and Cúmez, a group of indigenous leaders founded the Partido Indígena de Guatemala in 1976 to prepare for the 1978 national elections. The country's more established political parties and the national press roundly condemned the party as racist (for expounding antiladino rhetoric) and divisive (a primitive reaction to the sociopolitical integration mandated by the modernist proj-

FIGURE 4.2. Flyer produced by the Sociedad Ixim for the 1994 elections. Courtesy of Editorial Cholsamaj.

ect of development). Undeterred by this vehement response, yet cognizant of the need to present a nonthreatening image to the ladino power structure, the party quickly changed its name to Frente de Integración Nacional (FIN), and leaders began to speak more of national unity than of ethnic differences (*El Gráfico* 1976:8). Initially aligned with the liberal Christian Democratic Party, by early 1978 FIN had joined forces with the Partido Revolucionario, which had been courting its endorsement. In a politically fatal miscalculation, FIN then formally endorsed the successful candidacy of General Romeo Lucas García for president (Falla 1978b:454–455). Although he delivered part of his inaugural address in Q'eqchi' Maya, Lucas García quickly dashed any hopes of sponsoring pro-Maya policies; instead, he escalated the country's burgeoning civil war and targeted Maya populations as potential, if not active, subversives subject to eradication.

Whereas the early to mid-1970s had ushered in an era of increased Maya participation in national and local politics as well as the widespread emergence of peasant leagues and economic agricultural cooperatives, the civil war of the late 1970s brought a virtual end to such forms of organization and collective action. During the war years, many Maya were forced, directly or circumstantially, to take up arms in the great internationalist revolution or with the defenders of national sovereignty, as David Stoll (1993) vividly describes in his *Between Two Armies*. With war raging between communist revolutionaries and the U.S.-backed military, there was little political room in Guatemala for the pursuit of Maya identity politics during the early 1980s, and for both sides of the ideological war, ethnicity was a regressive force in social change. The state maintained its long-standing position that Indian culture was a drag on development and, even worse, lulled politically naive Indians into cahoots with the guerrillas. The revolutionaries followed a very conservative interpretation of communism within the Marxist-Leninist tradition, seeing ethnicity as a mystifying construct that bred false consciousness. The convergence of these views is not so surprising, considering that both developed from a common Enlightenment notion of rationality and logic.

With the democratic opening in 1985 and the concurrent scaling down of the violent counterinsurgency campaigns, Maya cultural activists began to pursue their agendas with renewed vigor. The Segundo Congreso Lingüístico Nacional held in 1984 (a much-delayed sequel to the conference sponsored by Chávez in 1949) was a watershed event in orienting postwar Maya activism toward the nonviolent pursuit of linguistic recognition and rights. One issue in particular galvanized participants' opinions and was to provide the rallying point for the pan-Maya movement's first lobbying offensive: the call for the creation of a unified alphabet for writing Mayan languages. To focus on such an issue in a country with myriad pressing social and economic problems might, at first, seem misguided. Is not orthography an innocuous topic compared to the poverty and violence of everyday life? Yet it is precisely this quality of innocuousness that made linguistic activism a subtly brilliant tactical move on the part of pan-Maya leaders. To begin the movement by demanding, say, massive land reform, would certainly have doomed its success in the charged political atmosphere of the mid-1980s: not only would individuals have been reluctant to offer support for such a potentially subversive cause, there can be little doubt that state and private paramilitary security forces would have methodically assassinated the movement's leaders. Thus, concentrating on linguistic issues was partially a politically tactical move on the part of Maya leaders, a path of least resistance in instigating institutional reforms. And it worked. Ladino politicians and elites largely perceived Maya linguistics as a quaint blend of folklorism and anthropological science, associating it most closely with rural development programs, missionizing, and bilingual education. Ladino perceptions of Maya linguistics as benign or esoteric were propitious for Maya activists. At a time when the state was under intense international pressure to broaden democratic participation, the demand for Mayan language reform was relatively well received as an innocuous concession to the country's impoverished Maya majority.

But linguistic issues were not pursued for purely politically instrumental ends. Language issues were and are historically important for Maya activists (one often hears that "language is the soul of our culture"), as language is the most widespread and apparent symbol of Maya self-identity (for men, at least, and for women also to large degree [see Otzoy 1988]). Both the academic and peasant views of language are markedly Whorfian, with language understood as being a key to cultural understanding. Interestingly, this has occurred at a time when Whorf's linguistic relativity hypothesis has been the subject of renewed interest with the Western academy as well (Lucy 1992a, 1992b; Gumperz and Levinson 1996). One of the movement's most distinguished spokesmen, Demetrio Cojtí Cuxil, states simply that "Maya people exist because they have and speak their own languages" (1990:12).

Further, the specific notion of a unified orthographic system had an illustrious Mayanist pedigree. Chávez had first set forth the notion in the mid-1940s, and more recently, linguists working with the PLFM in the early 1970s had developed a unified alphabet for writing Mayan languages. By the mid-1980s, Maya leaders saw the creation of a single unified alphabet for Mayan languages as a potential symbolic cornerstone of future Maya unity that could be parlayed into broad social and economic concessions from the government, even if these more widesweeping agendas remained implicit in public statements or confined to backroom politics. At the Segundo Congreso Lingüístico Nacional in 1984, a resolution was passed calling for the creation of an institution to preside over the creation of a unified alphabet for writing Mayan languages. Drafted around the time of the Segundo Congreso, Guatemala's Constitution of 1985 provided a legal framework for linguistic, and later cultural, activism by including a formal (if somewhat ambiguous) acknowledgment of Mayan languages and culture as part of the national patrimony, and as such, deserving of state protection.

In October of 1986, a meeting of all the groups working on Maya linguistics in the country was held. At this meeting, the Academia de las Lenguas Mayas de Guatemala (ALMG) was founded to promote a new unified alphabet for Mayan languages (based on the one developed by the PLFM and strongly opposed by the SIL) and to coordinate linguistic conservation efforts (see López Raquec 1989). The ALMG quickly rose to the forefront of the movement, and activists were able, within a span of only a few years, to obtain substantial legislative reform.

## The Pan-Maya Agenda

Contemporary pan-Maya activism seeks a culture-based solution to Guatemala's many ills. The approach is two-pronged: to work for the conservation and resurrection of certain elements of Maya culture while promoting broad-based reform in Guatemalan state structure and policy. The legal basis for many of the pan-Maya political demands of Maya groups comes from the 1985 Guatemalan Constitution, international treaties, and the 1996 Peace Accords (particularly the Accord on the Identity and Rights of the Maya People). The Constitution ensures the right of individuals and communities to have their own customs and languages (Article 58); promises to protect the cultures of native ethnic groups, especially the Maya (Article 66); and notes that, though Spanish is the official language of the country, indigenous languages are part of the cultural patrimony of the nation (Article 143) and should be taught in schools in areas populated mostly by Maya (Article 76). Focusing on these constitutional rights, the ALMG was instrumental in gaining early concessions from the government. In 1988 they successfully petitioned the legislature to adopt the unified alphabet for writing Mayan languages, and in late 1990 then-president Vinicio Cerezo signed into law a bill that grants the group 5 million quetzales (almost US$900,000) a year to support their programs in cultural conservation. Despite the fact that budget shortfalls and congressional maneuvering have prevented the ALMG from receiving its full allotment of funds, the monies received have enabled the organization to open branch offices in each of the linguistic communities it represents, and to begin extensive rural outreach programs to educate the Maya population about their cultural and linguistic rights. Although it receives its funding from the government, the ALMG retains a semi-autonomous status. Yet, partly as a result of their newly bureaucratic nature, the ALMG has retreated from the vanguard of the pan-Maya movement, fulfilling a fear voiced by several Maya leaders even before the 1990 allocation law was passed (Quemé et al. 1990).

The ALMG's important early role in loosely coordinating the efforts of many other national and regional Maya organizations has been taken over by the Consejo de Organizaciones Mayas de Guatemala (COMG), formed in 1989. COMG's membership is composed of fifteen independent Maya groups working throughout the country. Its stated purpose is to unite the many Maya organizations, relating their often disparate projects to a common set of goals as outlined in *Rujunamil ri Mayab' Amaq'* (Specific Rights of the Maya People; COMG 1991). COMG also acts as the Guatemalan liaison with the Coordinadora de Organizaciones y Naciones Indígena del Continente (CONIC), a group with strong ties to popular peasant organizations.

By the early 1990s, as international support rapidly diminished, both sides in Guatemala's armed conflict saw the end of their struggle as inevitable and they began peace negotiations in earnest, after years of fitful starts. In 1991 both sides agreed to the creation of a national body of Maya representatives who would develop an indigenous rights section for the Peace Accords. With funding from the European Community, the Mesa Nacional Maya de Guatemala (MENMAGUA) was formed in 1992 through an alliance between COMG (and its affiliated Mayanist groups) and Majawil Q'ij, an indigenous-rights spin-off of a leftist organization that is viewed with some suspicion because of its ties to the left. Tensions between pan-Mayanist and newly ethnically enlightened leftists proved too much to overcome, and MENMAGUA failed to draft a proposal by its 1993 deadline. Ideological divisions soon led to a splintering of MENMAGUA as popular representatives left to form their own group, and MENMAGUA's operation was largely taken over by COMG. (MENMAGUA still acts as a funding coordinator of European Community aid allocated to indigenous issues in Guatemala.)

The problem of incorporating Maya representatives in the peace process was tackled once again in 1994 with the creation of the Coordinación de Organizaciones del Pueblo Maya de Guatemala (COPMAGUA, also known by its Maya name, Saqb'ichil). COPMAGUA at first included only pan-Mayanist representatives from COMG, the ALMG, and other groups, although representatives of the popular/culturalist

Asamblea de Pueblos Mayas joined shortly thereafter. COPMAGUA proved vastly more successful than its predecessors in forging a consensus to draft a peace accord. Their wide-ranging Accord on the Identity and Rights of the Maya People was ratified by government, military, and guerrilla leaders as part of the peace process in March 1995, and it constitutes a binding component of the final Peace Accords signed in December of 1996. Bold in its aim, scope, and language, the Accord on the Identity and Rights of the Maya People is based on the *Derechos Específicos del Pueblo Maya,* a document first drafted by Demetrio Cojtí and later revised and expanded through committee work involving countless Maya leaders. The Accord first clarifies and strengthens rights provided for by the 1985 Guatemalan constitution in regard to education, language, and religion. For example, the Accord mandates that Mayan languages (at least a few regional languages — and this remains a volatile and unresolved topic) be made co-official with Spanish in matters of state. More radically, the Accord calls on the state to support and promote land-reform policies that will benefit the largely Maya rural peasantry and to take affirmative action to ensure that Maya gain proportional representation in political offices (for further detail on the 1996 accords and their impact on Maya activism, see Warren 1998 and Brown, Fischer, and Raxche' 1998).

Radical as these propositions are, it remains to be seen how they will be implemented. At present, a number of government and nongovernmental commissions are working on plans to operationalize the conditions of the Accord, but very little policy change has yet occurred; indeed, a 1998 popular referendum to amend the constitution in ways mandated by the Peace Accords was soundly defeated, although President Arzú has promised to implement the defeated proposition through other means, including presidential degree. It is estimated that the total cost of implementing the Peace Accord will exceed US$10 billion, a large portion of which must be covered by the government through projected increases in tax revenues. If these funds fail to materialize, the fate of the Peace Accords is unclear.

### *The Movement's Leadership*

It would be a mistake to characterize the pan-Maya movement as monolithic. Like all such movements, pan-Mayanism is actively and dynamically constructed by individuals, each with his/her own agendas, brought together because of perceived ideological affinity and the pursuit of a broad common cause. The pan-Maya movement is broad-based and made up of numerous organizations, many, but not all, of which are formally tied to one or more umbrella groups. The fundamental ideological goals of these groups are largely convergent. At the same time, each group, and ultimately each individual, holds what George Rude (1980) has called a "derived ideology" of the social movement. Rude is correct in acknowledging the internal diversity of a group that, at a macro (historical or sociological) level, may appear to be a homogeneous entity, but his use of the term "derived" is unfortunate. In fact, we might see the overarching movement ideology (the "inherent ideology," in Rude's terms) as derived from the temporal convergence of individual frameworks and intentions toward a common goal.

In those domains where community and individual interpretation vary greatly, such as religion, the pan-Maya movement takes its least strident, least controversial positions (although this too varies between pan-Maya groups and individual leaders). Indeed, one of the secrets to the success of the movement lies in the fact that its ideology appeals to individuals across religious boundaries, attracting Protestants, Catholics, and traditionalists alike. Of course, some religious tension exists, and a number of recently formed Maya groups have dedicated themselves to the promotion of traditional Maya religious values. Most often this takes the form of sponsoring and advertising ceremonies to commemorate Maya religious holidays, but Maya priests have also successfully pushed for legislation to protect sacred Maya archaeological and ceremonial centers. Most pan-Maya leaders are nominally adherents to Maya religion or syncretic Catholicism, although a few are practicing Protestants. There is, nonetheless, a notable absence of religious fervor, partly attributable to strategic bridge building, but also due to the skepticism associated with higher education. At the local level, however, pan-Mayanism seems to appeal to both Catholics and Protestants, each of whom interpret the meaning of cultural valuation and development slightly differently.[2]

Unlike the prototypical religious revitalization movements described by Wallace (1956), pan-Maya activism has no single charismatic leader. In part, this reflects a Maya model of group consensus building that diffuses decision making and power, and an abiding respect for age and experience as the primary sources of authority (at present the movement's elders are but in their early fifties). It also reflects the political reality in which the movement has had to operate. In the mid-1980s, being labeled as a Maya leader in Guatemala could have deadly consequences. A few pan-Maya leaders have confided that they are some-times followed, that their phones are tapped, and that they live in fear of being shot or, worse, kidnapped by either state security forces or private paramilitary death squads. In this context, Maya leaders do not feel that they have the luxury of pursuing apolitical scholarship, even if such were possible. Yet this does not mean that Maya scholar-activists are first activists and second scholars. The two roles are mutually con-stitutive and reinforcing in an integrated methodology of intellectual praxis.

State-level pan-Maya leaders come from a growing class of profes-sional Maya scholars, businesspeople, and activists. In many ways, these leaders represent an atypical sector of the Maya population: they are well educated, with most at some stage of university studies; they are overwhelmingly urban, with most living in Guatemala City, al-though an increasing number reside in Quetzaltenango (Guatemala's second-largest city) and in departmental capitals such as Chimalte-nango; and they are relatively affluent, increasingly so as the market for self-identified Maya professionals grows, fueled by demand from inter-national organizations and even a few Guatemalan state agencies such as the Ministry of Education. There are, of course, exceptions to this "essentializing" trait list of characteristics of pan-Mayanist leaders, but it well describes the general pattern found in leaders' biographies (cf. Warren 1998).

Most pan-Mayanist leaders have been trained in a social science. Pro-grams in linguistics at the Universidad San Rafael Landívar (funded through USAID) and the Universidad Mariano Gálvez (funded by the SIL) are aimed specifically at young Maya scholars. The Centro de Do-cumentación e Investigación Maya (CEDIM) established a grant pro-gram for Maya women to study in national universities in the early 1990s, and other scholarship programs have since emerged. Informal ties with foreign scholars have enabled a small but prominent group of Maya to study at universities in North America and Europe, and pro-grams in indigenous Fourth World studies have increased the demand for in-house natives in foreign universities.

The issue of foreign influence is a touchy one. A strong dose of xeno-phobia seems necessary in the creation of ethnic revitalization ideolo-gies; within the pan-Maya movement this is often expressed by the term *kaxlan* ("foreign," lit. "Spanish"). Originally referring to Spanish in-vaders and their culture (derived from the Spanish self-moniker of *castellanos*), *kaxlan* has come to mean anything non-Maya, or at least nonindigenous to the New World. It is the "them" against which a pan-Maya "us" is being constructed, and its utility lies in great part with its pragmatic flexibility. Though not inherently pejorative, *kaxlan* can easily carry negative connotations. Cultural items that can claim a purely Maya or purely indigenous pedigree are predisposed to acceptance in pan-Maya ideological constructions; ideas and items that are *kaxlan* are slightly suspect (they could be insidious tools of hegemonic oppression) and must be politically and empirically evaluated before earning acceptance. The fact remains, however, that individual foreign academics as well as foreign trends in academia have played an important role in the development of pan-Maya activism. Because of their structural position in the larger scheme of things, foreign scholars are always open to accusations of academic paternalism or imperialism. And rightly so, argues John Watanabe (1995), for anthropologists everywhere and always take the data they collect away from the community of study and use it toward their own ends. Yet foreigners did not create pan-Maya activism, as some ladino elites would like to believe, and it is certainly more than an academic construction.

All sectors of the Maya population are not proportionally represented in the pan-Maya movement's leadership. Maya leaders themselves acknowledge that the movement speaks only for "organized Maya" and not for all Maya (Gálvez and Esquit 1997:88–90; see also Warren 1998; Nelson 1999). Among the organized Maya, K'iche' and Kaqchikel speakers predominate in terms of both numerical majority and influence. Although the closely related K'iche' and Kaqchikel languages are, of Guatemala's twenty-one Mayan language groups, among those used by the most Maya (first and third respectively), this alone does not account for their speakers' early and sustained dominance in Maya cultural activism.[3] Rather, we must turn to their respective geopolitical histories and their histories of cultural contact, sustained outside imposition, and local intentionality.

The K'iche' and the Kaqchikel were the two most powerful groups in Postclassic highland Guatemala and were the objects of the Spaniards' most intense efforts to integrate them into the Spanish colony. During the Postclassic Period, the K'iche' polity, with the help of their Kaqchikel subordinates/allies, had steadily expanded their sphere of influence in what is today western Guatemala. Around 1470, the Kaqchikel Maya split off from their K'iche' benefactors, establishing their own kingdom centered around the capital of Iximche'. By the time of first direct Spanish contact in 1524, the Kaqchikel kingdom was expanding at the expense of K'iche' territory. In a grave tactical error common in the history of European expansion in the New World, the Kaqchikel rulers quickly aligned themselves with Spanish forces to defeat the K'iche' once and for all. The Spanish/Kaqchikel military defeat of the K'iche' was swift and decisive, although relations between the Kaqchikeles and the Spaniards promptly soured as the Spaniards turned their sights to Kaqchikel riches. Even today, when tensions flare between members of the two language groups, it is not uncommon for K'iche' speakers to remind Kaqchikeles of this fateful treachery (see Warren 1996).

Starting with contact, both groups have had close association with Spanish and Guatemalan political economic systems. Iximche', the site of the Kaqchikel capital, was also Guatemala's first Spanish capital, at least for a few months/couple of years, and even after the capital moved, first to Antigua and then to Guatemala City, the Kaqchikel area fell within the 30-league radius from which native labor was conscripted for work in the capital. Kaqchikel territory has thus always been in the sphere of direct influence emanating from the capital; the K'iche' are more closely aligned with Guatemala's second city, Quetzaltenango, and thus a bit more isolated from first Spanish and then ladino oversight—the provincial pseudocapital of Quetzaltenango being less stringent in its enforcement of state regulation. For centuries this pattern served the K'iche' well, allowing them to develop indigenously controlled regional commercial and political systems.

One Maya leader characterized the Kaqchikel/K'iche' distinction as one of ideological focus. Both groups, through their respective histories, have developed traditions of organized collective action. Yet, in his view, the K'iche' have traditionally been more oriented toward broadly leftist political goals, while the Kaqchikel have pursued a route of cultural activism. For whatever reasons, the K'iche' were certainly more caught up in the ground war of the late 1970s and early 1980s, and leftist peasant leagues were successful at organizing in the area both before and after the violence began. In the Kaqchikel region, organization during this time was more oriented toward cultural promotion, with active pro-Indian groups forming in Tecpán, Patzún, Comalapa, and other communities.

Another significant vector of diversity within the pan-Maya movement is generational. Pan-Mayanists are relatively young, given the traditional age-based criteria of leadership employed in Maya communities. As was the case with Catholic Action (see Warren 1978), this has created some generational tension in regard to authority, which has been largely mitigated by the overt valorization of traditional authority and knowledge among pan-Mayanists. There have even been attempts to formalize the influence of traditional elders in the movement through the creation of local councils of elders (Warren 1998).

Within the movement itself we may identify three distinct generations of activists. First, there are the "elders" born in the 1940s and 1950s. Many of these individuals were exposed to academics and identity politics through work with the SIL and Catholic Action groups, and a smaller number through the work of the Instituto Indigenista Nacional. Many members of this generation studied at one of the Catholic Church's Indian boarding schools, the Instituto Indígena Nuestra Señora de Socorro for girls located in Antigua and the Instituto Indígena Santiago for boys in Guatemala City. Funneled mostly through connections with rural parish priests, promising indigenous youths from across the country were accepted by these two schools for training as teachers. It appears that the Church was motivated by a sincere desire to promote development among the Maya. The goal was modernist: development through education. The result was postmodern: appropriating the tools of Western education for ethno-nationalistic ends through indigenous seminars, political parties, beauty pageants, and other cultural events.

A few members of this generation earned scholarships to study abroad at universities in Europe and the United States (particularly in the late 1960s), and these experiences are often credited with galvanizing an Indian ethnic consciousness. They often recall the ethnic awareness that accompanied living abroad, a context that both accentuated difference and romantically valued the novelty of being Maya. One man recalls studying English in Canada, the lone Maya among a group of ladino exchange students, and the English teacher who regaled students with the fallacies of the Spanish grammatical gender system ("stupid, stupid, stupid," he would repeat, arguing that objects have no natural gender). While his ladino classmates became indignant at this attack on their language, the young Maya man chimed in to agree, explaining that Mayan languages, like English, do not have such an illogical gender system. It seems that such foreign contexts, especially academic ones, are propitious for the development of ethnic self-consciousness. Living and studying abroad in a radically different cultural context accentuates ethnic difference, and the distance from the hegemonic structures in which one was socialized allows for a revaluation of subaltern alternatives.

A second generation is composed of those born in the 1960s and early 1970s. These men and women—and in this generation there is a growing minority of women leaders—occupy most of the movement's formal and informal leadership roles. Often younger siblings to the elder generation, these activists benefited from the advances of their predecessors. They were generally quicker to start and pursue studies, encouraged by the elder brothers and sisters. They also were exposed to a culturalist ideology early on by their elder siblings, often participating peripherally in the cultural groups active in the early 1970s. This generation experienced less influence from the SIL and Catholic Action (although these factors were not absent), and more contact with secular groups such as the PLFM, and later OKMA, in one of their ongoing capacitation seminars. Links to foreign scholars were better established, and a larger number than in the previous generation have studied abroad and hold graduate degrees from prestigious institutions. Both those who studied abroad and those who studied at home were instrumental in establishing the movement's momentum in the mid-1980s, and among them they formed a number of pro-Maya organizations.

Finally, there is now a third generation of Maya activists, largely the children of the elder generation, born in the late 1970s and 1980s. This is the first generation of children to come of age being exposed from their earliest years to the philosophy of pan-Mayanism. A large number seem to be following in the footsteps of their parents, pursuing studies in the social sciences and seeking jobs either with the government or with nonprofit organizations. A significant minority have chosen to pursue careers in business, medicine, computer programming, architecture, and other professional fields. I asked one father what he thought of his son's decision to study architecture. He replied that the movement has plenty of social scientists—what the Maya people need now are more self-identified Maya professionals, both as role models and as foundations of a Maya economic base not dependent on foreign assistance. Why, he asked, should a ladino architect be hired to create the impressive neo-Maya design of Tikal Futura, a luxury mall, hotel, and office complex built on the outskirts of Guatemala City in 1994? Would not a Maya architect such as his son, who has not only studied archaeology and iconography in school but who was also socialized in the Maya aesthetic, be better qualified? This same father explains that as his son was growing up he often worried about raising him in Guatemala City, removed from the traditional Maya values that permeated daily life in his hometown of Tecpán. To quell his fears, the father developed a number of neo-Maya socialization techniques, which he has since promoted among his peer group. When his son started working at odd jobs at about age nine, for example, the father made him contribute all of his wages to a household pool used for living expenses. As he grew older, the son could receive larger and larger disbursements from the common pool, but he still had to symbolically give all of his earnings to the family first. Such self-conscious socialization methods were reinforced through formal education, and the boy in question, along with his siblings, was sent to a cooperative Maya school run by pan-Maya activists for their children living in Guatemala City. Complementing a standard Western fare for primary schools, students were taught about Maya history, learned to write using the unified orthography for writing Mayan languages, and learned of the struggle of Maya identity politics. As a result, the man's son and his other classmates have a much less self-conscious internalization of pan-Mayanist ideological precepts and symbols. They are cognitively freer to expand the bounds of the *doxa* that they inherited, and thus are and will be an important source of change.

### The Xuyá Peres Family

Several members of the Xuyá Peres family have been active in national Maya cultural activism, and their family background illustrates a common pattern found in the life histories of Indian activists.

Don José, the father, was born in Xiatzam, an *aldea* of Tecpán situated along the edge of a deep ravine about 10 kilometers from the town center. His grandparents had migrated there from the K'iche' city Chichicastenango seeking a better life and land of their own. The rocky soils of Xiatzam were not ideal for farming, but the land was cheap, allowing Don José's grandparents to buy several hectares and set up their household. Don José grew up in the typical style of rural indigenous youths of 1920s Guatemala, never attending school and helping his father till the land. Over the years, his father extended the family plot, buying up various adjacent lands, and the family subsisted on the beans, maize, squash, and other foodstuffs they grew, in addition to the few head of cattle they maintained. The family would come into Tecpán every Thursday for the market, selling some of their produce and buying the few items they did not produce themselves; the family made their own soap and most of their clothes. Today Don José strikes an impressive image. Tall for a Maya, he stands about six feet and holds himself with a dignified stance, and though considerably weakened by his age, he still insists on overseeing his lands, which are tilled now by sharecroppers. He rises early every morning and dresses in the traditional garb of Tecpán males: long white pants, partially covered by a woven wool *rodillera* (or apron), a Western-style shirt, and a hat. When his parents died, Don José and his six brothers split the family land, and through the years he slowly bought up his brothers' shares and then some, expanding the family land considerably. Though Don José never attended school, he taught himself to count and to do the basic mathematical calculations necessary for buying and selling agricultural products. He also taught himself the alphabet while in jail in Tecpán: a relative had been operating a clandestine still on his land to make *cuxa*, the area's traditional moonshine, and when authorities discovered the still, Don José took responsibility to avoid implicating his relative, thus spending several months in jail in the 1940s.[4]

Don Jose's wife, Doña María, comes from the *aldea* Xuatzunu, not far from Xiatzam, and, being involved in several commercial enterprises, has long held land in the Patacabaj barrio of Tecpán itself. Doña María, who grew up in a family whose members were itinerant merchants as well as milpa farmers, and who had lived in Tecpán for many years, had difficulty adjusting to life in Xiatzam: drinking and cooking water had to be hauled from the river at the bottom of the ravine, a considerable task; and clothes had to be carried into Tecpán to be washed at a communal *pila*. Like Don José and most indigenous children born in Guatemala in the 1920s and 1930s, Doña María never attended school; because of her commercial background, however, she learned basic math and even gained a small degree of literacy for reading packaging. Don José and Doña María had their first child during the two years that they lived in Xiatzam. After two years, much to the delight of Doña María, they moved into the town of Tecpán, where Doña María opened a shoe store. The couple produced three more sons in rapid succession, and all four sons helped their father farm and care for animals. Don José was never in favor of his sons going to school, at least not for more than a couple of years, feeling that they should strive to be farmers like himself (and his father, grandfather, great-grandfather, and so on as far back as anyone could remember), for which he could teach them all they needed to know. The eldest two sons did not attend school until they were almost nine years old (going on to complete their secondary education and to attend university), but Don José relented to pressure from his wife and allowed the younger two boys to start first grade when they were six years old. The boys knew only Kaqchikel when they entered school for the first time, and they suffered through the trauma of total and hostile language immersion. Alberto, the third son, recalls his decision to continue with his studies after sixth grade:

> I worked our land in an *aldea* and went to school in Tecpán, having to walk a tiring eight kilometers each day to school. In sixth grade, my last year of primary school, my dad gave me the option of caring for the animals full-time or to continue studying. He wanted me to quit school and work in the fields with him. He gave me until the next day to decide; I didn't much care for school, but taking care of the animals day in and day out was such hard work, well, I decided to continue school. So my dad sent me to Chichicastenango to *básico*, but I couldn't eat the food they serve there and didn't like it, so after three months I came back to Tecpán and attended a private school there. But my dad got sick and couldn't pay the tuition and so I couldn't take the final exams. My mom even sold her pigs and other things, but it still wasn't enough money. After that I went to boarding school at the Escuela Pedro Molina in Chimaltenango, where I didn't even have a bed at first. I slept on the floor of a shack in back of the school. Finally, one of the teachers gave me a bed and food sometimes, and my mom and dad sent me money. But first through sixth grades were still the hardest.

Yet Alberto persevered, going on to the university and continuing his studies. Although he has yet to complete his degree, Alberto already has several publications under his belt. As a teenager in the early 1970s, he became involved in the Maya culture groups that were springing up around the country, primarily in Quetzaltenango, Tecpán, Comalapa, and Guatemala City. Despite this humble background — indeed, at least in part because of it — all the Xuyá Peres children, who in 1999 ranged in age from 32 to 59, have completed at least some university work, and several, including Alberto, are outspoken leaders within the pan-Maya movement.

Most other national Maya leaders come from similarly humble backgrounds. A significant number of them received their first exposure to pan-Mayanism during linguistic workshops hosted by the Proyecto Lingüístico Francisco Marroquín (PLFM). The PLFM recruited prospective Maya linguists through grassroots efforts, often going door to door in towns looking for interested individuals, who often turned out to be the children of petty merchants or farmers, as the prospect of poorly paid linguistic training did not attract the most prosperous sectors of the population.

Furthermore, a great number of Maya leaders are from towns such as Tecpán with a long history of activism. They were presented with educational opportunities, and they took advantage of these opportunities. Many started down a path of modernist development, much encouraged by their religious and scientific backers—but with outcomes that were unforeseen by the promulgators of development. And so it goes with such efforts: the subjects of development quickly become the agents of that development, interpreting and acting out their interpretations, which are informed by unique historical, cultural, and psychological circumstances. Similar circumstances gave us the memorable figures of Jomo Kenyatta, Handsome Lake, and Malcolm X.

Another significant vector of differentiation within the pan-Maya movement pertains to national and local levels of influence. Public pan-Maya activism has played an important role in demonstrating the possibility of voicing one's opinion without fear of being murdered; local activists are not, however, offshoots of national organizations, but are truly grassroots, local affairs. And whereas national leaders are often well educated and relatively affluent, local leaders are usually neither. At the local level, pan-Maya leadership is most diverse. Those who seem most attracted to the movement's ideology, and thus those most likely to actively participate in cultural activism, are young men, and to a lesser extent women, in their twenties, thirties, and forties. A greater percentage than is found in the general populace are single or divorced, although most are married and have children. They often have a formal association with a national or regional Maya organization, but retain close ties to their home communities and act as informal liaisons between national and local activities. Frequently they start cultural outreach programs, with Mayan language literacy workshops, historical lectures, and religious events held in private homes or, occasionally, in municipal buildings or schoolhouses. Their youth, and in the case of women, their gender, is a serious impediment to their effectiveness as local leaders. Traditional community leadership has revolved around both formal and informal age-grade hierarchies, and the relative youth of these leaders has led to a degree of resistance to their message of cultural pride and unity.

Local leaders are also sometimes accused of being self-serving opportunists, selling their cultural heritage for the chance of personal advancement. Interviews and life histories show the situation to be much more complicated. Take, for example, the case of Don Tomás.

### Don Tomás

I met Don Tomás, an eloquent and well-known local *aj q'ij* (day-keeper, religious specialist) in Tecpán, and my future wife, Mareike Sattler, on the same occasion. It was during the summer of 1991 while I was living in Tecpán studying Kaqchikel and conducting a market survey. A local family invited me, along with several other anthropologists (including Nora England, Carol Hendrickson, Lynette Melner, and Mareike Sattler), to a ceremony marking the transfer of the elderly father's land to his children. Held in a remote hamlet, the event, which included the ritual sacrifice of a sheep, a meal of fresh mutton stew, and dancing to the music of a marimba band, was attended by about twenty people.

Despite what for me was an auspicious introduction, after my wife and I moved to Tecpán in 1993, Don Tomás was aloof and evasive. Though we always took the time to exchange pleasantries when passing in the street or when we happened to be at a common social function, our exchanges with Don Tomás never went beyond shallow politeness, and at times he was almost hostile. On one occasion, we were attending the ceremony celebrating the Maya day Waqxaqi' B'atz' at the site of the Postclassic Kaqchikel capital on the outskirts of modern Tecpán. Don Tomás and several other *aj q'ijab* were directing the rituals, which included a number of prayer recitations as well as extemporaneous speeches by the organizers and attendants. During one such speech, the orator, an affluent Kaqchikel doctor from Tecpán, denounced the presence of voyeuristic gringos who hoped to capture a part of Maya sacredness, collect it as a folkloric relic, and commercialize it in publications sold in the U.S.; Don Tomás concurred with the doctor in questioning our presence and intentions. (We ultimately stayed, although not for too long, after several friends stood up and defended our goodwill, emphasizing that we were offering free English lessons to children and adults who signed up for local classes in Kaqchikel.) After this, our many overtures were rebuffed during our first year of residence, and it was not until we were preparing to leave that Don Tomás sought us out and invited us to his home for dinner. (On the occasion of extending that invitation, Don Tomás did mention that he was in need of a working shortwave radio, and inquired about what would be the fate of ours when we left.) After that dinner at his house, Don Tomás continued to seek us out in our remaining days of fieldwork, sharing his life history and offering his opinions on *la realidad maya.*

The night of our dinner we arrived at Don Tomás's house at dusk. Too punctual as always, we were kept waiting in the family's tiny living area for well over an hour as last-minute preparations for the meal were completed. Fortunately, we were kept company by Tomás's parents, who lived in an adjacent house. His father was an early convert to the Catholic Action movement and became a catechist in 1950. He recalled for us the first priests he ever knew, Catholic missionaries who arrived in his remote *aldea* following a devastating earthquake in the mid-1940s, and the lasting impression they had had on his life's direction. Throughout the meal and after dinner, the father kept up a running commentary on the merits of Christianity, all the while his son criticized the Church and its political stance, extolling instead the virtues of Maya religion.

Don Tomás was born in an *aldea* of Tecpán in the early 1950s. When he was eight years old, he left his parents' home and moved to Tecpán, where he worked as a laborer in a small family-owned weaving workshop. (Tecpán has long been home to a large number of weaving and knitting workshops, and Don Tomás recalls that many were started in the 1940s and 1950s by early Protestant converts.) At this time Tomás was devoutly Catholic, and he remembers being teased incessantly by his Protestant coworkers for his devotion. This torment acted to strengthen his faith, and he set his sights on becoming a priest. This ambition was encouraged by Father Dave, a parish priest from Louisiana stationed in the neighboring town of Santa Apolonia, whom Tomás had befriended. These plans changed, however, after Father Dave was transferred back to Louisiana before Tomás was able to master the national seminary's entrance requirements. Stung by this seeming rejection from the Church, Tomás turned to the Maya cultural groups that were springing up in and around Tecpán in the early 1970s. At first, he tried to join the Asociación de Profesionales Indígenas de Tecpán, but he was again rebuffed because of his lack of higher education. Inspired by the example of Adrián Chávez and undaunted by his rejections, in 1974 he and a number of other young Maya men and women formed the Círculo Cultural Ixmukane, a local group dedicated to cultural promotion that was active until 1980, at which time the violence forced its disintegration. Tomás himself was forced into hiding in 1981 as the violence escalated. On May 14, 1981, a Thursday market day, the priest assigned to Tecpán, a kind man sympathetic to Maya concerns with whom Tomás had established a rapport, was murdered in the crowded street outside the church's parish house, a killing meant to send a message to local groups. After the killing, Tomás and his family fled Tecpán and remained in internal exile for ten years, frequently moving around the country until their return to Tecpán in 1990.

After his return to Tecpán, Don Tomás started a new association of like-minded local indigenous leaders. Influenced by Don Tomás's years of living on the run, this group operates covertly, without obtaining the required legal recognition nor openly advertising its existence. Their goal is to focus not on language but on land, beginning with a reforestation project and ultimately aiming for revitalizing a system of communally owned lands. Despite their covert methods, the group and their efforts have run into resistance. As Don Tomás relates, Tecpán's current (in 1994) assistant priest (the one who administers the rural areas) is discouraging his flock from joining cultural groups. It is said that in one *aldea* where the ALMG's Comunidad Lingüística was giving literacy classes in Kaqchikel, this priest attacked such efforts as evil, shouting that "if you people join Mayan cultural groups, you want to bring back the pagan past, then you will be idolaters, and then you will die in a few years." We cannot know to what extent the priest was speaking metaphorically, perhaps of spiritual death; the fact remains that his words were interpreted locally as a very thinly veiled threat, implying that the army would soon retaliate against participation in such groups. Recounting this episode, Don Tomás provides another piece of supporting information that he had heard through an organizer of the popular group Mayawil Q'ij. The story (which I actually heard several times during the course of fieldwork) was that the U.S. ambassador spoke with a Guatemalan army general (in some versions it is General Otzoy, a Kaqchikel man from Comalapa). The general said the peace process was going along well and that the problem with leftists and Marxists would soon be solved. The new problem, he continued, would be with the Maya, and in the year 2000 there would be a war against Maya guerrillas. At this point in our after-dinner conversation with Don Tomás, his elderly father chimed in, saying, "yes! they say that the peace is coming!" all the while laughing madly.

And so, Don Tomás continues to pursue his various callings as an *aj q'ij*, as a milpa farmer, and as an occasional local organizer of cultural groups. The greatest challenge facing the national pan-Maya movement is reconciling the local concerns of Don Tomás and others like him with the broader goal of fostering pan-Maya unity and ethnic consciousness. Cojtí Cuxil writes that, with the exception of those thoroughly assimilated into ladino society, "the Maya *pueblo* is entirely Mayanist and thus anticolonialist, just with different degrees of consciousness and forms of action" (1997:51). He divides levels of Maya ethnic consciousness into three categories. First, there is the mostly illiterate Maya peasantry who have a fundamental (yet largely untapped) sense of themselves as part of the Maya *pueblo*, reinforced through the constant lived experience of ethnic discrimination and social marginalization. Second, there are the Maya peasants and workers incorporated into popular (i.e., class-based) organizations whose ethnic awareness is subsumed to class consciousness. Finally, there are the educated middle- and lower-class Maya promoting pan-Maya unity through "more authentic Maya practice" in their "initiatives in the fight against colonialism" (ibid.:52–53). Cojtí Cuxil concludes that the pan-Maya movement, of which he is a part, seeks

> the development of a Maya consciousness in, of, and for itself (*para sí*) and to fight for the rights of the Maya pueblo. Its primary obligation is logically to achieve clear and complete ethnic consciousness among all Indians, and to realize this it has to resolve the problems of communication and the diffusion of ideas encountered in a multilingual country such as Guatemala. (ibid.:53)

In the following chapter, I examine how pan-Maya leaders seek to raise the ethnic consciousness of Maya peoples through the construction of unifying cultural symbols. Included in the discussion are the problems that arise from competing obligations to their various constituencies and the controversies over authenticity that have emerged from their new constructions.

# Constructing a Pan-Maya Identity in a Postmodern World

### 5

**Ix Chumil:** *¿Por qué no se hemos dado participación cuando se toman decisiones por nosotros, Jolom B'alam?* [Why aren't we allowed to participate when decisions are made concerning us, Jolom B'alam?]

**Jolom B'alam:** *Porque existen personas que siempre piensan con la mentalidad de los colonizadores, Ix Chumil; es decir que ellos creen que somos pobres personas, no pensantes, que necesitamos muletas para andar.* [Because there exist those who always think with the mindset of the colonizers, Ix Chumil; that is to say that they think we are impoverished people, unable to think, who need crutches to walk.]

FROM A RADIO PLAY BROADCAST ON THE
PROGRAM *MAYAB' WINĀQ*

Bradd Shore (1996) notes that culture ultimately rests in the minds of individuals, thus models of culture must account for individual agency and intentionality. Theories of cultural construction are particularly compelling in this regard, focusing as they do on the mechanisms by which people actively construct the meaningful worlds in which they live. Such approaches acknowledge the important role of agency in cultural production while providing useful analytic techniques and representational strategies to document the workings of cultural imagination and invention. Constructivist analyses also serve as powerful tools of counterhegemonic critique, de-legitimizing dominant ideologies by uncovering power relations beneath the public facade of cultural representation.

Often overlooked in constructivist analyses, however, is the fact that subaltern critiques are themselves cultural constructions built on the same sort of claims to authenticity and legitimacy as dominant ideologies. This is ethically problematic ground for ethnographers, who see their primary obligation as resting with the peoples with whom they work; one would hardly wish to de-legitimize the precarious political position of a marginalized group seeking progressive reforms. Yet, acknowledging cultural construction need not undermine claims to authenticity and legitimacy. As this chapter documents, the efforts of Maya leaders to construct and promote viable elements of a pan-Mayan identity are fundamentally conditioned by received cultural norms and by desires to remain true to a perceived Maya past. Successful new elements are widely adopted precisely because they are seen as somehow continuous with an established tradition (if, perhaps, in ways that appear ironic to foreign observers), and thus essentially authentic.

Pan-Mayanist efforts to supplant community and linguistic group affiliations with a broader Indian identity have largely focused on (re)-constructing and mobilizing a number of cultural markers of Mayaness. Tellingly, these markers often mirror classic essentialist trait lists: language, dress, religion, and even hieroglyphic writing. While trying to remain faithful to a Maya past, activists are also self-consciously working to redefine meanings and connotations associated with these cultural symbols — harnessing essentialist scientism toward well-intended social engineering projects that most observers would characterize as "constructivist." Some see in this a textbook example of cultural constructivism, with cultural symbols being redefined and deployed as tools of ethnic resistance. From this stance, Maya cultural activism is portrayed not as an organic outburst of a tradition long submerged by powerful political-economic forces, but as a proactive contestation constructed in resistance to present contingencies imposed by a ladino Other (cf. Bastos and Camus 1993; Fischer and Brown 1996; Warren 1998). Critics of the pan-Maya movement have used such a constructivist perspective to argue that this sort of cultural creativity is somehow false, a savvy facade for a Maya elite's self-interested political and economic gain (Flores Alvarado 1993; Morales 1997).

In giving analytic primacy to the innovativeness of Maya cultural construction (and thus focusing on ethnic boundaries rather than the "cultural stuff" they contain), it is easy to dismiss the historically particular, culturally unique mechanisms of continuity; thus it is ironic that in concentrating on the microprocesses (by definition diachronic) of cultural construction one can lose sight of the macrohistorical context. The symbols being manipulated to promote the agendas of pan-

Mayanism are not randomly chosen; they are not constructed out of thin air. Rather, their effectiveness is contingent on calling into play the symbolic value with which they have been historically imbued. As van den Berghe (1981:27) notes, "Unless ethnicity is rooted in generations of shared historical experience, it cannot be created *ex nihilo*." The symbolic continuity produced in the ongoing construction of cultural symbols is indicative of cultural constraints that govern the process of innovation.

The pan-Maya movement bases its ideological position in large part on its historical legitimacy, and thus on its authenticity. If Maya culture today is inauthentic (if, for example, it is a derivative construction resulting from sustained Spanish contact; see Martínez Peláez 1971; Hawkins 1984), then pan-Maya identity politics fall into the same category as the use of scantily clad girls in ladino electioneering showmanship. Reduced to political tactics and stripped of moral and genealogical purity, pan-Maya self-representations then become easier for ladinos to oppose. Yet, for the pan-Maya leaders themselves, the movement is morally, and not merely materially, driven. They strive to remain true to a self-conceived vision of the past, and they do not take lightly their role as cultural bricoleurs.

## Traje

Dress serves as an important identity marker in cultures and subcultures around the world. This is due in part to its visibility, which makes it a convenient and nonintrusive (if not always 100 percent accurate) criterion for judgment: one need only look at a person to categorize him or her on the basis of dress—no further interaction is necessary. Though more plastic than language (clothes can be changed rather more easily than speech patterns), dress also reveals a level of commitment to a particular worldview. As Žižek (1997:33) observes, "Appearance is never 'merely an appearance,' it profoundly affects the *actual* socio-symbolic position of those concerned." For the Maya, traditional dress (*traje*) is a symbolically rich, polyvalent, and visually stimulating domain of representation for ethnic and gender identities. The use of *traje* has declined over the years, especially among men, but it remains a primary emblem of Guatemalan Indian Otherness; mention contemporary Maya culture to someone and the image likely invoked is that of a Maya woman dressed in a colorful handwoven *huipil* (blouse; *po't* in Kaqchikel) and *corte* (skirt; *uq'* in Kaqchikel).

The use of *traje* as a symbol of Maya-ness raises issues of gender and ideology. The pan-Maya movement often presents the autochthonous pattern of Maya gender relations as equitable, in contrast to the Spanish-ladino ideology of machismo. Lamentably, it is said, the Spanish system has corrupted Maya norms, introducing sexism into the cultural milieu. In this regard, then, the valuation of *traje* with the pan-Maya movement is also a valuation of the women who weave and wear it. Men are said to have been forced into abandoning their traditional dress through more intense and sustained contact with Spanish and then ladino society. In contrast, women are said to have been more valiant in their cultural tenacity, keeping alive traditions such as weaving and its iconography and passing them along to future generations. Recognizing weaving as a cultural art to be treasured, Maya activists hope to contribute to greater gender equality, placing women's work on par with that of men.

*Traje* styles have a long tradition of being community-specific, and although there is disagreement over whether this resulted from Spanish colonial imposition, the association between town and dress has been reinforced by centuries of practice (see Otzoy 1996). Thus while *traje* acts as a visible and readily recognizable marker of Indianness, it is even more closely associated with a sense of community. Distinctive designs in the *huipiles* and *cortes* of Maya women's dress have traditionally indicated the wearer's natal community, and anthropologists and savvy tourists often pride themselves on their ability to visually source particular pieces (and thus by implication their wearer). Community allegiances are therefore reinforced through dress, but pan-Maya activists would like to see such allegiances superseded by a broader concept of Maya-ness. In this project they have been aided by a number of innovations in *traje* design and use at the local level.

More and more Maya women are mixing and matching *huipiles* and *cortes* from various communities into a single ensemble, creating new aesthetic conventions that incorporate the beauty of other styles while subtly underlining notions of pan-Maya unity. Likewise, female activists such as Irma Otzoy (1988, 1996) stress the antiquity of the designs and techniques used in Maya textile manufacture, and many weavers have even begun to revive older designs and styles (see Hendrickson 1991, 1995, 1996). For example, master weaver Ix Ey conducts research at the Museo Ixil de Traje Indígena in Guatemala City to record patterns in older textiles that have fallen out of use. She uses these older, more "authentic" designs and colors in her own work. Such efforts at cultural revitalization in the material arts often converge with marketing strategies, as weavers capitalize on tourists' desire for authentic souvenirs.

Male leaders of the pan-Maya movement, most of whom long ago abandoned their traditional dress, have also developed new clothing markers of pan-Maya identity. The most widely seen clothing marker of male pan-Mayanists is a new Western-style jacket whose body is made of a dark fabric woven in Totonicapán (a K'iche' town) and whose trim comes from Tecpán (a Kaqchikel town). The idea for the jacket came to Raxche', an active pan-Mayanist and entrepreneur, in 1988. For a number of years distribution of the jackets was tightly controlled: only active and recognized pan-Maya leaders were given the opportunity to purchase one; in turn, the jacket was an unmistakable indicator of status within the movement. Over time the jackets began to be awarded to certain foreign scholars in recognition for substantial contributions to the Maya people; Linda Schele, Nora England, and Judie Maxwell, among others, were so honored. The jackets are well made and well designed, appealing to a Western aesthetic sensibility, and thus were in great demand not as symbols of ethnic consciousness but for their use value. By the mid-1990s, Raxche' and his associates had lifted distribution restrictions, and though the jackets continue to be symbols of the pan-Maya movement, their utility as a marker of participation in the movement has dramatically decreased. Once, my wife and I were returning to Tecpán from a trip to the German bakery in Guatemala City. About halfway back we saw a man wearing one of these jackets standing by the side of the highway hitchhiking. We stopped to pick him up, certain we were about to make a new contact within the pan-Mayanist leadership, only to find that he was an itinerant book salesman who had received the jacket in a barter with one of his customers.

Carol Hendrickson (1995:193) notes that for many Maya "there is an ideological and emotional identification with traje such that dress is inextricably associated with the person's very being," and that there is a felt "equivalence between dress and cultural heart." Hendrickson is not claiming that identity is somehow coequal with dress, but rather that dress expresses and reinforces generative cultural patterns underlying widely accepted Maya expressions of identity. This is most evident in the production process itself; as Hendrickson notes, "weaving is a means for making public Maya intelligence" (ibid.:153), and in this sense is closely tied to issues of language and communication.

## Political Linguistics

Maya scholars take a strong Whorfian view of the relationship between language and culture, asserting that only by speaking a Mayan
language can one understand Maya culture and worldview. This is a
political as well as a theoretical position, setting clear boundaries for
group affiliation and exclusion based on a historically important aspect
of Maya identity, and one that has been largely maintained by male
leaders of the Maya movement. Accepting a strong version of the linguistic relativity hypothesis (which holds that language structures
mold, in a largely unself-conscious manner, worldview), many Maya
scholars argue that the most effective way to promote pan-Mayanist
agendas is through directed linguistic change. Much Maya activism has
thus focused on language conservation and revival, a strategy that may
be termed "political linguistics" because of its self-conscious, opportunistic use of technical linguistics to promote explicitly political ends (see
Cojtí Cuxil 1984, 1990, 1991; COCADI 1985).

The goals of Maya political linguistics are, first, to produce scholarly
linguistic analyses and, second, to use these data to support the political
agenda of pan-Mayanism (see López Raquec 1989; Oxlajuuj Keej 1993;
Fischer and Maxwell 1999). Their work is thus both descriptive and
prescriptive. Maya linguists are constructing new linguistic markers of
cultural awareness and new grammatical standards. At the same time,
they are expanding Maya lexicons, resurrecting words found in colonial
documents but in disuse today and creating new words for technological items rather than borrow from Spanish or English (e.g., Oxlajuuj
Keej 1993:124; B'alam 1994).

Some of the most successful linguistic innovations have come from
the Comunidad Lingüística Kaqchikel's efforts to create Kaqchikel
neologisms. Linguists working on the project started with the basic assumptions that new words should respect the phonological and mor-
phological patterns of the language, and that new words should be
short — lexemes rather than phrases. After extensive experimentation,
linguists found that certain neologisms based on salient cultural metaphors were most readily accepted by native speakers. For example, the
word *kematz'ib* for "computer" (lit., "weaver-[of]-writing") found ready
acceptance, spreading quickly from the classroom to the general populace and inspiring a number of metaphorical extensions as *q'inotz'ib'* (the
warp of writing) for "computer programs" and *kemomtz'ib'* (woven writing) for "computer files." In contrast, *let'et'*, a proposed neologism for

FIGURE 5.1. Kaqchikel neologisms and their sources.

| Colonial Period Word | Colonial Referent | Refurbished Referent |
|---|---|---|
| *amaq'* | lineage-polity | nation |
| *ajpopi'* | council of elders | council |
| *ikiqinem* | respect, fidelity | officialization |
| *k'oxtum* | inner precinct | temple |
| *champomal* | work leadership | government |
| *teleche'* | slave | one exploited |

| Lowland Glyphic Form | Reconstructed Highland Cognate | |
|---|---|---|
| *winal* | *winäq* | 20-day period |
| *tetun* | *che'ab'äj* | stela, lit. "stone tree" |
| *xok* | *xök* | shark |

*Source:* Fischer and Maxwell 1999.

"bicycle," has not caught on in daily usage. *Let'et'* was a new formation, based on a nonproductive noun formative and reduplication of the last vowel and consonant; the root itself, *let'*, has no meaning. Although the proposed *let'et'* met the criterion of being well formed by the rules of language, most people still prefer the more metaphorically loaded terms *kaxlan kej* (Spanish horse) and the ubiquitous *ch'ich'* (machine; lit. "metal"; Fischer and Maxwell 1999).

Greater acceptance was earned by a number of new words refurbished from colonial sources (which are considered to be "truly" Kaqchikel) and words borrowed from glyphic sources, examples of which are in Figure 5.1.[1]

The purity of these words' etymologies makes them appealing as "authentically" Maya, and this connection is often emphasized in dictionary entries. The greatest rate of acceptance, however, is for neologisms built on certain salient cultural metaphors and models. Three in particular have provided the basis for a number of neologisms that have been widely accepted: metaphors of family, metaphors of color, and Western and Maya models of scientific knowledge (Fischer and Maxwell 1999).

Figure 5.2 lists some of the neologisms developed in the Kaqchikel

FIGURE 5.2. Examples of accepted Kaqchikel neologisms and their metaphorical bases.

### Extended Kinship Metaphors

| | |
|---|---|
| *qamama' q'ij* | our grandfather sun |
| *qate' rach'ulew* | our mother earth |
| *qati't ik'* | our grandmother moon |
| *ral ik', rume'al q'ij* | planets, lit. "daughters of the Moon, daughters of the Sun" |
| *ch'ipch'umil* | Pluto, lit. "last born of the heavenly bodies" |

### Color Metaphors

| | |
|---|---|
| *kaqatz'amil* | iodine, lit. "red salt" |
| *saqamaq'* | state, lit. "white nation" |
| *raxnaqil* | health, lit. "green-ed-ness" |

### Scientific Metaphors

| | |
|---|---|
| *eyalil* | fluoride (from *ey*-"tooth" and a noun formative) |
| *q'anaq'alil* | sodium (from *q'än* "yellow" and *q'aq'* "fire" and a noun suffix) |
| *chuwiläj ab'äj* | sulphur (from *chuw* "stinking," *-iläj* "superlative" and *ab'äj* "stone") |

*Source:* Fischer and Maxwell 1999.

project that gained relatively wide acceptance. The solar system was named after the family, since, though the glyphs do show visible planets, only a few current names are known. The known subsystem consists of Grandfather Sun, Mother Earth, and Grandmother Moon — thus, planets became sister worlds, and Pluto, the last, became the *ch'ip.* Color terms, especially as linked to cardinality and Maya cosmology, have also been important sources of neologisms, both for their descriptive properties (as in *kaqatz'amil,* "red salt," for iodine) and their metaphorical and metonymical associations (as with *saqamaq',* "white nation," for state and *raxnaqil,* "green-ed-ness," for health). The third major source was scientific knowledge, both Western and Maya. Fluoride was named *eyalil,* since it strengthens teeth; sodium is called *q'anaq'alil,* since sodium filaments give off yellow-tinted light; and sulfur is documented in colonial texts as *chuwiläj ab'äj,* "stinkiest stone."

The formation of such neologisms is aesthetically and intellectually pleasing for its parsimonious blend of linguistic theory and political praxis. Yet these neologisms are created to be used by Kaqchikel speakers, and if they are not adopted they are ineffective in their intended use, no matter how eloquent their construction. Given the lack of formal authority afforded Kaqchikel linguists in native communities, introducing neologisms is problematic. Adoption must be voluntary, and, moreover, adopters must be highly motivated to learn and vigilantly use new words. Because of this situation, the innovations proposed by pan-Maya linguists are kept in check by grassroots conceptions of cultural appropriateness (which in turn is based on notions of cultural continuity and authenticity). Neologisms must therefore be true not only to the precepts of "proper" grammatical construction and historical linguists, but also to the usage and cognitive schema of a large percentage (if not the vast majority) of native speakers. It is through such intersubjective negotiations of appropriateness that individuals reproduce, reinforce, modify, and correlate overlapping cultural models. In turn, this process is effective in times of cultural solidarity because it builds on a widely shared, relatively stable, and cognitively deep set of generative structures.

Orthographic revision has also been an important part of pan-Mayanist linguistic work. Terrence Kaufman, in his role as chief linguistic consultant to the pioneering Proyecto Lingüístico Francisco Marroquín (PLFM) in the early 1970s, encouraged the creation of a new orthography for Mayan languages, arguing that those developed by foreign missionaries and used by the government were inaccurate and ethnocentric because they relied on Spanish characters to represent Maya phonemes (Kaufman 1976). Maya linguists working with the PLFM quickly adopted Kaufman's strategy, seeing an orthographic system that highlighted similarities between languages and dialects as a potentially powerful force in fostering greater pan-Maya unity (Cojtí Macario 1984). The Academia de las Lenguas Mayas de Guatemala (ALMG) was formed in the mid-1980s to coordinate efforts to officialize a unified alphabet for writing Mayan languages, a move opposed by the Summer Institute of Linguistics (SIL), which had developed distinct alphabets for each language based on Spanish orthography. SIL leaders responded to the ALMG's orthographic challenge by sending out a call to their evangelical supporters in the United States for "prayers that the proposal [of the unified alphabet] either be dropped or turned down" (quoted in Stoll 1982:268). Alas, their prayers went unanswered, and in 1988 a bill making the ALMG's unified alphabet the official orthography for writing Mayan languages was passed into law. (This has turned out to be something of a mixed blessing, most Maya linguists would argue today: although the unified alphabet is superior to its predecessors, having it written into law makes it extremely difficult to formally codify the further revisions linguists are making to the orthographic system.)

Early colonial documents have become important sources on autochthonous Maya culture and provide the only first-person Maya accounts of the Spanish invasion. Maya scholars have begun to work with colonial documents, contesting earlier translations and interpretations by non-Indians. Tzaquitzal Zapeta (1993) has translated the colonial document *Título de los Señores de Coyoy,* giving a contemporary Maya commentary on this early Maya document, and Sam Colop (1991) references a number of colonial documents, written by both Maya and Spaniards, to deconstruct the history of contact espoused within the Western tradition in general and by ladino academics in particular. For example, a famous passage from the sixteenth-century Kaqchikel text *Anales de los Kaqchikeles,* as translated by a number of scholars into both Spanish and English, reads: "Truly [the Spaniards] inspired fear when they arrived, we did not know their faces, and the lords took them for gods" (Brinton 1969; cf. Recinos and Goetz 1953). Sam Colop (1996) argues, however, that the Kaqchikel word *kab'owil,* translated above as "gods," is more accurately translated as "idol" or "image." Maya scholars use this and other such examples to challenge conventional views of Maya history in Guatemala. (There can be little doubt that control over historical representations has very real implications in Guatemala; ladino elites, for example, often cite the violence of precontact Maya societies to rationalize the brutality of recent counterinsurgency campaigns.)

## *Hieroglyphs*

The pan-Maya movement has made effective use of the strategy of employing scientific data—the incontestable cornerstone of Western modernity—to fight the intended course of Western expansion. Hieroglyphs play an important symbolic role in this regard, being a definitively autochthonous Maya system so long elusive to Western observers who tried to break the linguistic/ideological code.

For Maya scholars, hieroglyphs provide concrete data on the workings of precontact Maya society while acting as powerful symbols of the splendor and literacy of that culture. For several years before her death in 1998, the epigrapher Linda Schele offered hieroglyphic workshops for Maya groups, and the syllabaries she produced are widely circulated among Maya activists, who use them to write their names and the names of their organizations (Schele and Grube 1996). These glyphic syllabaries were developed to record Classic Period lowland Mayan languages, and current Maya activists speak one of the modern highland Mayan languages. Because of the centuries of divergence between these languages (as well as the incomplete decipherment of the glyphs), glyphic syllabaries are incomplete in their ability to record modern highland languages, and pan-Mayanists have created new glyphic elements to represent the uvular stops /q/ and /q'/ and the liquid consonant /r/, sounds that were not present in the Classic Period lowland languages. Figure 5.3 illustrates such glyphic adaptation as used on the cover of the pamphlet *Rujunamil Ri Mayab' Amaq'* (Specific Rights of the Maya People), authored by Rajpopi' Ri Mayab' Amaq' (Council of Maya Organizations of Guatemala, best known as COMG). In transcribing the name of their group into hieroglyphs, the authors modified the glyphic symbol for /ya/, adding a wavy line to indicate that it should be read as /ra/ (the historically related, highland equivalent of /ya/); and a snail-like element was added to the glyphic syllable /k'a/ to make it /q'a/ (also the sound to which it is historically related). Although no changes were made to the glyph for /hi/, it is read in this context as /ji/, and once again these sounds are historically related. Thus, one who knows the system may read the Kaqchikel name of the group in hieroglyphs: RA-J-PO-PI' [ri] MA-YA-B' A-MA-Q'.

The layout of the cover shown in Figure 5.3 subtly reinforces COMG's valuation of Maya culture and the political agenda outlined in this pamphlet. Like many pan-Mayanist writings, the text is in Spanish to allow maximum accessibility across language groups. But note that the hieroglyphic representation of the group's name is placed proximately at the top of the cover page, followed by a smaller bold-face transcription into modern (Latin-based) orthography, and finally (in still smaller type) in Spanish translation; the Kaqchikel title of the book is likewise highlighted over the Spanish translation. This layout makes clear the authors' valuation of Mayan languages, their intended

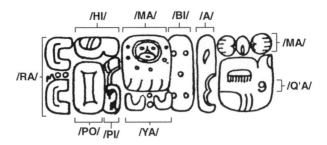

/HI/ /MA/ /BI/ /A/ /MA/ /RA/ moo /Q'A/ 9 /PO/ /PI/ /YA/

# RAJPOPI' RI MAYAB' AMAQ'

Consejo de Organizaciones Mayas de Guatemala
- COMG -

# RUJUNAMIL RI MAYAB' AMAQ'

Derechos Específicos del Pueblo Maya

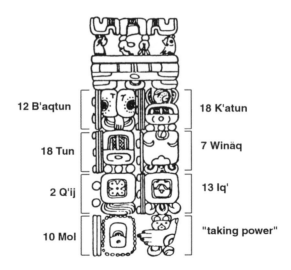

12 B'aqtun     18 K'atun

18 Tun     7 Winäq

2 Q'ij     13 Iq'

10 Mol     "taking power"

*... a pesar de 500 años... estamos presentes!*

FIGURE 5.3. The cover of COMG's *Rujunamil Ri Mayab' Amaq'*. Source: COMG 1991, annotations mine. Courtesy of Editorial Cholsamaj.

audience, and their own native language proficiency. The publication date of the book, which follows the title on the cover, is represented in the style of a Classic Maya hieroglyphic collocation using the Long Count and Calendar Round. Reading the bar (= "5") and dot (= "1") notations in the image from left to right and top to bottom, we arrive at a Long Count date of 12.18.18.7.2 and a Calendar Round date of 13 Iq' 10 Mol, which translates to September 7, 1991, in the Gregorian calendar. Following this date, the collocation concludes with a glyph that may be glossed as "taking power" (composed of a hand holding a lordly *ahua* face), reinforcing the view that publishing Maya scholarship is a form of empowerment. Sturm (1996) notes that such contemporary hieroglyphic texts may be read either literally or symbolically. Semantically specific readings are restricted to a small group of Maya activists and scholars literate in the modified hieroglyphic system. For most of their intended audience, these hieroglyphic collocations are read symbolically: recognizable as "Maya," they invoke political valences held by the individual reader. To make more explicit the message of empowerment encoded in the hieroglyphic text, the cover concludes with the following phrase in Spanish: ". . . despite 500 years . . . we are here!"

## *Maps*

Anderson (1983) notes the importance of maps (along with museums and censuses) in the construction of state-sponsored nationalist ideologies. Nations, after all, traditionally occupy clearly delimited territories, and cartographic representations give a sense of scientific exactitude (even "naturalness") to political boundaries. In Guatemala, production and control of maps does play an important role in state hegemony. In the 1980s and throughout most of the 1990s, all official maps of the country were produced by the Instituto Geográfico Militar, and their distribution was tightly controlled. Each map sheet had a unique serial number stamped on the back, and individuals who wanted to purchase maps had to travel to the Instituto's central office in Guatemala City, where their identification number would be registered along with the map's serial number. Presumably, if the maps were ever captured in the possession of guerrilla forces, the serial numbers would be traced back to their purchaser, who could then be questioned about their guerrilla contacts. Whether this ever actually happened I do not know, but the implied threat itself is revealing. The government clearly saw maps as important strategic and symbolic resources, and through the Instituto Geográfico Militar it sought to control access to maps of the country while exerting its authority to produce them. And herein lies the rub: these maps represented the country as it was seen by the powers that be, divided into administrative departments that reflect leaders' ideas of nation-statehood more than the country's ethnic geography.

Maya groups—in particular the publishing house Cholsamaj— have begun to contest the political implications of such government-produced maps by producing their own alternatives that have followed a telling development. Figure 5.4 shows the first in a series of maps produced by Cholsamaj and printed on the inside cover of notebooks distributed to Maya schoolchildren. Instead of the standard depiction of Guatemala's administrative departments, this map diagrams the territories covered by the country's Mayan language groups. In doing so, the map symbolically replaces technocratic ladino visions of statehood and national homogeneity with a graphic representation of Maya diversity and territorial expanse. The map identifies Mayan language groups using a key based on Classic Maya bar-and-dot numerals, and notes that Maya peoples make up approximately 60 percent of the Guatemalan population. In a nod to state sovereignty, the map includes the territory of Belize, long claimed by the Guatemalan state, as well as a prominent reference to the articles in the Guatemalan constitution that protect the right to use Mayan languages. In the lower left-hand side of the map, designers placed a variant of Cholsamaj's logo that, borrowing from Classic Period iconography of court scribes, shows a hand holding a writing brush emerging from the mouth of a vision serpent. This icon neatly captures Cholsamaj's self-envisioned role in the Maya movement as an outlet for contemporary visionary scribes while also lending a subtle sense of authenticity and ethnic authority to their publications. Opposite the Cholsamaj logo is the emblem of the United Nations International Children's Emergency Fund (UNICEF), which serves both to acknowledge that group's financial support and to legitimate Maya efforts through their association with an official international bureaucracy.

Figure 5.5 shows the next map in the series, which aggregates the areas where Mayan languages are spoken, thus accentuating the extent of the country's territory predominately occupied by Mayan-speaking peoples. The layout of the map subtly promotes the notion of pan-Maya unity while graphically conveying a sense of collective territorial

# PUEBLOS DE GUATEMALA

Guatemala la forman cuatro Pueblos claramente diferentes por su idioma, su cultura e historia: el Pueblo Maya ( + - 60% de guatemaltecos), el Pueblo Ladino ( + - 39% de guatemaltecos), el Pueblo Garífuna (- del 1% de guatemaltecos) y el Pueblo Xinka (en proceso de extinción). A su vez, en el seno del Pueblo Maya se distinguen varias comunidades lingüísticas porque hablan idiomas específicos:

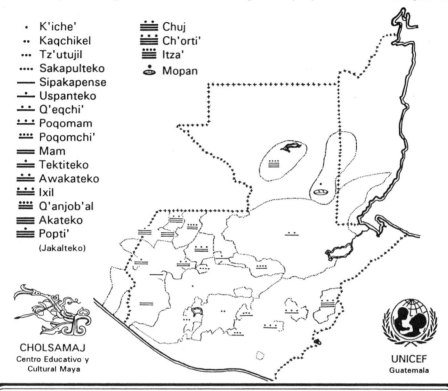

- K'iche'
- Kaqchikel
- Tz'utujil
- Sakapulteko
- Sipakapense
- Uspanteko
- Q'eqchi'
- Poqomam
- Poqomchi'
- Mam
- Tektiteko
- Awakateko
- Ixil
- Q'anjob'al
- Akateko
- Popti'
  (Jakalteko)

- Chuj
- Ch'orti'
- Itza'
- Mopan

CHOLSAMAJ
Centro Educativo y
Cultural Maya

UNICEF
Guatemala

*El Estado guatemalteco reconoce el derecho del Pueblo Maya, a mantener, desarrollar y disfrutar de sus idiomas.*

Ver Artículos No. 58 y No. 66
Constitución Política de la República de Guatemala
Promulgada el 31 de mayo de 1985.

FIGURE 5.4. "Peoples of Guatemala," the first map in a series produced by Cholsamaj. Courtesy of Editorial Cholsamaj.

| Pueblos de Guatemala<br>Porcentajes de habitantes, según los censos del INE y otras fuentes: | | | | | | | |
|---|---|---|---|---|---|---|---|
| | 1893* | 1950* | 1981* | 1981** | 1989*** | 1989** | 1993** |
| Maya | 64.7 | 53.6 | 41.9 | 60.88 | 37.1 | 60.88 | 60.88 |
| Ladino | 35.2 | 46.3 | 57.9 | 39.00 | 62.8 | 39.00 | 39.00 |
| Garífuna | ---- | ---- | ---- | 00.11 | ---- | 0.11 | 0.11 |
| Xinka | ---- | ---- | ---- | 00.005 | ---- | 0.005 | 0.005 |

* Censos INE.

** Pobl., Pueblos y Comunidades de Guatemala. Leopoldo Tzian, diciembre 92 (inédito).

*** Encuesta sociodemográfica, INE.

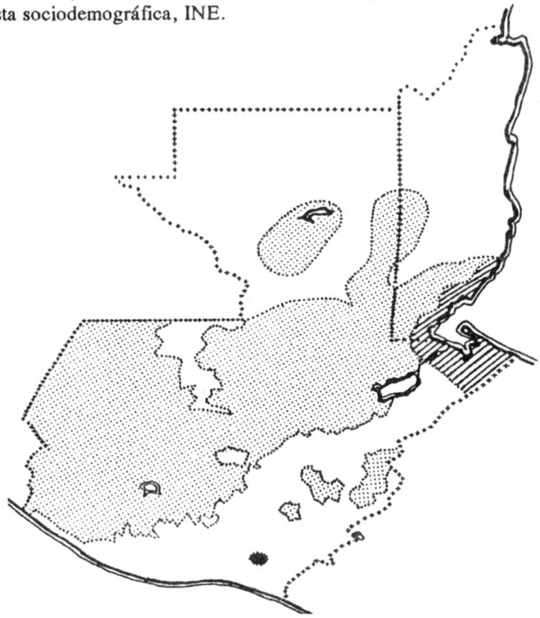

UNICEF
Guatemala

CHOLSAMAJ
Centro Educativo y
Cultural Maya

### AÑO INTERNACIONAL DE LOS PUEBLOS INDÍGENAS DEL MUNDO

*El 10-12-92, la Asamblea General de las Naciones Unidas ONU, en su 47 período de sesiones solemnemente declaró nominar 1993, como el AÑO INTERNACIONAL DE LOS PUEBLOS INDÍGENAS.**

Es un reconocimiento internacional a la existencia del Pueblo Maya, Garífuna y Xinka dentro del Estado guatemalteco, al que hace referencia el Artículo No. 66 de la Constitución Política.

*ONU, 10.12.92, New York.

FIGURE 5.5. "Peoples of Guatemala," the second map in a series produced by Cholsamaj. Courtesy of Editorial Cholsamaj.

expanse. At the top of the page revisionist census data from the work of Maya scholar Leopoldo Tzian are juxtaposed with much lower official figures from the Instituto Nacional de Estadística (INE). The disparity between the figures from INE and Tzian suggestively point to what Demetrio Cojtí calls the "statistical genocide" practiced by the Guatemalan state: undercounting Maya peoples in order to undermine their claims to power and representation. Tzian's revisionist count emphasizes the demographically dominant position of Maya peoples in Guatemala, hinting at the political possibilities this implies. This map again includes the UNICEF logo and further emphasizes ties to legitimating international bodies by quoting the United Nations' proclamation declaring 1993 to be the International Year of Indigenous Peoples. Such references to external authority act to buffer the rather radical notion of representing all Guatemalan Maya peoples as part of a single group that occupies about half of the state's territory.

The last map in the series, "Territory of the Maya People before 1492," goes even further in staking out the full expanse of Maya territories (Figure 5.6). Depicting all lands occupied by Maya peoples throughout their history, the map subsumes the state boundaries of Mexico, Guatemala, Belize, Honduras, and El Salvador within a unified notion of *el pueblo maya.* The inspiration for (and scholarly validation of) this map presumably comes from the quote at the bottom of the page by the archaeologist J. Eric Thompson, who observes that Maya peoples occupied an area equal to 325,000 square kilometers, including all of the current Guatemalan state territory. Yet the scene is being described by a Classic Maya figure seated at the bottom left of the page, with the entire map enclosed in a speech balloon (a hybrid style adapted from Classic Maya iconography, Central Mexican pictographs, and comic book dialogues). Using this technique to frame the map, Cholsamaj's designers imply that such a unified view of Maya culture was the vision of Maya ancestors, and thus represents an authentic and legitimate claim for current Maya activism. This point is further emphasized in the image of the Maya scribe, pictured in a much more aggressive pose than in the previous maps, who is envisioning (by way of thought balloons) the same image of pan-Maya unity as the ancestor figure. The development of this series of maps graphically demonstrates how Maya leaders' representations of pan-Mayanism are becoming increasingly inclusive: first highlighting linguistic groups, then aggregating Maya territory within Guatemala, and finally showing a transnational pan-Maya unity.

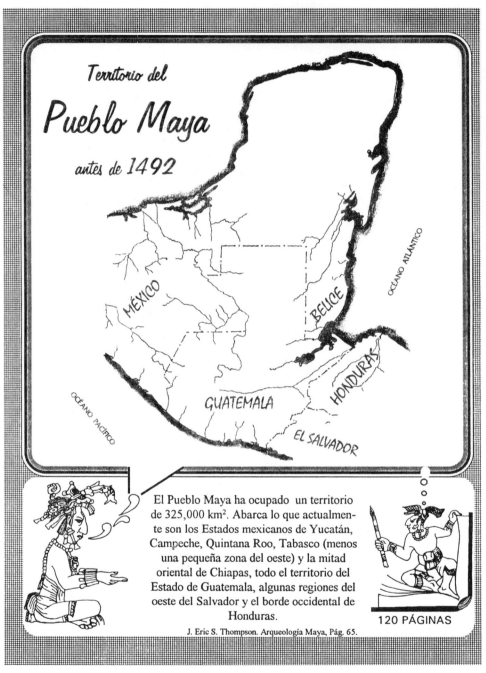

FIGURE 5.6. "Territory of the Maya People before 1492," the third map in a series produced by Cholsamaj. Courtesy of Editorial Cholsamaj.

## Communication: The Message of Pan-Mayanism

Pan-Mayanists have produced a wealth of scholarship and political analyses, and they have simultaneously had to develop new outlets for disseminating their work. The greatest barrier to effective Maya mass communication is an extremely high illiteracy rate among Maya peoples in Guatemala (over 80 percent in many rural areas) and the lack of technological infrastructure. For these and other social reasons, Maya culture places a high value on oral skill and dexterity; indeed, local political systems are traditionally based on a consensus model that favors persuasive orators. Building on this cultural bias, early pan-Maya activists distributed teachings and lectures about the value of Maya culture on audiocassette tapes. Families and small groups would listen to these and pass them along informal social networks within and between communities throughout Guatemala. And as televisions and video recorders have become more common, these same sorts of materials are being distributed on videotape.

Radio broadcasts have been especially effective at disseminating the pan-Mayanist message, particularly through the popular weekly program *Mayab' Winäq*. Sponsored by several Maya organizations and a few Maya-owned private companies, *Mayab' Winäq* is broadcast Sundays from 4:30 A.M. until 7:30 A.M. on Guatemala's Radio Nuevo Mundo. Mostly in Spanish, but with liberal doses of Kaqchikel and other Mayan languages, *Mayab' Winäq* combines music, political commentary, public service announcements, and short radio plays, all with a pan-Mayanist message. As intoned by the deep, booming voice of the program's host, Jolom B'alam,

> *Mayab' Winäq* brings together the roots of Maya culture: identity, music, and history. It is the voice of the people, of Maya sentiment and expression. It is the pure and sincere song of a peoples that hold dear the hope of future peace, equality, brotherhood, and justice for all. It is the musical expression of these words that carries our message of fraternity. It is the thought transmitted from our ancestral parents Xpiapok and Ixmukane.

Ironically for me, huddled over my portable radio at 4:30 in the morning, shivering from the cold Tecpán morning air and constantly adjusting the antenna to pull in the signal, *Mayab' Winäq* seems to have captured perfectly the style of popular Spanish radio programs, down to the richly inflected voice of the announcers and the catchy self-promotional jingoes (see Figure 5.7 for examples).

* "*Mayab' Winäq* — el raíz de todo el país."
* "Es la hora de venir a la cita y retornar el camino perdido."
* "*Mayab' Winäq* es la expresión de un pueblo que solamente pide una oportunidad para vivir."
* "Radio Nuevo Mundo los invita escuchar el programa más nacionalista en la radiodifusión guatemalteca: *Mayab' Winäq*, dirigido y producido por profesionales de la cultura maya."
* "*Mayab' Winäq* es de nuestras milenarias raíces mayas."

FIGURE 5.7. Promotional jingoes from the *Mayab' Winäq* radio program.

Each episode opens with a dramatic reading from the opening lines of the Popol Wuj: "Ha llegado el tiempo de amanecer, de que se termina la obra . . . se unificaron, llegaron y celebraron consejo en la obscuridad de la noche, descansaron y discutieron, reflexionaron y pensaron de esta manera salieron a la luz claramente sus decisiones [The time of dawning has arrived, for the work to be accomplished . . . they joined together, arrived at the appointed place, and took counsel under the cover of darkness. They rested and discussed matters at leisure; they reflected and thought. In this manner, their decisions came forth with clarity]."[2] Regular programming includes an ongoing series that gives mnemonic devices to remember Maya day names, educational plays that outline the constitutional rights of Maya peoples, and recorded speeches. *Mayab' Winäq* has arguably been the most successful effort by Maya leaders to reach out to the rural Maya masses. A number of friends in Tecpán and Patzún are fans of the show, and its producers say that they have received enthusiastic responses from across the country.

Although less widely received, several pan-Mayanist organizations have begun to produce newspapers, magazines, and other printed materials for the Maya public. Notable among these are the Centro Maya Saqb'e's newsletter *Rutzijol,* which presents stories about Maya cultural activities as well as reports the weekly prices of basic crops in regional markets. Maya Saqb'e also publishes a children's newspaper, *Kukuy* (for "the boys and girls of maize, the future of the Maya people"), and the very useful *Rutzijol Selección Quincenal de Noticias acerca del Pueblo Maya,* which reprints stories of concern to the Maya appearing in the Guatemalan national press.

The editorial house Cholsamaj has been the most prolific publisher of Maya work, producing scores of books (with an average print run of 1,500 copies). Established in the late 1980s, Cholsamaj has from its

earliest days taken advantage of desktop publishing and computer layout, and they have developed proprietary software that allows them to
quickly and easily set type in Maya hieroglyphs. Cholsamaj is reliant on
grants from international organizations and, increasingly, on publishing contracts from these same groups. Recognizing the vulnerability
brought about by this dependence, Cholsamaj spun off a for-profit subsidiary press, Maya Wuj; the nonprofit Cholsamaj owns 51 percent of
Maya Wuj and employees of the press own the other 49 percent. Maya
Wuj does a lively trade in private printing jobs, including books, diplo-
mas, posters, and wedding announcements. Its best-selling item is an
annual date book (*Cholb'al Q'ij/Agenda Maya*) that combines the hieroglyphic symbols for traditional Maya day names with Gregorian calendar dates and short essays about Maya cultural values and political demands. The 1999 print run produced 10,000 copies, and plans for the
2000 edition include an executive model packaged with an embossed
leather case.

Pan-Mayanists also use more traditional mass-media outlets to communicate with their constituencies, to sway *kaxlan* opinions, and to
make clear their vision. Cholsamaj produces *Jotaytzij*, a monthly bilingual supplement for the national newspaper *Siglo XXI*.[3] *Jotaytzij* presents translated summaries of news stories, original reporting on pan-
Mayanist activities, and editorials. In 1999, over 60,000 copies were
distributed each month, and the press has begun e-mail distribution of
*Jotaytzij* for readers abroad. Two of Guatemala's leading daily newspapers, *Prensa Libre* and *Siglo XXI*, have full-time Maya editorialists: Enrique Sam Colop, a lawyer who holds a Ph.D. in anthropology from the
State University of New York at Buffalo, writes for *Prensa Libre*, and
Estuardo Zapeta, a journalist and a graduate student in anthropology
at SUNY-Albany, has a regular column in *Siglo XXI*.

Zapeta's editorials in *Siglo XXI* have provoked controversy among
pan-Mayanists and ladinos alike, and they illustrate the diversity encompassed by broadly conceived pan-Mayanism (see Zapeta 1999 for
a compilation of his columns). A K'iche' man from Santa Cruz del
Quiché, Zapeta is an avowedly neoliberal pan-Maya activist, positions
that many see as mutually exclusive. But Zapeta claims that neoliberal
political reforms are good for the Maya, devolving power back to the
people from discriminatory and inefficient state bureaucracies. Seeing
the same forces at work that Friedman (1994) describes, Zapeta believes that neoliberal policies have allowed pan-Mayanism to emerge
and flourish, and that the movement should more whole-heartedly em-

brace further reform. For example, the 1996 Peace Accords call for the formation of a national Maya University in Guatemala to promote culturally appropriate higher education for the Maya peoples. In several of his columns and public speeches, Zapeta has argued that the Maya University should be a private institution, an idea that has met with fierce opposition. Many pan-Mayanist leaders see the notion of a private Maya University as elitist, and worry that it would continue to restrict higher education to a small percentage of the Indian population. Zapeta counters that an initial endowment from the government and international organizations combined with a higher-education voucher system would provide adequate scholarships for needy students, without the bureaucratic tangles and curricular meddling of a state institution. Such disputes are not easily settled, and the ideological stakes are high.

### Tactical Ethnicity and Cultural Constraints

For Maya activists, the symbols they mobilize are not mere political tools to be manipulated for any contingency. Maya leaders are constructing a new configuration of Maya identity, one that it is hoped can transcend community allegiances. In their construction, however, they are constrained by the tools at hand, and those tools are historically received symbols, meanings, and cultural constructs. This is a self-conscious constructivism, attempting to be true to perceptions of the Maya past — the sacredness of all that is deemed authentically precolumbian Maya. Such constructivism is fundamentally different from that described in much constructivist theory. It is a constructivism constrained by perceptions of the past and ideals of Maya authenticity as well as by less explicit grassroots perceptions. What Maya activists do must not only fit with their own historical interpretations but also with the myriad interpretations found in geographically dispersed communities.

Maya activists perhaps do feel less constrained than the "average" Maya by the weight of traditional usage in their tactical deployment of Maya symbols. It must be emphasized, however, that the symbols Maya employ are intentionally polyvalent, depending on the intended audience. Pan-Mayanist leaders are in the awkward position of having several constituencies, often with competing interests, to which they are beholden. Their primary obligation is to the country's Maya population, the vast majority of whom live in rural areas. Thus initial efforts have focused on raising the cultural consciousness of the masses, demonstrating and reinforcing the value of Maya culture, arguing for its role in the modern world, and recognizing it as a basis for concerted political action. Second, pan-Mayanist leaders must appeal to the powers that be in Guatemala — challenging racist opinions and lobbying for legal changes, certainly, but also portraying the pan-Mayanist agenda as primarily cultural rather than political (and thus nonthreatening and undeserving of violent reprisal). Finally, pan-Mayanists must also court the attention and favor of international academics and policymakers. Playing on the recent global valuation of all things indigenous, the recognition of indigenous rights as a subset of fundamental human rights, and the ideological commitment of many academics to support the empowerment of marginalized peoples, pan-Mayanists have been very successful at gaining material support for the movement from international organizations (including the United Nations, the European Union, the U.S. Agency for International Development, and numerous private foundations). In balancing the often competing intentions engendered by their diverse constituencies, Maya activists rely on fluid, and at times strategically ambiguous, representations of their positions. They have been particularly successful in domains such as language and dress, actively redefining what is meant by certain signifiers in a manner that promotes a raising of cultural consciousness.

The art of identity politics lies in the strategic and often self-conscious manipulation of received structures and norms toward situationally contingent ends. Yet the practice of identity politics is more than just politically instrumental opportunism, for actors also unselfconsciously reproduce the structures of implicit cognitive models. The following section examines the reproduction of such cognitive models as expressed through lived experience in Tecpán and Patzún.

PART

III

*Maya Identity as*

*Lived Experience in*

*Tecpán and Patzún*

# 6

# *Souls, Socialization, and the Kaqchikel Self*

Acknowledging the indeterminacies inherent in any social situation between act and outcome, one's intent and other's inference, improper eccentricity and acceptable rationalization, the moral logic of Chimalteco souls demands an existential eloquence of continual engagement with other individuals, predicated on established cultural precedents.

JOHN WATANABE (1992)

In this chapter I examine socialization in Tecpán and Patzún in relation to the formation of the heart-soul (*k'u'x*), arguing that cognitive models of *k'u'x* are an important mechanism of cultural commonality. A normal person is described as having a content *k'u'x*, and abnormal behavior is related to various states of the *k'u'x* (cold, hot, hard, in motion, and so on). Abnormal states may be fleeting reactions to specific events, but individuals are also predisposed to hold certain *k'u'x* traits. These predispositions are partly due to destiny (the unique conjuncture of animizing cosmic forces prevailing on the date of one's birth) but more significantly result from the shaping of one's heart during early childhood. I show how certain community norms concerning labor, gift giving, and filial piety are encouraged through values related to the *k'u'x*, and how these values and norms have adapted to changing material circumstances. I conclude by demonstrating how the cognitive schema of *k'u'x* and its variable states encode certain key aspects of a dynamic Maya cultural logic.

## Breast-feeding and the Sacred Mesoamerican Covenant

Building on Gillin's (1952) observation that infants are trained permissively, Colby (1967) suggests that Mesoamerican cultures are permeated by themes of orality that are, in turn, related through a Freudian logic to a concern with trust. The interrelationship between orality and group trust and cohesion is seen most graphically in accounts of Aztec ritual cannibalism, although Colby argues that this same psychological association underwrites commonplace traditions such as ritual feasting, the exchange of food and drink when negotiating a marriage, and the sealing of an agreement with a shot of liquor.

Colby might also have included that primordial object of oral fixation—the lactating breast—in his list. In Tecpán and Patzún, most Kaqchikel mothers have liberal breast-feeding regimes that usually last from one to three years, although it is not uncommon to see a toddler as old as four or five suckling occasionally, for comfort more than nutrition. Weaning is often precipitated by the birth of siblings, and Colby suggests that early weaning frequently results in unrequited oral desires and uncertainty over issues of social trust that must then be satisfied in later life through rituals with a prominent oral component, especially those involving food.

In widespread Mesoamerican cosmologies, food production and consumption is closely related to a sacred covenant based on reciprocal relations between humans and cosmic forces that animates the cycle of agricultural production and ensures the world's continual regeneration (see Freidel, Schele, and Parker 1993; Monaghan 1995; cf. Gudeman and Rivera 1990 on similar Colombian peasant views). Many traditionalist Kaqchikeles in Tecpán and Patzún explicitly hold such a view. For them, an abundant harvest reflects the strived-for state of equilibrium between cosmic and earthly forces; food exchange and sharing, as a sign of such abundance, both reflects and reinforces this harmony. Further, agricultural rejuvenation is not only symbolically but quite literally tied to corporeal existence and genetic posterity: individually, it is the gift of continued life, and in sustaining the family, it is the gift of everlasting life. Even many Catholic and Protestant Kaqchikeles (and to a lesser extent ladino farmers) interpret their church doctrine in a manner consistent with this traditionalist view. Christianity's focus on blood sacrifice and formal agreements between humans and their god are clearly convergent with the Maya view of a sacred covenant, and harvest ceremonies involving ritual sacrifice and offerings are commonly held in churches as well as at ancient ritual sites.

Watanabe and Smuts (1999) argue that ritual is a mechanism for expressing and reinforcing social cooperation and trust, and that food and drink have long been recognized by anthropologists as holding a singular position in the reciprocal maintenance of social relationships. Yet this need not be logically related to a shared psychological substrate conditioned by arrested oral development in early childhood. More than just oral gratification, it is the symbolic value of food before it enters the mouth and the material effects of food after it has been swallowed that give it a unique association with trust and cooperation.

Mother's milk is a primordial source of sustenance and life for the Maya, in the same class of animizing substances as maize and semen. It is seen as a food source par excellence, pure and natural while at the same time linked to metaphysical cyclic forces, and it plays an important role in early childhood socialization and the establishment of social bonds. In contrast to the European pattern of rigid timetables for feeding, Maya infants often snack throughout their waking hours in frequent feedings that last only a few minutes. Even infants raised on formula generally do not experience the crises of feeding characteristic of more rigid feeding regimes, leading to a sense of security closely tied, corporally and affectively, to the mother. This security is reinforced in swaddling practices. Infants are viewed as physically and metaphysically vulnerable in their early life and thus have to be kept tightly wrapped (preferably in red cloth that carries the metaphysical quality of heat to insulate the fragile soul). Most infants further spend virtually all of their day in close physical proximity to their mother or primary caregiver, most often literally tied to her back by a piece of cloth (an *ejqab'äl*). Travelers to Guatemala are often surprised when the bundle on the back of a woman standing next to them on a bus begins to move and wail, such is the nonchalance (naturalness) with which Maya mothers carry their young children.

Gillin's (1952) description of the Maya gestalt relates permissive childhood training to the ethno-psychological trait of seeking peaceful adjustment to cosmic forces. The Maya patterns of liberal breast-feeding and relatively liberal weaning initiate children into the sacred covenantal relationship between humans and vitalistic forces. Children are themselves the product of the covenant's continual rejuvenation of life; the giving of mother's milk metonymically symbolizes the larger process of metaphysical forces provisioning human existence. The relationship between humans and cosmic forces is based on reciprocity and cyclic reproduction, and so, too, is the relationship between mother and child. In part, the mother's return gift may be understood in terms of evolutionary fitness, the child providing a container for her genes to survive into the next generation (Dawkins 1976). Children are also conditioned to pay back this life-giving generosity through Chayanovian household labor, starting at a very early age. Children contribute labor to their parents' household throughout their lives, and male children often begin their own families as extensions of their parents', continuing the unspoken reciprocal labor agreements until they have enough savings to strike out on their own. Even after establishing a separate household, filial piety in the form of gifts (these days usually money) is expected, paying back one's parents symbolically and literally for the gift of life. The youngest male child, the *ch'ip*, is expected to live at home and care for his parents throughout their lives.[1]

Of course, circumstantial contingencies frequently alter such norms in actual practice. The youngest child may have a good job in another city, or one of the elder children may elect to stay at home. Likewise, an increasing number of mothers who work outside of the home in jobs where they cannot bring their infants must rely on less frequent breast-feedings supplemented by commercial formula. Some might argue that the frequency of deviation negates the validity of the norm; norms are still important, however, to the extent they are implicated in variations. If variant behavior is motivated and interpreted in relation to a normative model, then that model is still symbolically and practically valid, regardless of the frequency of non-normative instantiations. This is not to deny the primacy of practice as the subject of anthropology, but practice should encompass more than materially observable behavior, namely the culturally conditioned cognitive frameworks that give rise to concrete activity. Nor do I intend to reify the power of hegemonic construction. Through practice and the ongoing negotiation of consensual norms, subaltern variants can replace hegemonic norms; nonetheless, variants continue to be structurally dependent on the existence of a norm.

It is useful here to recall Lacan's (1981 [1956]) theory of the mirror stage of identity formation. Lacan argues that self-identity is first formed through a reflective and reflexive relationship between infant and mother (or primary caregiver). The primary narcissism of the mirror stage is due to the child's lack of an experiential social basis on which ego self-identity is based and is conditioned by the memory of seeming omnipotence in the womb. Building on the work of Freud and Piaget, Lacan posits that ego formation follows a sequence of identification leading to differentiation as one's consciousness expands. Though individuation may seem a "natural" psychological outcome of Western self-identity formation, Jonathan Friedman (1994:337) points out that "where the modern has his self, or ego, as the locus of his life-project's authority, the tendency in traditional societies is that the project and its authority exist external to the human subject, in the larger social network and its cosmological principles."

Most Kaqchikel children are conditioned from their earliest days by a close tie to their mother (reinforced through breast-feeding and swaddling practices), and the formation of their self-identity is certainly conditioned by this relationship. Nonetheless, the relationship of a child with its mother vicariously ties the child to larger systems of social relations and cosmic forces, including the family, the hearth group, and the community. Ultimately, the child is tied through the mother (and her sacrificial gift of milk) to the sacred covenant that requires sacrifice to ensure continued physical and cultural rejuvenation. Intergenerational cycles are but agricultural cycles writ large, and both are part of the larger cycle of creation.

## Socialization

Playing games occupies very little of Maya children's time in Tecpán and Patzún, although this varies significantly with socioeconomic position. From an early age, most children's play involves mimicking or actually helping in chores around the house and in the fields. It is through such work/play that Maya children are socialized in countless unspoken traditions and come to define themselves in relation to the conventions of their cultural community. Watanabe (1992:96–99) notes that in Mam child-rearing practices, most instruction and learning about how to act in the world remains tacit in the socialization process, supporting Bourdieu's (1977:167) assertion that "what is essential *goes without saying because it comes without saying:* the tradition is silent, not least about itself as a tradition." In the process of socialization, foundational cognitive schemas based on culturally received norms are laid down, and the basic structure of these schemas often remains remarkably resilient throughout one's life.

Socialization is composed of the unique conjunctures over time of individual cognitive models and biogenetic predispositions with available cultural resources (normative and otherwise). This view focuses on the idiosyncratic and contextually specific praxis of socialization (the interaction of the individual and the collectivity) to avoid portraying socialization as a homogeneous indoctrination of cultural values. Information received during the process of socialization must be reconciled with biocognitive predispositions. In the earliest days of life, biochemically produced instincts provide the individual predispositions reflexively indexed to the social and material world (demanding to be fed, for example), but in later weeks, months, and years these become overshadowed by cognitive models built on lived experience. Through repeated exposure to structurally similar social relations, certain cultural logics are deduced from and then induced upon social experience, with sociocognitive mechanisms conspiring (with varying degrees of success) to maintain consistency in action and representation. We may distinguish two broad phases of socialization, primary (or early childhood) and secondary (which takes on increasing importance in later childhood and continues throughout one's life). Primary socialization involves first and foremost an infant and his or her primary caregiver(s), who most often is a consanguineal female relation from the first or second ascendant generation. The inter-generational transfer of social norms remains important in secondary socialization, though over time it is increasingly replaced by generationally horizontal flows of information.

Socialization in both its forms involves reconciling new information with preexisting frameworks, and this occurs in a number of ways. Socialization occurs in a number of obvious ways, such as teaching children how to act and behave through inducements or punishments, as well as in a number of very subtle ways as children observe the myriad instantiations of social behavior to which they are daily exposed and extrapolate patterns from those behaviors. It is through such subtle means that the *doxa* is formed: the learning of unquestioned assumptions about the world, so fundamental that they must remain unspoken lest they be questioned. As Watanabe (1992:99) notes, "Learning never rationalizes conventions as the best choice between possible alternatives—indeed alternatives are seldom explicitly appraised." Through the reflexive praxis of socialization, children learn how to view the world, providing the foundation for future learning in a process Rogoff (1990) terms "an apprenticeship in thinking."

## *Metaphysical Balance and Identity*

The concept of reciprocal balance is an axiomatic feature of certain domains of Maya culture. (By this, I do not intend to negate the significant interpretative variation found in practice, but rather to focus on common points of reference that inform circumstantial variation.) Ethnographies from across Mesoamerica have pointed to the significance of balance in native cosmologies (e.g., López Austin 1988; Boremanse 1993, 1998; Monaghan 1995). Lévi-Strauss (1995) would likely see this as part of the dynamic dualism characteristic of native mythology throughout the hemisphere. A concept of balance has occupied a central role in Maya cosmology at least since Classic Period times (Freidel, Schele, and Parker 1993; Hill and Fischer 1999), and this balance has both spatial and temporal correlates in solar movements and the agricultural cycle (Hunt 1977; Watanabe 1983). For many Maya today, continued human existence is predicated on the maintenance of a cosmic balance that both affects and reflects earthly conditions, maintaining cyclic accumulation, agricultural rejuvenation, and procreation (see Tedlock 1982; Carlsen and Prechtel 1991).

Balance is conceptually related to centeredness. The center is definitionally midway, implying a balance of quantities (and these may be time, space, material goods, or anything else) in oppositional relation to the point of reference. This need not be conceived as a state of two-dimensional balance, such as with a see-saw. Indeed a three-dimensional model seems to better approximate the Kaqchikel conception. Balance, in the Kaqchikel conception, also requires grounding, an idea that again has precolumbian roots, for it was from the center of the primordial hearthstones that the tree of life, a maize tree, grew. The primordial maize tree thus was at the center of the cosmos, implying a propitiously balanced state, and yet, even as maize today, it was planted, grounded in the most literal sense.

Maya religious specialists have long been students of mathematics and numerology. Sacred calendars keep track of the passage of time and are used in native historiography and predictions. Calendrical equations mathematically represent the forces of the cosmos and their cyclic yet progressive nature: the perfect nature of cosmic harmony is mirrored in the precise balance of mathematical equations. Indeed the empirical essence of balance is a mathematical equation that works out; it is as simple as $1 + 1 = 2$. For example, the *tzolkin* (*chol q'ij* in Kaqchikel

Mayan) is the mostly widely used Maya calendrical system today. It measures a 260-day period; the *tzolkin*'s 20 named days (each associated with a certain conjuncture of cosmic forces) are complemented by numerical coefficients running from one to thirteen. Cosmic harmony is measured (and in part maintained) through counting of the progression of *tzolkin* cycles, and the balance of physical and metaphysical forces is mathematically demonstrable in the calendar's cycle (20 x 13 = 260). The number thirteen plays into numerous Maya equations; the primordial world tree was planted on the back of a turtle with thirteen platelets on its shell, associating thirteen with the primordial confluence of cosmic forces that produced the current creation. Words for twenty in Mayan languages (*winäq* in Kaqchikel) are cognate with words for human being (*winäq* in Kaqchikel). Finally, 260 days approximates the human gestation period, linking the human life cycle (including both cultural and biological regeneration) to the cyclic harmony of cosmic time and the confluence of cosmic forces acting upon individuals to result in their destiny. Thus this equation may be symbolically read as cosmic forces (13) acting on (x) individuals (20) regenerates human existence (260).

The day upon which one is born significantly affects one's fate, linking the self to the convergence of cosmic forces associated with a particular calendrical date. Though destiny is to some extent ascribed, it is also mutable, just as the mutability of cosmic cycles results in the irony of cyclic progression; events reoccur structurally without being identical in their contingent implications. The creation of the world itself resulted from cyclic progression, what Tedlock (1982:202) calls "accumulation"; for the Maya, three previous creations were destroyed because the beings created refused to perpetuate the covenants of spiritual and material reciprocity demanded by cosmic forces.

Such cyclic progression aptly captures the dynamics of a Maya cultural logic in which consensual norms are perpetuated in changing contexts. In part, this is based on the covenantal relationship between humans and cosmic forces and the dynamic cyclicity of history. Gary Gossen (1986:5) observes that mediation between cosmic and earthly realms is "key [to] intellectual, political, and religious activity, for with successful mediation come power, wisdom, and even personal health and community survival." Life on earth seeks to approximate cosmic harmony (or threatens to be destroyed through disjuncture with cosmic forces), both collectively and individually.

## *Maya Souls and the Self*

During the Classic Maya era, cosmic harmony was maintained through human blood sacrifices to the gods; today cosmic forces are appeased through acts of ritualized reciprocity. As related through hieroglyphic inscriptions and oral traditions, the primordial events that gave life to humankind and set the cosmos in motion were played out both on earth and in the celestial sphere, and the animizing force behind these events is linked to the eternal cycles of time as measured by the movement of the sun, the moon, and the stars. Conceived of in its perfect unitary state, the cosmic order is one of harmony and balance between natural and metaphysical forces. It is the duty of (Maya) humans to approximate cosmic harmony on earth, even if this end is known to be ultimately unattainable. Edmonson (1993:70) writes that

> like god, the human being exists in his or her self, his or her uniqueness (*t u ba, t u hunal*). The self (*ba*) or thingness (*baal*) of god and the human being lies in their relation to each other (*t u ball ba*), and this reciprocity is the inmost part (*ol*) of each. In various contexts this is identified with the heart, breath, mouth, eye or face, head, belly or womb, blood or semen, flesh and bone, but it is the center (*ol*) that is the seat of feeling, of thought, and of the soul (*pixan*).

Collective harmony is reinforced through adherence to rituals scripted to approximate cosmic equilibrium; individually, a balance should be maintained between aspects of the cosmic animizing force acting on the self.

Kaqchikeles view the self (and thus self-identity) as intimately connected to cosmic forces and phenomena, primarily through what anthropologists conventionally gloss as "souls," "spirits," or "animistic forces" (cf. Monaghan 2000: 44). This view is more overt among religious traditionalists, but it also permeates the hybrid beliefs of Maya Catholics and Protestants and even the social practice of many agnostics. Maya souls indelibly link the individual to the cosmic forces that animate the world, thus blurring the very boundaries that the modern (Western) conception of "self" seeks to delineate. Such a view of self was often problematic for Spanish missionizing. As Klor de Alva writes in his review of Nahuatized Christianity, "the boundary between the individual self (the sole object of a Christian-type salvation), other selves, and what Westerners would consider nonanimate objects was completely permeable. Human beings physically and supernaturally formed part of a universal continuum linking their fortunes directly to the cosmic order" (1993:185). This holds true for the Maya as well, among whom this link to the cosmic order is complex and multifaceted.

John Monaghan (2000) cautions against the creation of discrete categorizations of Mesoamerican soul concepts. Following Boremanse (1993), he prefers to see a singular divine force (*pixan* in Lacandón and other Mayan languages) that "takes on different aspects, depending on the context" (44). Edmonson (1993) similarly emphasizes the essential unity of the Maya soul and divine force as seen in the soul's "inner motives," though not necessarily transparent from the "outer clues" it gives. Such a concept of the unity of souls or soul-aspects follows logically from the Maya philosophical presupposition of fundamental cosmic connectedness—just as the individual is one with the cosmic order, so too are cosmic forces ultimately connected. The Maya penchant for seeing unity in apparent (to us) diversity is characteristic of a particular cultural logic diffuse enough to be transposable into various cultural domains while adhering to internal generative rules that render its instantiations intelligible (even if not sanctioned) by others.

In Maya and other Mesoamerican worldviews, cosmic forces act on the individual through a number of loci, including the mind, the liver, and the heart. For many Kaqchikeles, the concepts of *k'u'x* and *anima* are central to an understanding of the relationship between individuals and the cosmos.

### The Heart and Soul of Maya Culture

The notion of physical and metaphysical reciprocal balance underwrites key aspects of Kaqchikel socialization. The clearest explications of the logic of balance are found in the discursive domain of the heart and soul, and I will turn now to cognitive models of the Kaqchikel *k'u'x* and *anima*.

In a recent monograph, Wierzbicka (1997) advances a strong case for *Understanding Cultures Through Their Key Words.*[2] Key words are important in understanding other worldviews precisely because they index nonoverlapping domains of cultural logics. In Kaqchikel there are a large number of words with no adequate translation in Spanish or English. For example, *xrajowaj ruk'u'x* refers to becoming ill from eating something that because of its metaphysical properties and the time at which it was eaten (during a liminal stage of the day, particularly dawn and dusk) weakens a person's heart/soul (*k'u'x*). Any translation of *xrajowaj ruk'u'x* into English or Spanish is cumbersome, and it is through the use of such culturally relative terms that salient aspects of Maya worldview are reproduced in subtle yet fundamental ways. As Nora England (1996:180) points out in discussing the social theory underlying Mayan language conservation efforts, "while Spanish is of course an adequate code for daily expression, it certainly is not the *same* code as a Mayan language and can hardly substitute for it without loss."

*K'u'x* is a key word in Kaqchikel Mayan. Although I will make problematic simple translations of the word, it is useful to note from the outset that *k'u'x* is most often rendered in English or Spanish as "heart" (*corazón*), "soul" (*alma*), "center" (*centro*), or "essence" (*esencia*), and these translations give us a basic feel for the range of semantic variation the term encompasses. The concept of *k'u'x* is intimately related to that of *anima*.[3] *Anima* is most likely a loan word adopted from the Spanish *ánima* (spirit), and it seems to have replaced the Kaqchikel term *natub* found in early dictionaries (Hill and Fischer 1999). *Anima* denotes a vitalistic force unique to humans and located in the heart; "it is what makes us human," as one woman explains, "it gives us the will and power to live." These two terms come together in the phrase *ruk'u'x ranima* ("the *k'u'x* of one's *anima*," or the essence of one's being), a deep-seated metaphysical quality that both motivates and reflects expressions of individual identity.

*K'u'x* and *anima* are key words in Kaqchikel because they index a culturally specific paradigm that significantly affects the ways in which individuals view and act in the world. *K'u'x* and *anima* are thus significant because they implicate a larger system of symbolic relations. Examining their usage reveals the ways in which Maya conceptions of metaphysical balance are realized through lived experience.

## Anima

Conceptions of *anima* carry a sense of destiny, but a mutable destiny. The basic nature of the *anima* is laid down at birth, based on the cosmic confluence of forces associated with the day of birth in the sacred 260-day calendar, and yet one's *anima* is susceptible to the changing equilibrium of external (to the self) cosmic forces that act upon the self throughout one's life. One's *anima* is especially vulnerable when one is frightened (*susto*), described as *xb'e ranima* (the *anima* leaving). Stories of *susto* are common, such as that of the child whose *anima* left when a stray dog attacked her in the street. The *anima* of children, sick people, and the elderly is especially vulnerable to such events. When one's *anima* leaves, so does one's desire to live, and the condition can result in death. Death can be avoided through intervention, either by the work of a religious specialist such as an *aj q'ij* (day-keeper) or by bathing in a river, the water of which can bring back the *anima* of the afflicted. The ceremony to call back the life force of an afflicted person is termed *oyoj ruk'u'x* (a calling back of the *k'u'x*). *Anima* is closely associated with states of normality and abnormality, at least from an external vantage point. Individuals' behavior is often interpreted in terms of the condition of one's *anima*. A normal person is described as *nik'ikot ranima* (having a content or beautiful *anima*); an errant individual is *itzel ranima* (having an ugly *anima*) or *yalan kow ranima* (with a very hard *anima*, used to describe especially self-centered individuals). The *anima* survives death and lives on as a disembodied soul in the heavens and/or on earth.

There is disagreement among Tecpanecos on exactly when one is endowed with *anima:* some say at conception and others say at birth. All agree that the *anima* is weak in the earliest days of life. During the first nine days after birth, a child is in a dangerously cold state as its *anima* takes form. Newborns must be kept warm and are wrapped in heavy red cloth (the color red having the metaphysical quality of heat). Such swaddling has the added benefit of protecting the child from the harm that others could knowingly or unknowingly inflict through their emotional state and intentions (see Hendrickson 1995:102). The fragility of a newborn's *anima* is tied to an imbalance in vitalistic forces, described in terms of heat and cold. The hot-cold classification system is used in ethnomedical diagnostics throughout Mesoamerica. In Tecpán, as elsewhere, a "hot" state is associated with power, dominance, and potential harm, while a "cold" state is linked to weakness and physical and social vulnerability (ibid.:99). Pregnancy itself is a hot condition, which explains expectant mothers' mood swings, heightened sensitivity to metaphysical balance, and liminal powers.

Sipping sugary coffee and eating tortillas one day in her kitchen in Tecpán, Doña Eulalia told me of the unusual power of pregnant women with a story about her mother. Pregnant with Doña Eulalia's younger brother, the mother was frightened (*xb'e ranima*, "her *anima* left") one day as she stepped on a snake lying by the household well; she hurried indoors, urinated in a cup, and threw the urine on the snake, killing it instantly and restoring her *anima*. Doña Eulalia explained that so powerful is the heat of pregnancy, and so pervasive is it throughout the body, that the snake did not have a chance. Despite the heat of pregnancy, infants are born in a dangerous state of cold.[4] The work of balancing the child's cold state through infusions of heat begins even before birth. Prescribed treatments at various stages of pregnancy are conducted by a midwife, and many of these treatments take place in a *tuj*.[5] During sweatbath treatments, the midwife first massages her patient with various aromatic herbs, and then, after splashing water on the hot rocks to produce steam, blows hot, humid air at the patient's anus in order to warm the unborn child and strengthen its *anima*.[6] After birth, the infant is wrapped in swaddling clothes, and mother and child are kept isolated from visitors and even family for nine days. If the child survives the first nine days of life, his or her *anima* is considered sufficiently strong and the child is formally welcomed into the family in a ceremony designed to ground and center the child's *k'u'x*. During the ninth-day ceremony, the child's umbilical cord (coming from the navel, the center of the child's body, just as the navel of the earth is the sacred *axis mundi*) is buried inside the family *tuj*, if they have one. If not, a girl's umbilical cord may be buried in the ashes of the family hearth and a boy's cord at the base of a tree. In all cases, offering a sacrifice of part of the child's body to the earth (and thus to the vitalistic force known as *ruk'u'x ulew, ruk'u'x kaj*, the heart-soul-essence of earth and sky), the family perpetuates the covenantal relationship between humans and cosmic forces that ensures fecundity and agricultural abundance.[7]

## K'u'x

In contrast to the uniquely human *anima*, all things — humans, plants, animals, lakes, mountains, the earth — have *k'u'x*. This is not to say that every *k'u'x* is alike. The *k'u'x* of a mountain is quite different from that of a human, and among humans and objects *k'u'x* varies even interindividually. Meanings associated with *k'u'x* are also varied. It is most often translated as "heart" or "center." In this context, it has the connotation of a stabilizing force: *ruk'u'x che'* is the hard inner wood of a tree; *ruk'u'x ri ken* is the central rod used in backstrap weaving; and *ruk'u'x awij* is one's spine. In its metaphysical sense, *k'u'x* likewise has a centering function. Maintaining the metaphysical balance of cosmic forces requires that one's *k'u'x* be grounded or centered in those forces. In this sense *k'u'x* may be translated as "soul," as it is perceived as the point of contact between individuals and the cosmic animizing force behind the universe.

*K'u'x* also overlaps with Western concepts of "conscience." Kaqchikel cosmology views a close connection between one's *k'u'x* and one's self, and it is often invoked in categorizations of normality and abnormality. To have an ugly *k'u'x* (*itzel ruk'u'x*, to be a "bad person") is to be out of sync with the cosmos, a state with potentially dangerous consequences (for the individual and the collective). To have a big *k'u'x* (*nim ruk'u'x*, to be a "great person") is to be honest, trustworthy, and reliable; to have a small *k'u'x* is to be the opposite. A person possessing a hard *k'u'x* is insensitive to the concerns of others and thoroughly self-interested; at the same time, to have too soft or malleable of a heart is a sign of moral and physical weakness. To have one's *k'u'x* go (to another person) is to fall in love, a potentially blissful state, but one that can also threaten the equilibrium of the heart. A normal Kaqchikel is said to have a content (i.e., grounded and centered) *k'u'x* (*nik'ikot ruk'u'x*), denoting a deep-seated social and psychological stability.

Traditional Kaqchikel prayers normally begin by addressing the spiritual force *ruk'u'x kaj, ruk'u'x ulew* (often translated as "the heart of sky, the heart of earth"). A better translation of *k'u'x* and its metaphysical connotations in this context is "essence." The *k'u'x* of the sky and earth is the essence of the cosmic force that animates nature. The heart-center is, for the Kaqchikeles and other Maya, a spatialized representation of the ephemeral essence of an object or force. For the ancient and modern Maya, the *axis mundi* or cosmic navel is a powerful place where there is a confluence of primordial animizing forces (see Vogt's 1976 discussion of the *axis mundi* in the Tzotzil Maya town of Zinacantán, and Eliade's 1954 cross-cultural comparison of similar beliefs). Prayers addressed to *ruk'u'x kaj, ruk'u'x ulew* are calling on those same cosmic forces that continue to animate and often predestine life on earth, and are an explicit acknowledgment of the need for the world to maintain equilibrium among cosmic forces (i.e., to be centered).

The state of one's *k'u'x* is closely related to the ubiquitous Mesoamerican distinction between the physical and metaphysical qualities of hot and cold. Caves, where one descends toward the *k'u'x* of a mountain, are especially hot places. This is due to their symbolic proximity to the powers unleashed by cosmic convergence at the *axis mundi*. The *axis mundi* is often represented by hearthstones, which themselves have been converted from cold to hot by the primordial fire of creation. Hot conditions are powerful, and their power can be harnessed toward either benevolent or malevolent ends. A young man in Tecpán, for example, is said to have a hot *k'u'x* because he is impulsive and headstrong; though he is described as being very productive in his work and community obligations, he is seen as somewhat unstable (uncentered) and thus prone to rash unpredictable actions and starting projects that never get completed.

The *k'u'x* not only of humans but also of places are relationally analyzed and evaluated. Kaqchikel Tecpanecos recognize that the mountain of Pulchich, located in a neighboring municipality overlooking Lake Atitlán, has a grander, more powerful *k'u'x* than the mountain Ratzamut that is located just outside of Tecpán's city center (see Figure 6.1). It is a difficult journey over a steep mountain range from Tecpán to Pulchich. On crossing the last summit, the blue waters of Lake Atitlán announce pilgrims' imminent arrival. The area is surrounded by precipitous cliffs and soaring rock faces, and just below Pulchich's summit is a cave where rituals are performed. The importance of this cave is doubtless ancient; its first recorded mention is in the Annals of the Kaqchikeles, written in the sixteenth century. Inside the cave are mounds of multicolored wax, the remnants of countless candles that have been burned here, and the ceiling and walls are covered by a thick coating of black soot. The mountain of Pulchich, because of its majestic geological surroundings and deep historical significance, is a powerful place. Entering the cave mouth thus allows individuals to move closer, physically and metaphysically, to the mountain's center, its *k'u'x*. As the *k'u'x* of Pulchich is firmly grounded in the harmonious balance of vitalistic cosmic forces (being literally closer to the *k'u'x* of the earth, *ruk'u'x ulew*), rituals conducted there are better able to attune individuals to this harmony and thus to perpetuate or restore physical and emotional health, economic prosperity, and abundant harvests.

As sacrificial rituals at Pulchich attest, *k'u'x* is closely tied to the sacred covenant between Mesoamerican peoples and cosmic forces. In this sense, *k'u'x* is associated with balance and reciprocity, both material and social. A centered *k'u'x*, for example, leads individuals to participate in normative reciprocal labor exchanges and the ritualized exchange of sweet breads during Holy Week. To refuse to participate in such socially cohesive obligations is reflective of an imbalanced *k'u'x* and results in social censure. The reciprocal benefit of such relations and the consequences of social ostracization lead most, but not all, individuals to perpetuate these normative patterns. Social cooperation is highly valued as a sign of a great person (one with a large *k'u'x*), and it

FIGURE 6.1. Cave at Pulchich. Author photo.

is significant that a local agricultural cooperative decided to name its hardware store "Ruk'u'x Samaj" (The *K'u'x* of Work).

The concept of *k'u'x* is further tied to the covenantal relationship with cosmic forces through its meaning as "duplication" or "abundance." Kaqchikel farmers often refer to the *ruk'u'x nutikon* (the *k'u'x* of my planting), and in this context *k'u'x* signifies the regenerative nature of agricultural production and the cosmic harmony that predicates it. Likewise, *ruk'u'x rumerya* is a special coin that one keeps in one's pocket so that money never stops coming in. This meaning of duplication nicely links concepts of *k'u'x* to cultural notions of continuity through (re)generation.

### K'u'x *and Normality*

Having outlined the semantic domain of *k'u'x*, I turn now to how *k'u'x* is played out in practical activity, particularly in the behavior (*b'anob'al*) of individuals and its classification as culturally normal or abnormal.

The condition of normality is usually unmarked in Kaqchikel Maya. A normal person is just a person, *winäq*. In contexts that require the condition of normality to be marked, the phrase *nkikot ruk'u'x* (s/he has a tranquil soul) is most often heard. In his ethnography of the Mam town Santiago Chimaltenango (known locally as Chimbal), John Watanabe (1992) demonstrates the close relationship between the Chimbal conceptualization of the condition of normality and the perceived state of the soul. The soul, as Watanabe convincingly shows, is built around the "sense and sensibility" that common circumstance and socialization engender in Chimaltecos. Much the same holds true for the Kaqchikel Maya of Tecpán, who attribute a wide range of metaphysical, emotional, and physical attributes and causation to the *k'u'x*.

Of course there is a range to what is considered normal, both culturally and individually, a point that brings us to the heart of recent debate in anthropological theory concerning the relationship between individual idiosyncrasy and what we call culture. For our purposes, we may define normality as the exhibition of culturally unmarked behavior, that is, observable action (or inaction) that is explainable post hoc (if not predictable) through salient, contextually variable cognitive models. Individual variation plays into both sides of the equation of normality. The actor who produces the observed behavior certainly influences the way he is perceived by others, and consciously so to the extent that he knowingly plays off salient cultural models. A Tecpaneco who refuses to speak Kaqchikel, even to his age mates and elders, feigning forgetfulness of his maternal tongue after having completely adopted Spanish, the language of formal political power and prestige, is seen by others in town as abnormal: though not necessarily evil, he is considered a troubled person whose identity crisis leaves him metaphysically uncentered. He has symbolically rejected the Tecpaneco Maya communitas by rejecting the primary vehicle for that sense of solidarity — a unique language unintelligible to the town's non-Indians — and he has cast his lot with an Enlightenment-inspired philosophy of individual self-improvement and advancement (ironically by adopting the hegemonic principles advanced within Guatemala's elite non-Indian class). The man in question is quite aware that his actions lead to censure among Maya Tecpanecos, so the perception of him as somehow less than normal owes much to his own self-conscious rejection of expected behavior.[8]

But any condition (or action, or thing) does not itself produce an objective cultural significance; that significance is ascribed to it by other cultural actors (and in cases such as these that have fortuitously caught an anthropologist's eye, ascribed once again in the writing of ethnographic texts). Thus it is that the observers who interpret behavior also take an individually variable role in the classification of actions and individuals along the continuum of normality and abnormality, and indeed in the construction of the cognitive and cultural models upon which that continuum is based. As one might expect, among Tecpanecos there is not always consensus on what behaviors constitute abnormality or whether an instance of abnormal behavior is an aberration or indicative of a fundamentally abnormal individual. To illustrate, let us take the example of Pedro, a schoolteacher and part-time farmer whose wife tragically died in a 1993 bus accident. Grief over the loss of his wife, compounded by a general unhappiness with his teaching job, propelled Pedro into a deep, year-long depression, a condition exacerbated by periodic bouts of excessive drinking. Pedro lost his job, refused to fulfill obligations of reciprocal aid to his neighbors, and was alleged by some to be involved in financial misdeeds to support his newly reckless lifestyle. Among his family, friends, and neighbors there was much discussion about his state and what it indicated. His family and a small circle of friends argued that although his behavior (*b'anob'al*) was onerous, it was understandable given the circumstances; the man's *k'u'x* was uncentered, resulting in a loss of *anima,* a dangerous state with potentially permanent effects if allowed to progress. Here we see *k'u'x* closely associated not only with normality but with self-identity as well. Indeed, Pedro's crisis of *k'u'x* was largely an identity crisis, resulting from his abrupt and complete alienation from the person with whom he had long most closely identified. His wife had, early in their acquaintance, "taken his heart" (*xb'e ruk'u'x chi rij xtan*), as the Kaqchikeles say of falling in love. The couple had gone beyond the grudging fulfillment of expected duties that seems to hold many marriages together to integrate their lives and their livelihoods. It seems that Pedro's vicarious self-identification through his wife was more pronounced than hers through him. Nonetheless, as a couple, their souls had conformed to one another (*xkuqur ruk'u'x*), and the loss of this close and constant point of reference left his *k'u'x* uncentered and his self-identity uncertain.

It was the considered opinion of his immediate family and close friends that this crisis of individual self-identity and its potentially dire consequences could only be subverted by grounding the man once again in a strong sense of common social identity. An important point of self-reference had been lost, and a healthy readjustment required that it be replaced by the stalwart and dynamically normative (being as much deduced from the norms of practical behavior as determinant of those norms) anchors of community and kin. This was realized practically by making special efforts to sympathetically exercise "normal" relations with the troubled man, including him whenever possible in the myriad daily tasks that foster a sense of communal integration. Perhaps the most important of these daily efforts was sharing a family meal around the kitchen hearth. The location of this perhaps seemingly mundane event symbolizes the centering effect of the action, for the kitchen hearth is known as the mother of the fire (*rute' q'aq'*), and the traditional three hearthstones surrounding the fire represent the *axis mundi*, the center of the world where the primordial life forces came together to produce the current creation.[9] Symbolically, then, the hearth is associated with the balance of cosmic forces (which act simultaneously on the physical world, the social realm, and individuals) that is implied in the conception of "center." Anthropologists have long noted that the sharing and distribution of food in nonmarket contexts often follows different rules than the sharing and distribution of other goods. There is something special about sharing food; at one level, for the Kaqchikeles of Tecpán, it is the daily practical and symbolic continuation and affirmation of cosmic, agricultural, and life cycles: physical sustenance received from the cyclic bounty of the agricultural cycle that is governed by the confluence of cyclic cosmic forces. A greater sense of mutual empathy is created in sharing food around the hearth than in any other daily activity of the life cycle; the filling of the stomach seems to stimulate mutual goodwill as expressed in open stories about one's daily activities and thoughts. As I argue in Chapter 7, this empathy creates a strong sense of mutual identification, and the hearth group serves as a primary nexus of identity in Tecpaneco society. To jolt us out of any unmerited romanticization, I should note that the hearth in question where our troubled protagonist shared his meals with his immediate family was not built around three hearthstones. Very few hearths in today's Tecpán are, a side effect of the modernization of house construction (in which a cinder-block stove is de rigueur) that followed the 1976 earthquake. Elder Tecpanecos lament this change of design, seeing it as detrimental to the maintenance of family ties. Nonetheless, even in houses with modern stoves, the symbolic value of the hearth is retained. This symbolic value is reinforced through practical activity, as the kitchen hearth remains a center of household activity and common meals continue to be important events in interpersonal integration. It was through practical activity such as sharing meals that Pedro's family and friends exercised kinship ties and affective relations to provide Pedro with a stable reference for self-identity to fill the void that he had experienced so that his *k'u'x* (and his self) could once again be centered, returning him to a state of individual normality.

A number of more distant friends and neighbors believed that Pedro had become chronically unbalanced, and that his behavior was indicative of a fundamentally flawed *k'u'x*. This analysis led them to adopt a strategy of distancing themselves from him, cutting their social and economic losses before he dragged them along on his downward spiral. Past behavior was reinterpreted based on this new characterological interpretation, and evidence was found to support the diagnosis of a chronically unbalanced, ugly *k'u'x* (*itzel ruk'u'x*). Here we see the clear but not always unwavering distinction made between an abhorrent abnormal behavior and chronic abnormality, and the ways in which such distinctions can be self-reinforcing if not self-fulfilling. Distancing an already alienated individual from important social relations heightens that individual's alienation and thus can promote the very antisocial behavior characteristic of the diagnosis. Conversely, a group-therapy approach to social integration of an uncentered *k'u'x*, akin to early childhood socialization, can re-center the *k'u'x* in terms of social identity. And this has largely been the outcome in Pedro's case. He has dedicated himself anew to his teaching career, he now participates actively in family and community life, and he has given up heavy drinking. At times he is struck by waves of melancholy ("sometimes I sigh," as he says in Kaqchikel)[10] that he now self-consciously recognizes as a dangerous uncenteredness and that he combats by seeking out situations of conviviality to counter his feeling of alienation and isolation.

Despite the importance of differing constructions of normality and abnormality in the dynamics of local Tecpaneco society (variation that might be employed to argue against the concept of shared culture), it is telling that there is more often than not a general consensus about what constitutes abnormality. Drinking too much, crossing an ill-defined threshold of excessive domestic violence, cheating friends and relatives in financial dealings, and many other such behaviors are almost uniformly condemned as being abnormal, and this abnormality is explained through reference to the state of one's *k'u'x*. Consistent with the reflexive nature of such cognitive models, *k'u'x* simultaneously models observed behavior and conditions individual agency. The application of the cultural logic underlying the *k'u'x* model is not uniform; indeed the generative quality of cultural logics allows for infinite variation. There is no uniform agreement on what specific contextualized behaviors reflect an unsettled *k'u'x;* as we have seen in the case study above, there are often competing logically rigorous cultural interpretations of specific behaviors. For the most part, however, these competing interpretations are mutually intelligible, for they are based on common logical principles. Whether or not it was believed that the man whose wife died possessed a fundamentally unbalanced *k'u'x,* all explained his state of ab/normality in terms of *k'u'x* and the situationally unique conjuncture of social and cosmic forces acting on it. Further, the man in question, in recovering from his emotional depression, consciously seeks to live up to the social standards indicative of a stable *k'u'x.* Less dramatic realizations of individual agency are likewise informed by the fluid and idiosyncratically perceived social standards of *k'u'x,* although often not in such a self-conscious manner. In acting on cognitive models of *k'u'x* through concrete activity and in applying the *k'u'x* paradigm to observed behavior and relations, these standards are constantly modified in light of circumstantial contingencies. Still, continuity is maintained through the logical transposition of salient cultural schemas. Maya men no longer pierce the foreskin of their penises to offer blood to the god(s), yet the covenant between humans and cosmic forces is perpetuated through ritual sacrifice to the *k'u'x* of earth and sky and through individuals striving to maintain metaphysical centeredness, grounding their *k'u'x* in the balance of the cosmos.

## K'u'x, Anima, *and the Logics of Cultural Change*

The cognitive model indexed by the usage of *k'u'x* and *anima* lays clear the workings of the concept of cultural logics. It is a model that allows for the idiosyncrasies that have been the focus of constructivist theory and at the same time reaffirms an essential continuity and authenticity within the Maya cultural tradition. As we have seen, the state of one's *k'u'x* is idiosyncratically and contextually variable, shaped by the contingencies of lived experience. At the same time, cognitive models of *k'u'x* are socially maintained through consensual interpretations of behavior and categorizations of normality.

It is significant that the Kaqchikeles have a word for the essence of identity, *ruk'u'x ranima* (the heart-soul-essence of one's being). The *ruk'u'x ranima* is the foundation for individual agency and intentionality as well as a product of social interaction. Although Kaqchikeles are born with *k'u'x*, in childhood the *ruk'u'x ranima* is not yet fully formed. Events affect the individual's *ruk'u'x ranima* and thus in part mold its formation, shaping the future outlook of individuals based on affective sentiments. There is an enduring quality to *ruk'u'x ranima* as well; as the essence of one's being, it is much less variable than the outward manifestations of the *anima* and less affected by the ups and downs of daily life. One close friend in Tecpán told me of the trauma caused by her father's drinking problem when she was a young girl. She has vivid memories of her father getting drunk and unruly while watching soccer games, and ever since she has had a powerful disdain for soccer. In her words, her father's behavior pushed into her *ruk'u'x ranima,* changing it in a negative way.

Predicated on practice as it is, *ruk'u'x ranima* may change over one's lifetime. Often noted in this sense are military veterans, as the intense brainwashing and indoctrination of military recruits in Guatemala has been well documented. Conscripts are taken far away from their natal communities and trained in Spanish to highlight the break with community; those selected for service in the elite Kaibil corps are reportedly given a puppy at the beginning of their training to care and provide for until graduation, at which time they must cut the dog's throat and drink its blood in a rite of passage. Not surprisingly, men often return from military service changed in some fundamental way, suffering from what we might term post-traumatic stress syndrome. On returning to their hometowns, veterans frequently suffer severe crises of identity as they find themselves again enmeshed in local systems of ethnic politics while carrying the stigma of association with the military and its violent campaigns. They often have little patience for the machinations of established tradition and are more comfortable with rigid command chains than the consensus model of negotiation and governance long characteristic of Maya communities. One man I know well was said to have been a kind, gentle soul before he was shanghaied by the military, but upon his return he drank heavily, abused his wife and children, and alienated his family and friends through his antisocial behavior; it is said that the army changed his *ruk'u'x ranima*.

Constructivist analyses of culture and identity have long focused on such idiosyncratic change, showing how individuals adapt to changing contingencies through innovative cultural interpretation and transformation. Certainly, humans as symbol makers exhibit the qualities of Lévi-Straussian bricoleurs; individuals are innovative and constructive given the material and ideological resources at hand. Accepting this observation, we must then turn our attention to a consideration of not only how available resources are rearranged and symbolically redefined but how they are themselves changed through the process of ongoing reflexive practice. Cultural logics do not merely facilitate the interpretation of novel situations; their very organizing principles are changed through cumulative micro and macro situational conjunctures of idiosyncratic intentions and collective actions. In the preceding discussion I have stressed the symbolic conservatism built into cultural logics as well as their idiosyncratic internalization in the context of ongoing social interaction. But idiosyncratic interpretations and actions may, given conducive and overlapping structural contexts, result in the emergence of new normative patterns. Most dramatic in this regard, perhaps, is the wave of large-scale violence that swept through highland Guatemala in the late 1970s and early 1980s. Not only did the violence create new social groups such as the returned veterans and the large groups of internal refugees, it also fundamentally altered the contours of the material and political space open to Maya individuals and groups.

In some areas, preexisting cultural templates were transposed onto the new realities (see Carmack 1988; Wilson 1995); in other domains, cultural and cognitive templates proved less resilient. For example, from the army's counterinsurgency perspective, the consensus model of group interaction became suspect as a communist device, and it was therefore abandoned or curtailed by local Maya groups throughout the highlands to avoid persecution. Effective consensus building requires a degree of moral transparency, and with the infiltration of military and guerrilla *orejas* (spies, literally "ears") in Tecpán and other Maya towns, the ability to accurately divine the intentions of others was greatly reduced. This new darkness of the *ruk'u'x ranima*, which could result in torture and death for the targets of bad intentions, was not easily discernible through traditional criteria. Furthermore, inter-subjective interpretations of the state of an individual's heart-soul were themselves dangerous activities (one can imagine the interrogation beginning, "So, they say that you are worried that Señor X may be collaborating with the forces of state security . . . why is that? What would you have to fear, compatriot?"). Despite their internal resilience, cultural logics do not perform like rubber bands, stretching to accommodate present contingencies and snapping back to their original form when oppressive mechanisms are curtailed. The violence has fundamentally changed the way Maya peoples view the world, expanding the realm of the *doxa* by bringing that which was formerly unthinkable into the realm of cognizant possibilities.

### Comparisons

The cultural logic of *k'u'x* (and *ruk'u'x ranima*) is not unique to Tecpán or the Kaqchikel region. Cognate foundational paradigms based on soul concepts are reported in a number of ethnographies of other Maya communities. John Watanabe (1992) eloquently relates a cultural logic of soul to the ways in which the Mam of Santiago Chimaltenango learn, gossip, envy, and maintain local forms of knowledge. Watanabe focuses on two important concepts for the Mam, *naab'l* and *aanma*. He poetically glosses *naab'l* as both "sense" and "sensibility": "if naab'l means 'sense,' as in general sense perceptions or awareness, it also means 'having sense' as in being humanly sensible to oneself and to others" (ibid.: 82). *Naab'l* plays an important normative function in Chimalteco culture, and its various meanings "thus define general human social capacities and characteristics in reference to the conventional normality of particular communities" (ibid.: 84). *Naab'l* is intimately related to the soul, or *aanma* (cf. the Kaqchikel *anima*). As Watanabe notes, the concept of soul is largely self-referential, but "this does not mean that Chimaltecos can do whatever they please and call it 'soulful,' because . . . the propriety of having soul must be recognized and affirmed by others, not simply self-asserted (ibid.:90–91). Similarly, among Kaqchikel speakers, the concept of *k'u'x* provides a stable cultural logic with a transcendental point of reference, realized through practical activity, that centers identity. An emotional episode or period may indicate an uncentered heart, but that does not translate into an ugly soul. As Watanabe points out in an earlier article, "a linguistically derived model of Maya space and time need not depend on any particular historical constellation of cultural traits but can represent a more fundamental cognitive order which underlies these traits" (1983:711).

Carlsen and Prechtel (1991) find a similar logic at work in the Tz'utujil cognitive model of *jaloj-k'exoj*. *Jal* refers to life-cycle change, metaphorically associated with the maturation of maize as seen in its changing husk. *K'ex* refers to cyclic generational change and is associated with the rejuvenation of seeds in maize agriculture. As with *k'u'x*, the *jaloj-k'exoj* cognitive model is based on the sacred covenant between humans and vitalistic cosmic forces that perpetuates the progressive cycle of earthly existence. But, as Watanabe has pointed out, such cognitive models do not blindly reify received wisdom, for they are predicated on lived experience. It is through habitual practical activity, such as the reciprocal social relations implicated in models of *naab'l*, *k'u'x*, and *jaloj-k'exoj*, that the cultural logic underlying these models is reinforced and transformed. As Carlsen and Prechtel write, *jaloj-k'exoj* refers to a process of "change within change: a single system of transformation and renewal" (ibid.:27). As with the Kaqchikel model of *k'u'x* and the Mam model of *naab'l*, the cultural logic underlying the *jaloj-k'exoj* paradigm "guide[s] the transformations of the local Maya cultural configuration" (ibid.:38). Further, *jaloj-k'exoj*, like *k'u'x*, is spatially associated with the *axis mundi*, the center of the world. Such metaphorical and metonymic modeling of nature may well describe the etymology of such conceptions, but doubtless, as with *k'u'x*, their ongoing expression and logical transformation is based on social and cultural as well as natural contingencies.

Similar cultural logics related to the soul have been reported from other areas of the Maya region (Nash 1970; Vogt 1976; Boremanse 1993; Wilson 1995) and other parts of Mesoamerica (López Austin 1988; Sandstrom 1991; Monaghan 1995, 2000). In all of these cases, the logic appears to be based on conceptions of metaphysical balance and a sacred covenantal relationship between individuals and cosmic forces. That such conceptions are found in widely divergent contexts across both time and space in Mesoamerica belies the strong constructivist position that cultural forms are developed and deployed solely in relation to circumstantial contingencies. Cultural elements, and the logics that bind them, are used as tools of resistance, yet their power largely derives from their unifying quality — a quality based at least as much on continuity as on resistance to an Other.

# 7 *Hearth, Kin, and Communities*

All associations of place, people, and culture are social and historical creations to be explained, not given as natural facts.
AKHIL GUPTA AND JAMES FERGUSON (1997)

If you take an Indian out of his village, he stops being an Indian.
A LADINO JOURNALIST (QUOTED IN NELSON 1999)

Body metaphors provide salient, transposable cognitive templates for
many domains of Kaqchikel culture, including household architecture,
kinship terminology, and religious affiliation (Lolmay 1999).[1] I once
asked a Kaqchikel linguist active in the pan-Maya movement about
such body metaphors. He explained that they were related to a Maya
perspective that all aspects of the human condition and the material
world are interrelated, and thus one's family, house, and environment
are seen as organic extensions of the individual. Such metaphors also
reveal, he continued, a Maya cultural proclivity for group cohesion —
what affects the larger group is clearly seen to affect the individual —
and thus provides a solid cultural basis for pan-Maya unity. On first
hearing this explanation, I frankly wrote it off as a romanticized view
of indigenous peoples at one with nature and the world. At the same
time, I began to ask people in Tecpán and Patzún about their view of
humankind's relationship to others and to nature. Their responses varied greatly, influenced by occupation, religious beliefs, and particular
life histories, among other variables. Most farmers were simultaneously
more pragmatic about agricultural production (having an intimate
knowledge of the particulars) and more romantic (in a spiritual sense)

about cyclic rejuvenation (being so reliant on and vulnerable to cyclic environmental changes); conversely, schoolteachers and other educated professionals tended to romanticize the process of farming and its communion with nature while holding a more scientific understanding of seasonal change. Yet significant recurring elements and structural relationships, common threads, appeared in the responses I recorded.

Central metaphorical models condition the way individuals look at, think about, and act in the world (Lakoff and Johnson 1980; Lakoff 1987; D'Andrade 1995). Though these metaphors are differently internalized and their usage is highly context-dependent, their utility as tools of communication depends on the existence of certain shared structural relationships. As the native-speaker/expert informant I questioned suggested, the salience of corporeal metaphors to conceptualize the household and kinship relations in Kaqchikel indexes a significant unitarian principle of a Maya cultural logic, as does the *k'u'x* concept (cf. Johnson 1987).

Sociobiologists point out that conceptualizing kinship as an extended body is but an emic recognition of the genetic facts of relatedness. From this perspective, overtly highlighting degrees of biological separation serves as a convenient shorthand for calculating cost-benefit ratios for acts of altruism and reciprocity. Van den Berghe (1981) argues that movements of ethnic nationalism are further extensions of overtly marking relatedness, and that even if they occur only in historically specific circumstances and forms, they are but superorganic mechanisms deployed to increase reproductive success. Such reductionism should not be dismissed out of hand, but it seems inadequate to explain the complexity and fluidity of Maya identities.

Identity is elusive and ever fluid, being both context-dependent and built upon a lifetime of socialization. Individuals construct an enduring core of self-identity, laid down in significant ways in early childhood but also constantly modified through lived experience. Stemming from common circumstance and overlapping structures of socialization, widely shared indices of identity take on a superorganic quality in the form of cultural models held by both cultural outsiders and insiders. Ethnicity—in Guatemala as in much of the rest of the world—has become an increasingly important vector of self-identification over the last thirty years, but it is but one among myriad others, including religion, gender, age, kinship, and immediate community. In this chapter, I argue that self-identity is formed from these foci of allegiances. Hearth-group affiliations carry the strongest obligations, but individuals are also tied to extended families, religious groups, and particular barrios. These social ties are constantly in flux (being refined and renegotiated), and they are, in many contexts, subsumed by municipal allegiances.

### *Kinship, Residence, and Hearth Groups*

Kaqchikel kinship is cognatic with a patrifocal bias, and postmarital residence is preferentially virilocal. This is to say that inheritances most often come from one's father, and that male children most often bring their wives to live in their family's house or nearby. Naming practices follow the Spanish custom of having two family names, that of the father followed by that of the mother, with the latter being dropped by females at marriage (cf. Restall 1997). This naming practice reinforces the bilaterality of the kinship system as well as its patrifocal bias, and it also allows for some flexibility in terms of kin-group association. For example, a man named Juan Morales Xpantzay could choose to offer either his Spanish or his Maya surname when asked (although in this case, the Maya name would be a marked construction), thus emphasizing one or the other of his primary kin-group affiliations.

It is common, though not overtly prescribed, for children to be named for one of their grandparents, a practice termed *nuk'exel* (substitute). Such substitution symbolically and materially reproduces the lineage and the blood (and genes) of the ancestors, which seems to be a comforting thought for those in the twilight years of their life. And the generational rejuvenation of the lineage is itself tied to larger cycles of cosmological regeneration going back to the very beginning of time.

Sons generally receive the bulk of household property upon their father's death, although it is not uncommon for daughters to receive small plots of land and even occasionally full shares of the inheritance. Depending on the nature of her marriage, the daughter may keep these lands in her name and under her control, or she may integrate them with the holdings of her husband and pass along to him management of the holdings. For many women, this inheritance acts as a dowry, and a financial safety net for herself and her children in case her husband is unable to provide for the family. The household compound itself usually passes to the youngest son, as it is he who is expected to live with his parents until their death.

FIELDNOTES — TECPÁN, NOVEMBER 20, 1993

Leonel, an industrious young Kaqchikel man we know, had to drop out of the university, where he was studying computer science. His father recently died, his mother is unable to keep up the household and milpa

plots by herself, and his siblings have all left home. And so, at 22, Leonel, the youngest son, is taking on the responsibility of maintaining the
family household. He is disappointed at having to interrupt his studies,
and worries that he may become trapped by his obligations in Tecpán,
unable to return to the capital, where he hopes to make his career. But
a strong sense of filial piety keeps him here, for now at least, and he is
making the most of his time here by taking English and German classes
from Mareike and me and preparing to work on the 1994 census.

Given situational contingencies — an opportunity for study, a lucrative
job in another town — it is not always the youngest son who stays with
his parents, and individuals adapt and creatively redeploy the social
structural principles involved to novel circumstances. Such variation
does not, however, negate the validity of the norm itself, at least as long
as the norm continues to be socially recognized as such by the members
of a society.

Once land has been transferred across a generation, there frequently
occurs a period of liquidation and consolidation. In the latter, siblings
or other relatives with land in the same area will buy recently inherited
land to expand their own (often contiguous) plots, and this may be combined with a liquidation of more distant plots. The ideal in consolidation
is to acquire a maximum number of contiguous or almost contiguous
plots as close as possible to the household compound, thus maximizing
the efficiency of labor inputs. This ideal is rarely met, and most households own land in two or more, often distant, locations. In selling one's
land there is a clear preference to deal with other relatives. Selling a
plot of inherited land is not undertaken lightly, and I have frequently
heard stories of individuals being forced to sell land only to return some
years later to buy back that very land, so strong is the affective tie.

Among Ego's siblings, Kaqchikel kinship terminology distinguishes
both relative sex and relative age (see Figure 7.1). The term *nunimal*
refers to an elder same-sex sibling (be it brother or sister) and *nuchaq'*
is used for younger same-sex siblings. (*Nuchaq'* may also refer to the
children of siblings, regardless of relative age or sex.) Males use a single
term (*wana'*) to refer to a sister, regardless of her age, and females likewise use *nuxib'al* to refer to their brothers. Speculating on the source
of such distinctions, it seems likely that they developed as both reflection and ideological reification of familial authority structures. It is
traditionally valued and indeed very commonly practiced for the first
children born in Maya households to quickly assume certain duties of

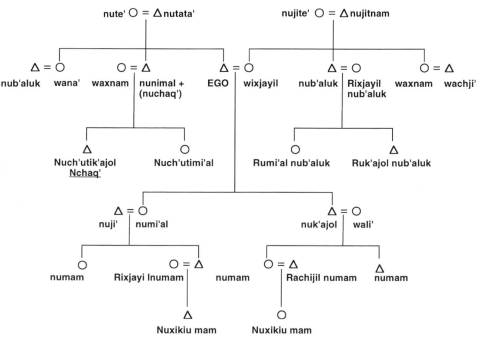

FIGURE 7.1. Kaqchikel kinship terminology, male ego. Illustration by the author.

adulthood. As Chayanov (1966) has pointed out, this is a demographic necessity for peasant households, as the first child (*nab'ey alaxel* in Kaqchikel) is almost never the last, and a rapid succession of births dramatically alters a household's producer/consumer ratio.

In Maya households that depend primarily on subsistence production, elder sons quickly make the transition from babies in diapers to farmers, setting out with their fathers almost as soon as they are able to walk to the fields and carry a hoe. Elder daughters assume many of the responsibilities of caring for younger siblings and, except for breastfeeding, might often be considered the primary caregivers for the younger siblings. The sacrifices of the older children are culturally recognized and evident in the fact that younger children are much more likely than their elder siblings to attend school and obtain good jobs. With this sacrifice comes both obligation and authority: an obligation to look out for the best interests of the family's children, and the authority to impose their will as befits a caregiver. As the sexual division of labor is rather rigid, it is most common for elder children to take a more active role in the socialization of their same-sex siblings, and therein lies the utility of reinforcing the status of relative age among same-sex siblings through kinship terminology.

More often than not, two or more related nuclear families will live in a single household compound; in Tecpán, households have an average of 1.27 nuclear families, and in Patzún, the average household contains 1.38 nuclear families. An individual's primary social ties and obligations are to family members in the same household, those who share the empathy that can only accompany living together and sharing food on a daily basis. Eating together, specifically around the same hearth, is especially important within Indian families, as I point out in Chapter 6. Membership in a hearth group, which is most often although not always coequal with a nuclear family, carries with it most of the rights and obligations of kinship ties within a nuclear family.

The layout of Maya houses is conceived of in terms of the human body, reflecting the organic nature of this social group. *Ruxkin jay* (ear of the house) is the bathroom, *ruchi' jay* (mouth of the house) is the door, *ruwi' jay* (hair of the house) is the roof, and the kitchen hearth is called *rute' q'aq'* (mother of the fire); even soil, *ruwäulew* (face of the earth), is anthropomorphic. This system of nomenclature reinforces the interrelatedness of household members and emphasizes the roots metaphor of the body as applied to kinship relations.

In some house compounds there are two or more kitchens, and in these cases, households are clearly divided into separate groups, each associated with a particular hearth. Figure 7.2 diagrams the house compound of one of my key informants and illustrates one local pattern of residence. Three nuclear families live in the compound: (1) the mother (M) and father (F); (2) Ego (my informant), his wife (W), and their four children (C); and (3) Ego's sister (Z), her husband (ZH), and their seven children (ZC). Within the household compound there are two kitchens. The older and larger one is used by the mother, father, Ego, and Ego's wife and children; a newer, smaller kitchen is used by Ego's sister and her husband and children. Ego is the youngest son (*ch'ip*) in his family, and it is his duty as *ch'ip* to care for his parents until their deaths. His residence in the household is thus dictated by kinship obligations, and he moved back to Tecpán from Guatemala City in order to help care for his parents. His sister and her family, however, would normally live with or near her husband's family. Ego's sister did live with her affinal relatives for a short time after her marriage, but because of domestic problems and the fact that his family is economically

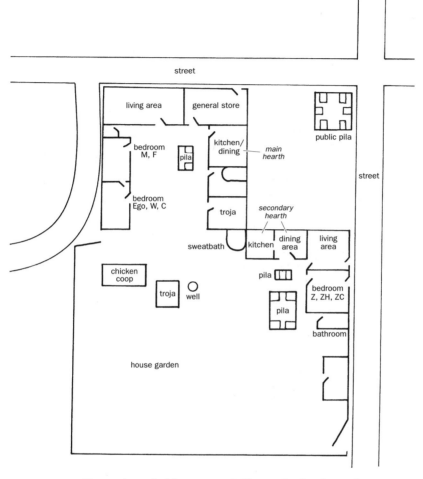

FIGURE 7.2. Tecpán household compound. Illustration by the author.

less successful than her consanguines, she moved back to her parents'
house. Her husband could not convince her to return to his home and
so eventually moved in with her family. They have since built several
rooms for themselves, connected to, yet set slightly apart from, the
rooms of her mother and father's house, and they have their own entrance opening onto a side street. This compromise in residence allows
Ego's sister to live with her consanguineous relatives while maintaining the degree of independence from them that her husband desires.

(Although Maya families in both towns generally prefer patrilocal or neolocal postmarital residence, matrilocal residence is surprisingly common.) Within this household compound, then, there are two hearth groups: one with Ego and his wife, children, mother, and father; the other with Ego's sister and her husband and children.

Hearth groups and households act as communal economic units, and within them resources are pooled, almost on a daily basis, and financial obligations are shared. Between them, the hearth groups share the rent for house, taxes, and the cost of parties, the well, the household garden area, and maize and beans from the common *troje*. Resources are thus shared, and gifts and loans constantly flow between the hearth groups in the household, but these gifts and loans are marked by a greater overt expectation of reciprocity than is found within the hearth group. Households are generally homogeneous in terms of economic class, social status, and religious beliefs.

Of course, the bonds of kinship extend outside of households to relatives living in other locations. Beyond the household, however, social obligations are open to a greater degree of negotiation. Close relatives — siblings and parents and even aunts, uncles, and cousins — are treated much as household members, as long as they are willing to reciprocate and do not distance themselves from the family. More affluent individuals are expected to be generous with their kin, providing jobs, loans, food, and housing when needed, and in this way fortifying the crucial balance that symbolically, and here materially, perpetuates the cycles of Maya cultural development.

### Barrios and Towns

Relatives in separate households often live close by, reflecting the divisions over time of larger ancestral holdings. As a result, related households tend to cluster together in the same barrio (a section of town known as a *cantón* in Patzún). This commonality of place also brings together unrelated households in a number of ways.

Urban Tecpán is divided into four barrios, the boundaries of which extend out from the town's central park. These are Poromá to the northeast, Asunción to the southeast, San Antonio to the southwest, and Patacabaj to the northwest (see Figure 7.3). Fuentes y Guzmán, who visited Iximche'/Tecpán in the late seventeenth century, describes the old town as divided into four distinct sections (1933:353). Guillemin (1977:246) also found evidence for this quadripartite structure in his

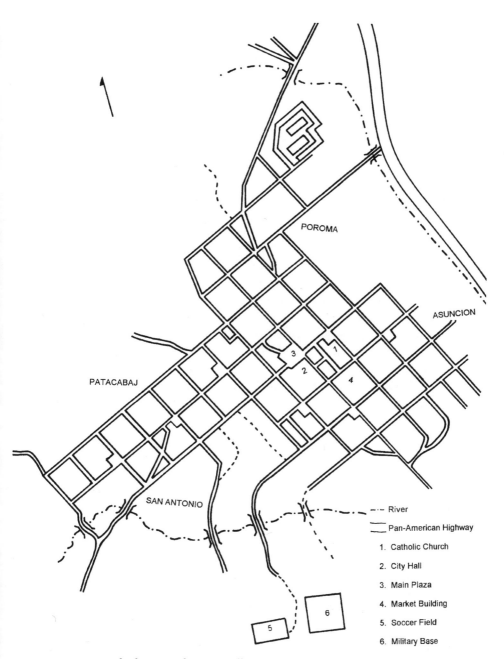

POROMA

ASUNCION

PATACABAJ

SAN ANTONIO

- – - River
═══ Pan-American Highway
1. Catholic Church
2. City Hall
3. Main Plaza
4. Market Building
5. Soccer Field
6. Military Base

FIGURE 7.3. The barrios of Tecpán. Illustration by the author.

excavations of Iximche'. Guillemin cites personal communications with persons who claim to have read a document in the ecclesiastical archive of Guatemala (a document now lost) that reports that Tecpán's four barrios were originally named Naveahpop (First Leader), Rucanah-pop (Second Leader), Ispansay, and Poromá; the last two were family names of prominent local Indians. Thus, Guillemin writes, "the four barrios of Tecpán were in the hands of four dignitaries, just as the four palace and ceremonial complexes of Iximché were in the hands of its hierarchs" (ibid.:246).

Two of the current barrios have Spanish names (San Antonio and Asunción), and two have Maya names (Patacabaj and Poromá). In Kaqchikel, *pa* means "in," *taq* is a diminutive plural used with inanimate objects ("many small" things), and *abäj* means "rock"; thus Patacabaj is "place of the many rocks," and the barrio, which is where we lived during our stay, is covered with pieces of pumice. Guillemin's sources report that Poromá was the name of a prominent Indian family, though no such surname presently exists in town. When asked why the barrio is thus named, several people told me the following story: Once upon a time (*ojer, ojer kan*), Jesus appeared to the barrio's residents in the form of clouds above their houses; he is known as Jesús de Poromá, and the barrio has since been called Poromá. However, just why he was called Jesús de Poromá in the first place I was never told. According to Guillemin, another barrio was named Ispansay in the early colonial period. Ispansay clearly refers to the Xpantzay family, noblemen from before Spanish contact (see Recinos and Goetz 1953; Oxlajuuj Keej 1992) and important Indian leaders throughout the colonial and postcolonial periods (for examples, see AGCA A5 3957 6062, fol. 30v–44r [1658]; and AGCA A1 4896 167, fol. 2r [1868]). Although their fortunes have since declined, Xpantzay family members now live almost exclusively in Poromá. Hill (1989, 1992) relates Tecpán's barrio structure to the colonial system of *parcialidades*, which itself is related to the precontact social, territorial, and political unit (*chinamit*). He shows that as late as the mid–eighteenth century, the Kaqchikel people of Tecpán maintained a *chinamit/parcialidad* system divided into eight territorial units: Xpantzay, Poromá, Chikbal, Kantioy, Nimak Achi, Xaxbina, Tubalik, and Nima Kay (Hill 1989:180). By 1806, however, the *parcialidad* organization of the town and its outlying villages had been reduced by Spanish decrees to the present quadripartite barrio structure extant today (ibid.:186).

The changing social significance of barrio organization points to the fact that barrios serve as foci of local politics and, to a certain extent, are seen as extensions of kinship relations. This is seen clearly in Patzún's structure of *cantones* (the equivalent of Tecpán's barrios), where close ties extend out from the household to other family members who are coresidents of the same *cantón*. Patzún is divided into four *cantones* (North, West, South, and East), the boundaries of which extend out from the town's central park (see Figure 7.4). Sections of town, however, are still referred to by a number of older names, mostly associated with families who live there. For example, in Cantón Poniente there is a section called Chi Coyoti', largely inhabited by members of the extended Coyote clan.

The town or municipality serves as an important nexus of social obligations and group affiliation above the level of household and barrio (Tax 1937, 1941; Wagley 1941; Adams 1957; Warren 1978; Watanabe 1992). As Nelson notes, "Most ethnography, foreign and Mayan, agrees that indigenous identity is community-bound. . . . It is a sacred tie that links fertility, gender, food, ethnicity, relations to the dead and the living, the unseen world, and right living and forms the basis for the categories and 'cognitive mapping' that make sense of lives. It is the basis for cooperation and thus survival in an uncertain world" (1999:131).

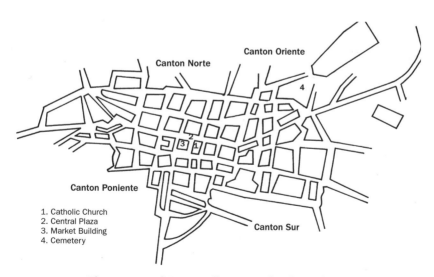

Canton Oriente

Canton Norte

4

Canton Poniente

1. Catholic Church
2. Central Plaza
3. Market Building
4. Cemetery

Canton Sur

FIGURE 7.4. The *cantones* of Patzún. Illustration by the author.

Yet, this is a two-edged sword. Nelson goes on to point out, "viewing 'Indian-ness' as bound to a particular place can become an incarceration and a double-bind, so that any indigenous person who leaves their community, the rural area, and the manual labor associated with the village is vulnerable to accusations of inauthenticity and ladinoization" (ibid.; cf. Campbell 1994).

Differentiating between those who leave and those who stay is but one among several salient markers that can act to delimit community identities. Another important distinction in Tecpán and Patzún is between the more cosmopolitan and prestigious urban life of the town centers and the slower pace of rural living in their dependent *aldeas* in the *campo* (countryside). Lévi-Strauss has argued that such distinctions are ubiquitous throughout the Americas, distinguishing the village from the wilds, cosmopolitan city life from country backwardness, and culture from nature.

*Aldea* residents usually come into the town centers once a week or once every two weeks for the town's large market, selling raw and processed agricultural goods (maize, beans, squash, cheese, chocolate, honey, broccoli, mushrooms, greens, chickens), as well as simple manufactured goods (wood furniture, woven textiles, pottery, metates). (The primary market day in Tecpán is Thursday; it is Sunday in Patzún.) For many town-dwellers, despite their own often close ties to *aldeas*, *aldeas* and the countryside (*campo*) are associated with rural poverty and backwardness, which reflects an internalization of modernist ideas of development. A Patzunero schoolteacher who considers himself to be Indian complains that the Indians of the *aldea* in which he works treated him badly, as if he were a rich government official from the city (a *kaxlan* if not a ladino). In Tecpán, our landlord, an elderly carpenter, was alarmed when we let grass and weeds (*monte*) take over our patio rather than maintaining it as packed dirt. We simply did not want to get our feet dirty after bathing in the *pila*, but our landlord feared that we were letting the *monte* take over, turning his plot of urbanity into *puro campo* and exhibiting a backwardness surprising in presumed cosmopolitanites like ourselves.

Styles of *traje* and dialectical differences as well as local political interests act to accentuate the community-based identity of Tecpanecos and Patzuneros. Such identity is often expressed through local pride. Patzuneros, for example, are quick to point out that their church is older than Tecpán's (a debatable claim), that a prominent cypress tree in town is more than four hundred years old, and that after its reconstruction, the town hall will be the most impressive in all of Chimalten-ango. While several Patzuneros reported that their town was once an *aldea* of Tecpán, they see themselves as distinct from Tecpanecos, and in some ways (purity of language, for example) as better. Tecpanecos are generally proud of their town's role as an important regional eco-nomic and political center. The luster of being a capital city (first of the Kaqchikeles and then of the Spaniards) has never quite worn off, and the historical memory of grandeur is often interpreted as a sign of great destiny as well. Such interpretations, however, go beyond reactive in-terpretation; internalized in subtle and implicit ways, they inform cog-nitive structures that direct proactive behavior.

## *Religion*

Religious association provides an important sense of community for many Tecpanecos and Patzuneros, and it is often discussed using met-aphors of the body (the church body, the flesh and blood of Christ) and kinship (the Virgin Mother, Fathers, brothers and sisters in Christ). At the same time, with the rise of various forms of Protestantism, religion has come to be seen by many locals and more than a few anthropolo-gists as a source of division within Maya communities. Like most Maya communities, Tecpán and Patzún are religiously diverse. A number of traditional religious specialists (*aj q'ijab'*) live and work there, and both towns are home to large Catholic churches, dozens of evangelical Protestant congregations, Mormon tabernacles, Seventh Day Advent-ist groups, and, in Tecpán, a Mennonite colony and the Central Amer-ican Agnostic Movement. This balkanization of religious affiliations leads to some tension within the communities as sects seek to expand and to exert their moral standards on the community as a whole (cf. Warren 1978). Evangelicals in particular are noted for their opposition to public ceremonies that involve drinking and pagan rituals. For the most part, however, Tecpanecos and Patzuneros do not let religious animosities get in the way of everyday life. Catholics and Protestants do business with one another; voters in local elections are not easily swayed by the religious association of candidates; and Maya Protes-tants, Catholics, and traditionalists alike participate in local forms of cultural activism.

Kaqchikel Tecpanecos and Patzuneros frequently explained to me that the state of religious coexistence in the town is due to the fact that there is really only one god, although s/he is differently conceived by religions and individuals. Such an ecumenical perspective plays down the differences in the forms of religious expression to emphasize a fundamental commonality. Individuals are judged by their behavior (which is reflective of the state of their soul) more than by the church they attend. It is not surprising, then, that traditionalist day-keepers appear to use the terms *ahua* ("lord" or "god"), *ruk'u'x ulew, ruk'u'x kaj* ("the *k'u'x* [heart/soul/essence] of earth, the *k'u'x* of sky"), and the Spanish *dios* ("god") interchangeably in their prayers and ceremonies. Each addresses the same divinity, and the diversity of terms plays nicely into the Maya rhetorical style of using couplets and repetitions based on synonyms in formal discourse. That Catholic saints and other figures from the Judeo-Christian tradition are also invoked alongside deities and mythical figures from the Maya tradition further points to the encompassing hybridity of Maya religion. The monotheistic-polytheistic distinction breaks down in its application to traditionalist Maya beliefs. As day-keepers repeatedly informed me, there is but one "god" in Maya religion, best conceived of as a cosmic, vitalistic force rather than the corporeal entity "god" denotes in the Western tradition. This force has various aspects and is manifest in various manners that may appear as distinct "gods" (cf. Montejo 1991). Despite having different names, different symbolic associations, and different contexts of activity, these "gods" are described by most *aj q'ijab'* as aspects of a single, unified force that animates the cosmos. Viewing unity in diversity is characteristic of Maya cultural logics in a number of domains, and such unity is conceptually associated with balance and harmony within and between both the physical and metaphysical worlds.

Tecpán and Patzún are, generally speaking, nominally Catholic. In both towns the Catholic church holds a prominent position in local life, an importance reflected in the central position the church occupies in each town's layout. Tecpanecos and Patzuneros alike are proud of their churches, and Catholic saints have taken on the role of shibboleths in many ways (see Watanabe 1990b). My 1994 survey found a slight majority of Catholics in both towns (58.3 percent in Tecpán, 52.7 percent in Patzún).[2] In both Tecpán and Patzún, a greater percentage of ladino respondents than Indian respondents claimed Catholicism as their religion: in Tecpán, 52.2 percent of sampled Indians were Catholic while 70.9 percent of sampled ladinos were; in Patzún, 50.3 percent of Indian respondents were Catholic compared with 84.6 percent of ladinos (see Figure 7.5). Protestants ("*evangélicos*") made up 36.3 percent of the Tecpán sample and 39.4 percent of the Patzún sample. No one in either

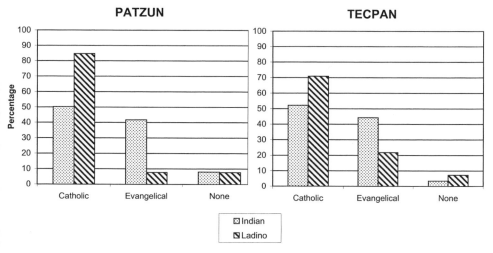

FIGURE 7.5. Religion and ethnicity in Tecpán and Patzún. Illustration by the author.

town claimed affiliation with an indigenous religion, although 11.5 percent of surveyed Tecpaneco Indians and 13.7 percent of Patzunero Indians reported having recently attended a Maya religious ceremony. A surprising 4.8 percent of Tecpaneco and 8 percent of Patzunero respondents claimed no religion at all.

Catholicism in Tecpán and Patzún is by no means homogeneous. The term "Catholic" encompasses a great deal of ideological diversity. In both towns, the mainstream, conservative (i.e., closely following the teachings of Rome) Catholic doctrine is espoused by the towns' priests from the pulpits of the main churches. There are two priests in Tecpán. The senior one, a man in his mid-forties, is a ladino from San Martín Jilotepeque; his assistant priest is a Kaqchikel speaker from Patzún in his early thirties. The older priest presides over all of the most important church rites, speaking exclusively in Spanish. His sermons often rail against contraceptives, Protestantism, and the perversities of global pop culture, and simultaneously exhort Tecpanecos to overcome their backward ethnic animosities and live together as one community in Christ. In private conversations, he claims to admire many aspects of Maya culture, while arguing for ethnic harmony through assimilation. He has a reputation among the town's Indians for being unkind and even abusive. He has reportedly commanded supplicants to bathe more often and has ridiculed illiterates. The younger priest, in contrast, conducts his ceremonies in both Spanish and Kaqchikel. Although he does not carry the administrative authority of the older priest and mostly works in *aldeas*, he has a reputation among Indians for being sympathetic and helpful.

The priest in Patzún does not speak Kaqchikel, but indigenous sacristans translate much of the service. The sacristans, all older Kaqchikel males who wear the white pants and *rodillera* of traditional men's dress, also help the priest by lighting candles, preparing the incense, and aiding the preparations for the Eucharist. Because of this prominent indigenous participation in the workings of the church, Catholic Kaqchikel residents of Patzún generally feel a stronger allegiance to the church than do Catholic Indians in Tecpán.

Both Tecpán and Patzún have a number of *congregaciones* (formal subdivisions of the church parish) to serve residents of the *aldeas*, although in Tecpán *congregaciones* in the town center play a more important role than in Patzún. It is through these much smaller congregations (made up of from five to one hundred member households) that Catholic diversity is locally expressed. Congregations take various approaches to Catholic doctrine. Some take a charismatic approach, with their services closely resembling those of evangelicals; some focus on improving family relationships; some concern themselves primarily with liberation theology; and at least one congregation in Tecpán is made up exclusively of women and addresses women's issues.

*Cofradías* (religious brotherhoods), reportedly strong just twenty years ago, have lost much of their former importance in Maya communities and exist only in abbreviated form today in Tecpán and Patzún. In Tecpán there are eight active *cofradías*. Patzún reportedly has seven active *cofradías*, although only three still have public activities. In both towns, the *cofradía* associated with the local patron saint (Saint Francis of Assisi in Tecpán and Saint Bernard in Patzún) is the most vigorous. In Tecpán, members of the *cofradía* of San Francisco are mostly from *aldeas*, although they rent space in the town proper to house their saint's images and ceremonial paraphernalia. The structure of their *cofradía* is the most elaborate of those found in the two towns; the organizational structures of the other *cofradías* are simply abbreviated forms of the pattern found within the San Francisco *cofradía*.

The senior *cofradía* official is called "Tetata" (or "Cofrade"), and under his direction are four *mayordomos*, each with his own specific duties (or *cargos*). The Tetata is in charge of organizing all *cofradía* functions, maintaining contact with the priest, and ensuring the financial stability of the group. The *mayordomo* positions are ranked, with each post carrying specific duties. The First Mayordomo is in charge of the keys to the *cofre* (the chest that holds ritual paraphernalia and clothing for the statues). The Second Mayordomo keeps the saints' images clean and makes sure fresh flowers are always at their feet. The Third Mayordomo is supposed to sweep the church (although Tecpán's priest complains that he never does), and the Fourth Mayordomo serves as the personal aide to the Tetata. The wife of the Cofrade and the wives of the *mayordomos* form a parallel structure, called simply *texela* (the women). The *texela* also have certain prescribed duties, including taking incense to the saint images, preparing meals for *cofradía* functions, and making new clothes for the saint's images. The wife of the Tetata directs these activities. In addition, there is a parallel set of five couples (*säkalej*) paired with the couples of the *cofradía* proper. Their job is to aid the member couples in carrying out their tasks, and the structural position of these auxiliary posts is at the bottom of the *cofradía* hierarchy.

Adherence to the traditional protocol of behavior for *cofradía* members is waning. It is said that until twenty years ago, the *texela* wore their ceremonial outfits whenever they made a public appearance, even when just going to the market. Today the use of ceremonial finery is confined to certain processions on and around the feast day of Saint Francis (see Figure 7.6).

We lived next door to the house in Tecpán where the images of San Francisco were kept. Frequently we would hear the melodious sound of the flute and drum, punctuated by the explosions of fireworks, as ceremonies were carried out at the house. On September 16 of a year long forgotten, the wounds of Christ are said to have appeared on San Francisco's body, a sign of his sincerity in wanting to suffer as Christ did. On that day, Tecpán's *cofradías* all turn out to "look" for the wounds. In the late afternoon, the two images of San Francisco, accompanied by the alcaldes of all the *cofradías* in town and the women auxiliaries, lead a procession to the church, where the images are left overnight. On October 4 the images traditionally change houses, as another person takes on the role of Tetata and the corresponding obligation to care for the saint all year. In 1994 the position of Tetata did not change hands; the great expense of buying candles, incense, fireworks, and liquor, as well as paying for the Masses, left no one willing to assume the respon-

FIGURE 7.6. The procession of Saint Francis of Assisi, Tecpán, 1994. Author photo.

sibility. The *cofradía*'s drum and flute players come from San Andrés Itzapa, as there are no longer any local musicians (see Figure 7.7).

Like the *cofradía* of San Francisco in Tecpán, Patzún's *cofradía* of San Bernardino is much weaker than town elders remember it being (see Hill 1992 for a discussion of the economics of Patzún's *cofradías* from the mid–seventeenth century to the mid–nineteenth century). Made up of five elderly men and their wives, the *cofradía* of Patzún's patron saint is organized in a hierarchy much like that of the *cofradía* of San Francisco, but its only public function comes on the day of San Bernardino. Patzún is said to have six other *cofradías*, although most of them reportedly have only one remaining member who takes care of the saint's images. In Patzún, membership in one of the town's two *hermandades* is much preferred by younger people to participation in the *cofradía*. The *hermandades* (one Indian and one ladino) are responsible for Holy Week festivities; and because of their more widespread support, Semana Santa festivities rival those of the day of San Bernardino. This trend away from *cofradía* participation is lamented by some Kaqchikel Patzuneros as an ill effect of Westernization. As one elderly man told me, "The youth no longer have time to work for such customs—they would rather use their time working and making money."

The importance of the *cofradía* in the social life of Mesoamerican Indian communities has been well documented. Eric Wolf (1957) saw the prevalence of *cofradías* and the cargo system as mechanisms for maintaining the inward focus of "closed corporate peasant communities." This idea, later elaborated by Waldemar Smith (1977) and George Foster (1965), viewed Indian communities as having developed as mechanisms to maintain economic and social isolation from national systems and to redistribute wealth within communities. Wolf (1986) and others have come to question the validity of this concept as it has been widely applied to modern Indian communities. Most analysts recognize the many ties that Maya communities maintain with national and international political and economic systems. Regardless of its role in the past, it is undeniable that the *cofradía* system has eroded significantly over the last forty years. Indeed, the future of the *cofradía* system in both towns is uncertain. With little interest in them among the under-30 population, they seem doomed to die out with the current generation of older adherents. Economic factors are most often cited as the cause in the decline of *cofradías*. Membership is expensive, and younger Indians, striving for upward mobility, are unwilling to pay the costs of member-

FIGURE 7.7. *Cofradía* drum and flute players in front of Tecpán's Catholic church. Author photo.

ship. Furthermore, the spread of evangelicalism and Catholic Action, both of which define themselves in opposition to the traditionalism embodied in the *cofradía* system, has eroded the former position of *cofradías*. Maya activists in both towns express an interest in maintaining the *cofradía* tradition, but they have made little progress. In both towns, social distinctions hinder the process. *Cofradía* members often come from *aldeas*, have little formal education, and maintain a tightly closed social network. The more cosmopolitan and better-educated Maya concerned with cultural revitalization are often distrusted by *cofradía* members. In Patzún, one local Maya author tried to bring together the town's surviving *cofradías* to form an organization that would provide mutual support between the groups and serve as a means of introducing prospective members to the system. *Cofradía* leaders, however, were unenthusiastic — even given their groups' dire predicaments — and nothing came of the effort.

My 1994 surveys found that 11.5 percent of Indian respondents in Tecpán and 13.7 percent of those in Patzún had recently attended a traditionalist Maya religious ceremony. Both towns support several full- and part-time religious specialists (*aj q'ijab*) and maintain a number of altars at sacred sites in the surrounding forests and hills. An altar kept in a remote corner of the archaeological site of Iximche' is the closest, most important ritual site. It has the great advantage over sites such as the cave at Pulchich of being easily accessible, even by vehicle if one adequately compensates the *guardián*. On several occasions my car was commandeered to haul people from Tecpán to Iximche' late at night. As a result of this accessibility and the luster of its place in Kaqchikel history, the Iximche' site has become an important regional center, and Maya priests from across the Kaqchikel and K'iche' area come there for important ceremonies. The Waqxaqi' B'atz' ceremony, which took place on September 23, 1993, at the Iximche' altar, was attended by more than two hundred people.

Over the centuries, Maya priests have successfully internalized much Christian doctrine, and their ceremonies often reflect this hybridity. For example, one *aj q'ij* in Patzún told the following story:

> Jesus Christ came to Guatemala, he lived here, and thus he knows the situation of the Maya here. Jesus Christ is an intercessor for the Maya people, equivalent to one's dead relatives. The Bible speaks of Jesus' life from his birth to when he was 15 years old, and then from when he was 30 until his death. Where did he live between 15 and 30? It does

not say, but certainly he was here. The Bible is incomplete, or more likely, there were other parts written here that the Spaniards burned. And there are no Maya saints, only Spanish ones. Why? Well, it is not logical. Of course there were Maya saints, but their writings were destroyed by the Spaniards.

Although this was the only time I heard mention of precontact Maya saints, many Catholic Maya would agree with my informant in principle: Christianity is important, but alone it is incomplete. I was frequently told that Maya *costumbre*, Catholicism, even Protestantism are but different ways to worship the same deity. Many see no incongruity in taking communion and professing their faith while also participating in native rites.

Protestantism is an important social force in both towns, and according to my surveys, a greater percentage of Indians than ladinos are "*evangélicos*." Most Protestant churches are small grassroots congregations of the charismatic variety of Christianity (marked by an emphasis on the "gifts of the Holy Spirit," including speaking in tongues and healing). The emotional release of dramatic religious services seems to appeal to a broad segment of the stereotypically reserved Maya population. The most prominent markers of Protestant belief are actually found in the absence of certain traits: *evangélicos* are expected to abstain from alcohol and tobacco—and they often do so aggressively—and they oppose, sometimes vehemently, *cofradía* rituals and other "pagan" aspects of town fiestas (including saint veneration). Many Catholics see *evangélicos* as more materialistic, and since it is usually less expensive to be Protestant than Catholic (Annis 1987:85), many *evangélicos* do have more capital available for investment.

One would expect *evangélicos* to be ideologically opposed to the philosophy of pan-Mayanism. Nationally, the Instituto Lingüístico de Verano (ILV, or SIL), perhaps the single most influential Protestant group in the country, strongly opposes the unified alphabet and in general the activities of groups such as the Academia de las Lenguas Mayas de Guatemala. Furthermore, *evangélicos* in the two towns oppose participation in traditionalist Maya ceremonies and the perceived paganism of certain pan-Mayanist activities. Unsurprisingly, then, most local pan-Mayanists had been raised in the Catholic Church. Nonetheless, there are Protestants in both towns who have been able to reconcile their faith with pan-Mayanist activities. For example, one Protestant Indian man in Tecpán, who had long pursued a path of cultural assimilation, began in 1993 to accept some of the ideas promoted by pan-Mayanists, especially in those areas where he perceived pan-Mayanist goals would help his business, which caters to foreign tourists. Whereas he had previously not allowed his wife and daughters to wear *traje,* he began to encourage its use, and though he had formerly feigned ignorance of a Mayan language, he began to speak proudly in his native tongue in certain contexts. Although he refused to attend shamanistic ceremonies, and he discouraged alcohol and tobacco use, this man nonetheless began to support local cultural revitalization.

Perhaps the most surprising fact about religion in the two towns is that it does not manifest the extremely divisive role that it plays in other highland Maya towns (see Sexton 1978; Warren 1978; Annis 1987; Hill and Monaghan 1987). At the same time, religion has been a troublesome point for many pan-Maya activists. In many ways, religion presents the greatest threat to Maya unity, highlighting ideological differences with the weight of religious fervor. Protestant evangelization, in particular, has been the subject of much criticism from pan-Maya leaders for destroying local bases of culture and encouraging ladino-ization. Yet, in Tecpán and Patzún at least, religious affiliation is not necessarily incompatible with any particular ethnic affiliation. Indeed, ethnicity is the most pervasive vector of self-identity and plays a more prominent role in shaping individual agency.[3]

# 8    *Local Forms of Ethnic Resistance*

Maya cosmology—its agrarian ontology, sacred cycles, social preoc-
cupations, and syncretic aesthetics—has been selectively used by a
variety of interests as a marker of the intimacy of community in the
countryside and as a common moral language for trans-community
movements. Thus, these ethnic "post-peasants" continue to reaffirm
religious meaning and cultural distinctiveness through an idiom that
reflects their Maya-agrarian roots.

KAY WARREN (1998)

No ethnic marker, even the most essential, exists independent of lived
experience, for it is only through sensually repetitive experience that
such markers and the schemas they represent are produced and reproduced. They are reproduced across time and space, yet they are also
tailored to historically and sociologically particular circumstances, and
herein lies the conundrum presented by postmodern theorization. A
theoretical zeal to correct the errors of our ethnographic forbears by
focusing on the situationally contingent production of culture has led
us to be too bold in our rejection of the sort of "essentializing" analyses
that look at the historical reproduction of culture. Certainly culture is
produced and reproduced in the innumerable real-world encounters of
daily life, but even situationally contingent meaning cannot be divorced
from history. Cognitive structures and cultural models do change in the
practice of being indexed to "real" world (social and cultural) circumstances, but to accept the fact of such change entails also accepting the
important role of a presupposed meaning derived from precedent and
valued for historical continuity (Sahlins 1976; Bloch 1985). Even in

circumstances in which meanings are radically changed and symbols reinterpreted, even in the frenzied heat of postmodern constructivism, there remains for ethnic activists a sincere sense of continuity and a driving quest for authenticity (see Conklin 1997). In the trenches of ethnic activism, in Guatemala at least, there is little room for the luxury of postmodern irony; a palpable desire to change society for the better gives Maya activism a quasi-religious fervor that makes many foreign academics nervous.

In this chapter I turn to the explicit practice of identity politics in the daily life of Tecpán and Patzún, a lived experience that mirrors in many important ways the strategy of national pan-Maya activism. I am concerned mainly with ethnic markers and their mobilization in local contexts. Ethnic identity is the self-conscious manipulation, articulation, and reification of perceived cultural differences, and is thus built from the "stuff of culture," but it is not coequal with it. The relationship between culture and ethnicity is complex, for ethnicity is inherently defined relationally (oppositionally) and yet ethnic presentation is also conditioned by the associative patterns, presumptions, and predispositions of culture—in short, by cultural logics.

### Beauty Queens and Identity Politics

Observers often take ironic delight in the juxtaposition of cultural symbols characteristic of identity politics in these postmodern, transnational times. I am thinking particularly of the famous images of Kayapó cameramen working alongside BBC filmmakers (see Turner 1991), but also of Maya writing hieroglyphs on their notebook computers or talking on cell phones in the middle of a crowded bus. We must remember, however, that the irony is ours, not theirs, and that such irony can be a seductive and insidious means of distancing ourselves from the contradictions of theoretical praxis (see Fabian 1991; Collier 1997; Herzfeld 1997; Nelson 1999).

Beauty pageants constitute one aspect of Maya activism that is rich with potential ironies.[1] In many ways, beauty pageants epitomize popular essentialism, equating beauty and authenticity through the commodification of an identity. From a critically humanistic perspective, Miss America, Miss Universe, and the other well-known Western beauty pageants reinforce implicit hegemonic ideals of gender roles—orthopedic devices to keep women in their place. Maya activists have taken this tool of hegemonic imposition and redeployed it as a sublime weapon of resistance. Yet Maya beauty pageants are not parodies in any sense, and they are taken quite seriously by both participants and Maya academics (a fact that I embarrassingly discovered after my few initial attempts at beauty-pageant jokes received only uncomfortably muted laughter and more than a few mean glares from Maya friends).

Since the early 1970s, beauty pageants have played an important role in the development of Maya activism. Gálvez and Esquit (1997) emphasize that the early pageants provided both physical and ideological space for incipient Maya leaders to meet, as well as fertile ground for discussing issues of cultural relevance. They write that

> the elections of the Indian beauty queens — an imitation of the ladino beauty contests, became a central part of the work of many community organizations. Nevertheless, these activities transcended the touristic purposes of the state and were turned into means for channeling concerns and demands, and which permitted gatherings with representatives of other Mayan regions. These elements were reflected in the speeches of the indigenous queens with an increasingly political content. (ibid.:30)

Beauty pageants provided an ideal vehicle for incipient pan-Mayanists' efforts, combining a concern with the beauty of authenticity (and the authenticity of beauty) with a public forum for expressing ethnic pride that would be interpreted by most outsiders as "touristic" and "folkloric" (and in that sense, nationalistic). Carlota McAllister (1996:107), in a lucid exegesis of the interplay between symbols and meanings in the national Rabín Ahua beauty pageant, notes that "an authentic representation is one in which the relationship of form to content, of signifier and signified, is intrinsic and therefore eternal," and yet, she proceeds, "the very claim to authenticity recognizes the possibility of inauthenticity . . . authenticity, thus, is always emergent and never more so than when the authentic representation is not an artefact, but a person, a producer of representations." In this context, beauty pageants present the possibility of examining the dynamic relationship between symbols and meanings as they are performed in the public practice of identity politics.

### Negotiating a Common Identity

Identity politics is a messy business. Coming together for the common good is not as easy as some philosophers and economists suggest: culture is always idiosyncratically internalized in an individual's cognitive models, and so interacting, even with other cultural insiders, is problematic. First, the common good must be inter-subjectively defined in a manner equal to the task of motivating compliance and even enthusiasm. Second, structural conditions must be conducive — or at least perceived as being conducive — to the form of cooperation proposed.

The stakes are often high in negotiating local identity politics. It is an ideal arena for the playing out of long-standing or recent social animosities between families and individuals, and it forces one to define one's beliefs and construct an acceptable common historiography. It is here that religious tensions (between Catholics, Protestants, and traditionalists) stand out, although I was constantly surprised at the degree of consensus that is reached, a testament to Maya cognitive models that value consensus. While tempers may flare and opinions diverge widely, Kaqchikel confrontations are most often circumspect.

Tecpán's town beauty queens are crowned in early October as part of the preparations for the town's annual fiesta on the day of San Francisco. The fiesta is a major event in local life, at once bringing the town together in a common celebration while reifying local social boundaries. It is also an important public forum for presenting images of cultural pride and negotiating new patterns of ethnic relations. For the 1994 coronation ceremony in Tecpán, several local Maya activists formed a group to participate in the presentations, hoping to communicate a positive and pluralistic message of ethnic awareness to the town's ladino and Indian populations alike.

FIELDNOTES — TECPÁN, SEPTEMBER 27, 1994

Last night we went to a meeting with eleven local Maya who want to plan an event to be included in the coronation of the town's two queens next week. It was supposed to start at 7:00, but really did not get under way until after 8:00. Present were Don Raymundo (an *aj q'ij*), José and Eugenia (both fervent Catholics sympathetic to Maya activism), Ignacio (the man who had stopped us last week while drunk and explained that he had built a cane fence around his house to be truly Maya), Víctor (who organizes the traditional dances, and who is married to a ladina), J'olom (a prominent local Maya activist) and Juana (a self-possessed woman from El Quiché who had recently married J'olom), Polo (the son of the president of the women's artisans association and a volunteer fireman), and Ix K'ot, Oscar, and K'ot (three locals in their late teens or early twenties with an interest in cultural issues). Juana had already talked to the committee of the town fair and they offered the group thirty minutes to put on a cultural activity. The first order of business was to decide what to present, and there was quick agreement that it should be a dramatization of a Maya religious ceremony. It was noted that the Maya ceremonies still much practiced are those for the construction of a house, the construction of a *tuj*, the birth of a child, marriage *pedidas* (requests for marriage), and rituals related to maize. In the general discussion, Eugenia said that they should do something to give the ladinos the view that Maya ceremonies are not all bad: "Who brought the five hundred years of evangelization? The Spaniards, but what was our evangelization? Maya priests pray to gods — our god, our gods, the owners of the sun, the rain, the wind, the earth. They do not pray to the devil. They are not witches." K'ot then spoke, saying that they should not say, as school texts do, that X is the god of water, but rather that it is god in water, because it is the same god, just present in, just represented through, the water. Don Raymundo then spoke about what a shame it is that there is so little participation in cultural activities here these days, not like there was twenty years ago: "It is because of fear, nothing else, and the church and the army [*ri poop*, a word derived from the Kaqchikel name for "blow-gun"], who say that to involve oneself in these cultural activities is bad. Language and ceremonies are very important, but the Maya of Tecpán also have other necessities." It seems that he felt uncomfortable saying any more than this on the subject, but his meaning was clear: what we are doing is but a first step. Eugenia then took the floor again, and discussed the possibility of portraying the *pedida*: "Long ago parents chose spouses for their children, but we do not want to portray that since 'they' say it is a bad example." Raymundo broke in to ask who thinks that it is bad, and Eugenia responded that it just was "not educational." A compromise was finally reached after several hours of discussion, and it was decided to dramatize a maize ceremony: it was said that today only the ceremony of the storing of the maize was widely practiced, so that would be the theme of the presentation. It was decided that daily meetings would be held to further elaborate the props and script. Got back home around 10:30 and fell into bed.

Subsequent meetings followed much the same pace of group consensus building, which, I must admit, I found to be an agonizingly slow process. Most potentially explosive was the subject of religion, as the group was composed of religious traditionalists such as Don Raymundo, devout Catholics such as José and Eugenia, and family members of Protestant households such as K'ot. This potential point of contention was implicitly acknowledged by all, however, and pains were taken to work around it in group discourse. In carefully worded orations, members outlined their own beliefs and largely worked toward a relativistic theory of religion: individuals may approach the higher being in various ways, none of them inherently right or wrong. In terms of theory and practice, this is heady stuff indeed: subaltern praxis seemingly organized around the tenets of postmodern theorizations of multivocality. But postmodernism of this sort is nothing new to the Maya, and epigraphic and iconographic data show that intentionally polyvalent symbols have long been employed by the Maya for strategically political ends.

The confrontations that did occur were muted, such as that between Don Raymundo and Eugenia over the value of arranged marriages. Eugenia resisted including an arranged marriage ceremony in the presentation, saying that it sets a bad example, obviously speaking from her experience as a woman. Conservative Don Raymundo began to counter Eugenia's portrayal of a traditional Maya custom such as arranged marriages as bad—and indeed I had heard his arguments in favor of arranged marriages on other occasions—but thought better of it and strategically backed off, choosing not to leverage his social capital in what might likely have been a losing battle. Similarly, in subsequent meetings there was much discussion on how to treat the issue of drinking. It is customary to drink ritualized shots of maize liquor throughout the *entrojada* (maize storage) ceremony, and the same holds true for most Maya ceremonies. Don Raymundo and several others felt that in the spirit of authenticity this must be explicitly included in the performance. The few Protestant teetotalers in the group as well as a number of liberal Catholics felt that including ritual drinking would set a bad example and further solidify the ladino stereotype of Indians as drunks. In the end, it was decided that the ritual consumption should be included, but that the drink be identified only as a ceremonial beverage prepared for the occasion from maize.

The play was presented with barely a hitch and received a warm round of applause. Watching the performance, I scanned the audience, looking for people's reactions. The ladinos mostly appeared at first amused and toward the end bored, but showed no visible malice in their facial expressions and body language. The Maya audience members were generally more engaged in the performance, often keeping up a running commentary on the authenticity of the portrayal. Few if any spectators left the Tecpán auditorium that night with a radically changed perspective on Maya culture, and doubtless the performance reinforced certain stereotypes for both Maya and ladinos alike. For the organizing group itself, however, the experience was an empowering one, and it was subsequently often cited as a concrete example of what grassroots organizing can accomplish.

### Vilma I and Ixmukane

Beauty pageants play an important role in the titular saints' feasts of Saint Bernard in Patzún and Saint Francis in Tecpán. Each town has two queens, one Indian and one ladina, each elected by their respective ethnic group. Telling of the pervasiveness of ethnic segregation, townspeople are nonplused by such separate but equal standards.

Tecpanecos say that the system of having two queens began in the 1960s, with ladinos selecting an Indian young woman to serve as the "Princesa Iximche'" alongside the town's official "Reina Franciscana." By the 1980s, Indian leaders had established a separate committee to run the Indian elections, and they gradually broke ties with the ladino fair committee and started their own election and coronation ceremony. Interestingly, the Indian committee continued to crown their beauties "Princess" as opposed to "Queen" (a title reserved for the ladina winner). It is reported that after the break, attendance at the ladina queen pageant dropped dramatically, a fact deeply resented by local ladino elites. After the violence began, the organizers of the Indian pageant were reportedly among the first placed on the "black lists" kept by army assassins, and the indigenous committee therefore dissolved.

Hendrickson (1995:82) reports that Tecpán's Indigenous Fair Committee reemerged in 1983, when it sponsored (along with Maybelline Cosmetics) the Primera Fiesta Folklórica de Tecpán, and in 1994, I was able to witness the crowning of both the Reina Franciscana and the Princesa Iximche'.[2] The pageant began in the streets of Tecpán with each candidate riding through town atop a float constructed by her supporters. The floats, which are built on flatbed trucks, generally have themes such as "local flowers" or "Tecpán's industries." Schools, clubs, and other local organizations all proposed candidates for either ladina or Indian queen, and some groups, including the local military base, proposed a candidate in each category.

In the 1994 competition, the military base nominated Vilma I for Indian queen, and employed a precolumbian theme in its float design.

FIGURE 8.1. Vilma I, the Tecpán military base's candidate for Indian Queen in 1994. Author photo.

Queen Vilma, draped in a cloak made of the distinctive rich brown fabric of Tecpán ceremonial clothing, was seated atop a miniature white-washed pyramid and was flanked by two girls and two boys wearing local traditional dress. From her vantage point atop the pyramid, Queen Vilma looked out over a scene of ritual human sacrifice. Wrapped in a full-length blood red cape, a young army recruit played the role of the Maya priest/executioner who chopped at the neck of the young woman tightly wrapped in bright white sheets (see Figure 8.1).

That the notorious local military base, responsible for the death of hundreds of local residents just over a decade earlier, chose to portray a scene of precolumbian human sacrifice on its Indian queen float is a disturbing sign of the army's entrenched power. We cannot know the intentions of the float's designers, and it is likely that they were making a good-faith effort to support the indigenous queen's crowning ceremony, just as they had long done with the ladina queen ceremony. At the same time, it seems highly unlikely that the implications of showing a brutal scene of ritual sacrifice were completely lost on the military officials charged with designing the float. Richards (1985) writes of a dichotomous worldview into which military recruits become indoctrinated, positing a stark contrast between the progressive, modern, urban world of ladino society and the untamed, regressive chaos of the rural Indian world. In this scheme, Indians represent the animal ignorance and brutality that threatens modernizing development, and an explicit link is developed between Maya cultural values and savagery. The military base's float makes this link explicit and thus traces its origins back to an image of a hedonistically pagan and blood-thirsty Classic Maya civilization. It takes a heavy hand, the float's iconography seems to imply, to control a people capable of human sacrifice.

The 1994 competition included a candidate (the Princesa Ixmukane) put forth by a local women's weaving cooperative with ties to pan-Maya activists. The cooperative's float design focused on precolumbian Maya culture, but with a predictably different interpretation of life than that presented on Vilma I's float. The Princesa Ixmukane wears the women's ceremonial dress distinctive of Tecpán. (Vilma I, in contrast, wears an approximation of a royal cape made from the same fabric.) A Classic Maya temple is visible in the painted background, topped by a brilliant yellow rising sun. The candidate herself is seated on a low chair, under a large maize stalk in the midst of young girls and boys sorting the colored kernels of maize. One young girl weaves a Tecpán-style *huipil* on a backstrap loom attached to the maize hut. On the large background painting and flanking the sides of the flatbed truck are the hieroglyphic signs for the days and months of the Maya calendar (see Figure 8.2).

The float's design is a rich symbolic statement, all the more pronounced because of its juxtaposition with the army base's entry. The scene that unfolds on the float is set against a backdrop of precolumbian symbols, a beautiful rendering by a local artist of the grandeur of the Classic Maya. The inclusion of hieroglyphic calendrical day names conveys both specific information about Maya cosmology (ordered, as they are, above the rising sun) as well as a more general reminder of the scientific expertise of the precolumbian Maya. The inclusion of such symbols emphasizes the chain of relationships that grants the modern Maya an essential authenticity rooted in an autochthonous past, while subtly valuing that tradition over the Western alternatives (organizers were quick to point out that the Maya calendar was more accurate than the Julian calendar used at the time of conquest). The staging of the float's centerpiece, with its symmetrical props and blocking, further re-

FIGURE 8.2. Princesa Ixmukane, the weaving cooperative's candidate for Indian Queen in 1994. Author photo.

inforced the concepts of cyclic regeneration (as measured by the sacred calendar) and cosmological balance. The juxtaposition of an ancient Maya backdrop with contemporary customs theatrically brings the past into the present. For ladino onlookers, this likely reinforced cognitive models that classify Maya culture as primitive and antimodern, a living folklore (and as [McAllister 1996:112] points out, "folklore is the fetish of Guatemalan-ness"). For the Maya spectators with whom I talked, the meaning was quite different, and they saw the float's representation as a valuation of elements of their cultural heritage dismissed and misunderstood by ladinos. The Princesa Ixmukane's float was the product of a truly grassroots effort, although some of the committee members were familiar with the pan-Mayanist agenda. In stressing peaceful themes of traditional Maya culture, members of the weaving cooperative were presenting a view of Maya culture geared toward the local context of Indian-ladino relations. Despite its local origins, the float was highly convergent with pan-Mayanist representations of Maya historiography, the result of commonly based cultural logics acting within similarly perceived contexts.

After the parade of candidates, elections were held later that same night in Tecpán's municipal auditorium. Despite the admission charge of two quetzales (which entitled the ticket holder to vote on the finalists), there was a standing-room-only crowd of over five hundred. Every group that had proposed a candidate tried to pack the audience with their supporters to gain votes, but many members of the artisans association did not show up, put off by the two-quetzal ticket price. The ceremonies began late (even by local standards), with each candidate being presented by her sponsoring group. After being introduced, the young women walked up a ramp onto the stage and sat in their assigned places; the ladinas all sat on the left side of the stage and the Indians on the right. The military's Indian candidate was accompanied by a girl walking in front who swung a smoking incense burner and a boy following behind dressed in *traje* with a black mustache painted on his face. The ladina candidates seemed to be striving for the most exotic and flashy dress they could find or afford, and the preferred style sparkled with sequins and beads and clung tightly to their figures. The Indians all wore ceremonial *traje* from Tecpán, including an older style of brown blouse (the *xilon huipil* discussed below) and an indigo skirt with white stripes.

In their prepared speeches, the Indian candidates all spoke in both Kaqchikel and Spanish, stressing traditional Maya culture and values. The military ladina gave an impassioned speech on the role of the military in Guatemalan democracy, and called for a future of ethnic harmony in Tecpán, seemingly given without irony in regard to the segregation of the event itself. After their speeches, each candidate was asked a question supposedly unknown to her in advance to elicit an impromptu response. Many spectators, however, commented on the fact that certain well-connected candidates seemed to have prepared their answers ahead of time: for example, the volunteer firemen's candidate was asked about deforestation, and she quickly reeled off amazingly precise figures about the number of trees cut down around Tecpán in recent years; and the candidate for Nivi Industries (a manufacturer of propane gas containers and the largest local employer) was asked about local industry, and she gave what appeared to be a memorized spiel about Nivi's pioneering role in Tecpán's economy. Finally, three ladinas (the candidates from the military base, the volunteer firemen, and Nivi) and three Indians (candidates from the artisans association, the military base, and a government-run agricultural cooperative) were selected by the panel of ladino judges as finalists. Ticket holders then voted on the final winners, electing the two candidates (ladina and Indian) sponsored by the army. The commanding officer from the military base then crowned the two women as the new Reina Franciscana and Princesa Iximche'.

## *Language*

Tecpanecos, Patzuneros, and Maya in general regard language as an important and somehow essential part of Maya-ness. In Chapter 5, we saw how pan-Mayanists have actively promoted the use of the unified alphabet for writing Mayan languages, prescribed new grammatical standards, and introduced a large number of neologisms in Kaqchikel. This linguistic work has been instrumental in effecting political change at the national level, and its innovative application of linguistic methodologies is certainly intellectually compelling. Yet, the extent to which this initial flurry of success can be sustained is largely dependent on the acceptance of the pan-Mayanist ideology at the local level. Without the ability to mobilize the constituency they presume to speak for, Maya leaders have little hope of retaining their leverage with the government; and more than a few ladino elites would be pleased to reveal the pan-Mayanists as self-serving opportunists with few ties to the Maya masses (see Nelson 1999).

Cultural change is both underwritten and constrained by cultural logics. Pan-Mayanists are "free" to innovate in the construction of linguistic markers of ethnic awareness. Their innovations are first constrained by the idiosyncrasies of their uniquely internalized cultural logics (the boundaries of their cognitive *doxa*), but these same idiosyncrasies provide the basis for innovative logical extensions. Simply put, overlapping cultural-cum-cognitive structures constrain, largely subconsciously, the possibilities for creativity. Yet this is but the first test of appropriateness, for innovations must then be accepted by others. This means that innovations must index cultural models that are intersubjectively salient, and do so in a manner accepted as culturally logical by others. This process is normally not merely one of development, testing, and acceptance or rejection. Rather, there is constant discursive dialect in which individuals explain their logic, persuade others of its legitimacy, and adapt its structure based on their perceptions.

Language provides a measure for examining the acceptance of pan-Mayanist ideals in local settings. Maya linguists have self-consciously and strategically — opportunistically — presented their linguistic research in a manner that appeals to non-Indian sensibilities. Yet, the creation of neologisms and new grammatical structures also rests on conventional norms in Maya communities. Neologisms must be accepted by the language's speakers if they are to be effective. Certain new constructions are more likely to be adopted by local populations, and these accepted constructions index culturally salient semantic domains. This reality demonstrates the grassroots constraints on the instrumental constructivism of Maya scholars and their political agendas.

In Patzún one hears Kaqchikel spoken more frequently and in more contexts than is the case in Tecpán. Market transactions, municipal business, and even church services in Patzún are often conducted in Kaqchikel, whereas in Tecpán, Spanish has become dominant in many of these domains. For example, the Indian mayor of Tecpán in 1994, who is fluent in Kaqchikel, used Spanish as the language of first resort even when speaking to other known Kaqchikel speakers; Patzún's mayor, in contrast, preferred to conduct much of his business in Kaqchikel. Tecpanecos refer to Patzún as a place where a pure, original (thus "more authentic") Kaqchikel is still spoken.

My survey data show that 96.6 percent of Indians in the Patzún sample spoke Kaqchikel fluently and 98.3 percent spoke at least some Kaqchikel. In the Tecpán sample, only 60.2 percent of Indian respondents claimed fluency in Kaqchikel, though 99.1 percent reported speaking at least some Kaqchikel. Thus, although the overwhelming majority of Indians in the two towns report some level of Kaqchikel proficiency, fluency in the language is significantly more widespread in Patzún (see Figure 8.3). The degree of Kaqchikel fluency found in Patzún does not, however, translate into a relatively lower degree of Spanish fluency. In the Patzún sample, 48.6 percent of Indians reported speaking Spanish fluently, whereas in the Tecpán sample, 35.4 percent of Indians claimed fluency in Spanish. (In both towns, slightly more than 94 percent of Indian respondents reported at least some use of Spanish.) Thus, conservation of Kaqchikel has not led to a rejection of Spanish in Patzún, but rather to higher levels of bilingualism.

By itself, the use of Kaqchikel does not, however, indicate adoption of a pan-Mayanist philosophy. Indeed, there seems to be little acceptance in either town of specific linguistic changes promoted by pan-Mayanists. For example, native linguists are encouraging the use of *rin* as the first-person-singular pronoun in Kaqchikel. There are four primary dialectical variants of the first-person-singular pronoun in Kaqchikel Maya: *in re', yin, yïn,* and *rin.* All these forms are historically derived

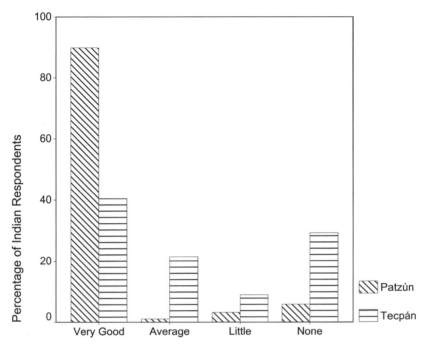

FIGURE 8.3. Kaqchikel language proficiency among Indians in Tecpán and Patzún. Illustration by the author.

from a contraction of *ri in,* with *rin* being the first derivation, and the others following. Maya linguists working to standardize the language have thus chosen *rin* as the preferred form because of its etymological primacy, even though most of these same linguists are from areas that use *yin.* Nonetheless, when asked for the first-person-singular pronoun in Kaqchikel in my survey, speakers of the language in both towns responded *"yin,"* the local variant, with only one exception. The single respondent who said *"rin"* is a Tecpaneca woman who has studied linguistics for several years and who has ties to pan-Mayanist organizations. Directed linguistic change is a difficult task made harder by strong allegiances to the local dialects found in Maya communities. Even those individuals in the two towns who adopt the new structures often fall back on old forms and frequently resort to self-correction.

In their efforts to expand the use of Kaqchikel and to purify the language, pan-Mayanists encourage the use of Kaqchikel numerals, an important lexical domain in which many Kaqchikel speakers resort to Spanish. Not surprisingly, given the extent of Kaqchikel use in Patzún,

my survey found that only 91.3 percent of Kaqchikel speakers in Patzún knew at least some Kaqchikel numerals; most knew ten or less,
but 26 percent could count to one hundred. In Tecpán, 75.6 percent of
Kaqchikel speakers knew some Kaqchikel numerals, and only 5 percent
could count to one hundred.

Related to their encouragement of the use of Maya numbers, pan-
Mayanists also promote the use of Maya day names as an alternative
to the Western/Spanish system. Maya day names, however, are rarely
used in either town. In the Patzún sample, only 4.5 percent of Kaqchikel
speakers knew any Kaqchikel day names, and in the Tecpán sample,
only 5 percent of speakers knew a Maya day name. Despite this lack
of knowledge, however, I found that many Indians in both towns are
interested in learning Maya bar-and-dot notation and day names (as
well as their Classic Period symbols). Thus, in regard to the use of
Maya numbers and day names, as with the other linguistic innovations
mentioned, pan-Mayanist forms of expression have not been widely
adopted in the two towns, although Indians in the two towns are not
actively opposed to the new forms. Indeed, informal workshops conducted in Tecpán on Maya numeration and day names have been well
attended. At least six such workshops were offered in 1994 and attended by between ten and thirty individuals. They would sometimes
take place in private homes, but were more often held in public rooms
in the town hall or in classrooms of a public school. Based on this interest, it seems likely that the use of Mayan languages in these lexical domains will increase.

In addition, receptivity to the philosophy of pan-Mayanism can be
measured by the growing acceptance of the unified alphabet for writing Mayan languages. Only a small number of individuals literate in
Kaqchikel in both Tecpán and Patzún are familiar with the unified alphabet. Nonetheless, there is much interest in learning it, and workshops on the alphabet sponsored by the ALMG have been well received
in both towns. Owners of stores that carry Maya names are slowly
changing their signs to conform to the new orthography, many evan-
gelizing Protestants and Catholic catechists are using the alphabet in
their work, and when classroom instruction in the towns' schools is conducted in Kaqchikel, teachers employ the unified alphabet. Thus, the
evidence from Tecpán and Patzún suggests that the predictions of supporters of competing orthographies that rural Maya would vigorously
resist adoption of the unified alphabet were unfounded.

These data show that although Indians in Tecpán and Patzún have not extensively adopted the linguistic markers of pan-Mayanism, neither have they actively resisted them. The small degree of acceptance that we have seen suggests that the process of directed linguistic change is just beginning in the two towns and that more widespread adoption of pan-Mayanist markers will likely follow. Further, the data from Patzún supports the hypothesis put forth by many Maya linguists that fluency in Kaqchikel need not be accompanied by a lesser degree of Spanish proficiency.

When asked their opinion of the Kaqchikel language, 67.8 percent of Indians in the Patzún sample and 71.7 percent of Indians in the Tecpán sample said that it held much importance for them. In Patzún, a further 21.6 percent of Indian respondents stated that Kaqchikel and Spanish are equally important, and 10.5 percent said that Kaqchikel was no longer important in today's society. In Tecpán, only 5.3 percent of Indian respondents said that Kaqchikel and Spanish hold equal importance, but 23.3 percent claimed that Kaqchikel was no longer important. These differences of opinion between the two samples reflect a greater degree of general cultural conservatism in Patzún than in Tecpán, and a correspondingly greater degree of receptivity to locally realized pan-Mayanist projects. Nonetheless, it is significant that a majority of Indian respondents in both towns see the Kaqchikel language as an important part of local and national culture. In their responses, Indians from both towns stressed the practical utility of Kaqchikel — it facilitates communication — as well as its historical-cultural significance: it has value because their ancestors spoke it. Thus, although language use in the two towns does not closely follow pan-Mayanist prescriptions, it is nonetheless convergent in many ways with the pan-Mayanist ideal. It is precisely such convergent processes — one arising from grassroots efforts, the other developing within national Maya activism — that characterize certain domains of Maya cultural logics.

### *Education*

Building on the observations of Foucault, Nelson (1999:5) argues that "powerful practices such as the law, schooling, and the use of language work with individual bodies to produce the body politic rather than simply repress an already-existing self. Thus identification is produced through constant repetition in sites of power that themselves are historically overdetermined, as well as through unconscious investments and resistances." In Guatemala, the state has long made use of the public education system to promote a modernist vision of acculturation and development—that is, to "fix" the Maya population. Yet, as Nelson elsewhere notes, "in those sites meant to 'fix' them, to turn them into ladinos, the Maya are repairing their communities, *formando* activists" (ibid.:162); indeed, "the goal of many Mayan activists is to fix, in the sense of *repair*, th[eir] culture, to renew people's pride in their indigenous identity" (ibid.:132). Education in Tecpán and Patzún illustrates these fluid agendas, and schools serve as important orthopedic devices for both the state and grassroots Maya activists.

By law, all children must attend school through the sixth grade, although, for various reasons, many do not. *Primaria* (first through sixth grades) is followed by *secundaria* (sixth through twelfth grades), and upon graduation from *secundaria*, students receive a certification that qualifies them for jobs in their specialty (e.g., accounting, teaching, construction). The mean number of years of primary and secondary education within the Patzún sample (3.52) is just slightly higher than the mean of the Tecpán sample (3.28), and in both towns roughly 36 percent of respondents did not attend school at all. On average, the residents of Patzún have slightly higher levels of education than do Tecpanecos, but in both towns women have lower levels than men and Indians have much lower levels than ladinos. In Patzún, Indian respondents averaged 3.15 years of primary and secondary education, whereas ladino respondents averaged 8.46 years; in Tecpán, Indian respondents averaged 2.5 years of education compared to 4.87 years among ladinos. Nonetheless, of respondents in Patzún, only 1.6 percent ($n = 3$, one of whom was Indian) had attended university, while among Tecpán respondents, 4.2 percent ($n = 7$, three of whom were Indians) had completed at least some university study. These figures certainly underestimate the extent of university education of individuals born in the two towns because many, if not most, who attend university do not return to their natal communities, opting instead to remain in the urban centers where they studied (although this is said to be less true of Patzuneros than of Tecpanecos).

Public schools are financed and operated by the national government through the Ministry of Education. The state's curricular policy for Indian areas has long been based on a philosophy of *castellanización*, or "Hispanizing" — linguistically and culturally — the students, so that they would grow up to be assimilated Guatemalans rather than isolated Indians. This in turn was based on the idea that Indians and their culture hinder progress and prevent Guatemala from becoming a homogeneous nation-state in the Western tradition.

In Tecpán, the municipal supervisor of education is a Maya man who has recently begun to espouse pan-Mayanist ideas in limited contexts. In the *cabecera* of Tecpán he presides over three national schools: the Escuela Nacional Mixta Miguel García Granados, the Escuela Nacional Mixta 25 de Julio 1524, and the Instituto Nacional Experimental. In 1994, none of these schools had a program in bilingual education, though there were a number of bilingual schools in the *aldeas*. With instruction given only in Spanish and using only state-produced textbooks, the local education system did not cater to the needs of Maya students, much less promote pan-Maya ideals (although female students were allowed to wear *traje* to classes). By 1999 this situation had changed somewhat: the Instituto Nacional Experimental now offers bilingual courses, many Maya teachers now feel more empowered to cater to the cultural needs of their Maya students, and two private schools catering to Maya students have opened.

In Patzún, the formal education system is more attuned to the needs of Maya students and the goals of pan-Mayanism. The supervisor of education is a Maya man from Tecpán who has studied linguistics for several years and who is an outspoken proponent of pan-Mayanism. He oversees three public schools: the Escuela Oficial Urbana Mixta Felipe López, the Escuela Nacional de Niños, and the Escuela Nacional Mixta Indígena Justo Rufino Barrios. The Barrios school has long offered bilingual programs, providing instruction in Kaqchikel for the first three years of primary education and then gradually switching to exclusive use of Spanish in the following three years. The school's bilingual textbooks are produced by the Programa Nacional de Educación Bilingüe (PRONEBI) with funds provided by the U.S. Agency for International Development. In these texts, Kaqchikel is written in the unified alphabet, although the books have been criticized by pan-Mayanists for simply translating Western concepts into Kaqchikel and not including purely Maya content. Although the other schools give instruction only in Spanish, most teachers are Kaqchikel women who ease the transition to Spanish for monolingual Kaqchikel-speaking children by providing occasional translations.

Public school teachers in Guatemala are often assigned to work in schools away from their home communities. These assignments have been viewed by many as an attempt to divide and conquer: minimizing the role of local teachers and leaders to promote allegiance to the state. In a similar fashion, military recruits are always stationed in areas far away from their homes. Nonetheless, the national educational system has actually aided the pan-Maya movement in several ways. First, regional workshops offer a chance for teachers (mostly Indians and often the most educated members of their communities) from around the Kaqchikel region to get together and discuss common problems and solutions. With the encouragement of PRONEBI officials, these teachers are becoming more sensitive to the ethnic dimensions of their work. Furthermore, relationships usually form between host communities and the teachers from other towns who are assigned to work there, and these relationships crosscut intercommunity rivalries and animosities. The effect has been to encourage and maintain intercommunity solidarity.

Both Tecpán and Patzún have a number of private schools (*colegios*). In both towns, the two largest private schools are associated with the Catholic Church and a Protestant church. In Tecpán these are the Colegio Mixto Bethesda (Protestant) and San Vicente de Paúl (Catholic). In both schools, instruction is given exclusively in Spanish, although only the Catholic school allows its students to wear *traje*. The third-largest *colegio* in Tecpán is the William Booth School, associated with the Salvation Army, which has been an important Protestant force in town since the 1976 earthquake reconstruction efforts. The curriculum employed in these schools is decidedly oriented toward *castellanización*, although concessions have been made for the use of *traje*.

These private schools, then, also act as orthopedic devices, in many ways convergent with the larger state agenda of modernization. Yet, as in Patzún, schools have also become important tools for local cultural activists. In 1993 a group of parents formed a vacation school to teach Kaqchikel, traditional skills, and the pan-Mayanist view of history to local children. Twenty-five students attended that first year, and in 1994 the group had plans to open a year-round private primary school (as yet unrealized in 1999). Also in 1993, a local man involved in pan-Mayanist activities opened Data K'ot, a vocational institute that offers instruction in computer science. The institute's curriculum combines coverage of personal computer basics with explications of pan-Maya philosophy, and homework assignments are often centered around Maya themes. By 1999, two other bilingual and bicultural schools were operating in Tecpán, the Escuela Bilingüe Iximche' and the Escuela Ixmukane school, reinforcing the town's image as a center of education.

Patzún has one private Catholic school, San Bernardino, which gives instruction in Spanish, but also allows students to wear *traje*. Patzún also has two nonreligious private schools: Colegio Luz del Saber and Colegio Mixto Renacimiento (run by a local cooperative). Both of these schools offer instruction in Kaqchikel as well as Spanish, actively encourage *traje* use, and employ some pedagogical materials developed by pan-Mayanist organizations. Finally, Patzún's Centro de Aprendizaje Maya offers classes exclusively in Kaqchikel and bases its curriculum solely on pan-Mayanist teachings; the school has produced a number of educational materials that have been adopted by Maya schools in other communities.

Maya-oriented education in Tecpán and Patzún also takes place in other contexts. For example, the Academia de las Lenguas Mayas de Guatemala gives occasional courses in both towns on the use of the unified alphabet for writing Mayan languages. Thus, increasingly, grassroots efforts in the two towns have been able to subvert the national education agenda, just as that agenda itself has become more culturally sensitive (see Richards and Richards 1996).

## Traje

Most Indian women in both Tecpán (98.9 percent) and Patzún (97.9 percent) wear *traje*. A much smaller percentage of Indian men in both towns use traditional dress. In Tecpán, 26.3 percent of Indian men sampled wore *traje*, and in Patzún, only 13.8 percent of men sampled did. (I should note that my surveys were conducted during the day, biasing the male sample toward older men who are more likely to wear traditional dress; the mean age of male Indian respondents was 47.2 years in Tecpán and 41.2 years in Patzún.) Male *traje* in the two towns consists of commercially produced white pants, a brown-and-black woven wool *rodillera*, and a Western-style shirt; many men who wear *traje* also use homemade sandals. Women's *traje* consists of a woven or embroidered blouse (*po't* in Kaqchikel, *huipil* in Spanish) and a woven skirt (*uq* or *corte*). Each town has its own distinctive pattern for the *po't*, and seasoned tourists and urban ladinos alike pride themselves on their ability to provenance *traje* and the humans who wear it. In Tecpán, there are four different styles of *po't*s associated with the town, as well as a distinctive ceremonial *rij po't*, or overblouse. Each of the *po't* designs consists of woven patterns, although one style is designed to imitate the look of cross-stitching (see Hendrickson 1995 for a more nuanced discussion of Tecpán's *traje* styles). In contrast, Patzún has only one distinctive *po't* pattern, characterized by embroidered designs on a woven base cloth.

In 1994, Rosa, the wife of one of my key informants, was attending the private Instituto Tecpaneco de Educación Media, which is owned and directed by Don Paco Coral, a prominent local ladino. One of Rosa's teachers, Don Paco's daughter and the assistant director of the school, tries to prevent any of her students from wearing *traje*. In the past, most women have simply accepted the rule, but Rosa, under pressure from her husband, who has ties to the pan-Maya movement, resisted. She wrote a formal letter of protest to the municipal supervisor of education in which she cited sections of the national constitution that protect expressions of Indian culture, specifically *traje*. Upon learning of this letter, the teacher became extremely agitated, yelling at Rosa, "Don't cite the constitution to me!" After much arguing, the teacher gave in, allowing Indian girls to wear a Tecpán-style *po't* with a white background and an indigo *uq*, an outfit that resembles the school's official blue-and-white uniform.

Such stories are frequently told by Tecpaneca Indian women. Maya women, generally, recall the experience of being forced to give up their *traje* for school as traumatic. Recently, women such as Rosa have begun actively to resist such rules, and as a result, school policies are slowly changing. Even the unspoken prohibitions against *traje* use in white-collar settings are being overturned. In Tecpán, the Indian woman who manages the local branch of Granai y Townsend Bank always sports a stylish-yet-traditional outfit of *traje* from various communities.

In Patzún, the use of *traje* is acceptable in a wider range of social contexts, and the schools there have a longer tradition of tolerating the use of local dress. Tellingly, it is rare to see a teacher in Tecpán wear *traje*, although this seems to be the norm in Patzún. Increasingly, young women in both towns are wearing *traje* in styles associated with other communities, although in Patzún, there is a greater allegiance to local styles. My survey of Patzún found that only 2.7 percent of sampled Indian women wore *traje* from other communities. Patzún's *traje* designs also appear to be rather conservative compared to Tecpán's changing styles, although, as Carol Hendrickson points out, stylistic innovations in Patzún may simply be more subtle than those found in Tecpán. One notable exception is a *po't* that incorporates the Classic hieroglyphic day names of the Maya calendar round embroidered around the collar. I first saw a *po't* in this style in 1993, and in response to inquiries, I was

told that they were being produced by members of a Patzún cooperative. Nelson (1999:201) attributes the original innovation to a Patzún
woman who studies law and works as a congressional secretary in Guatemala City, noting that she learned the hieroglyphic design "through
a Mayan cultural studies group." By 1997 the design was sufficiently
common for me to commission one from a *po't* vendor in Tecpán (see
Figure 8.4).

Regardless of who first developed the style, this hieroglyphic *huipil*
design is emblematic of larger processes of cultural change. It is an innovative idea — something objectively "new" — but it is also a culturally
logical reconciliation of received local norms and the contingencies (and
opportunities) presented by larger systems. The design works particularly well with Patzún's traditional style of *huipil*, as the glyphic symbols
for the calendar round simply replace the embroidered floral patterns
that usually circle the neckline. In creating it, the embroiderers have
built on the tradition of textile innovation documented by Hendrickson
(1995) — imaginative but within the bounds of socially acceptable novelty — while employing a symbolic code promoted as a marker of cultural consciousness by pan-Maya activists.

Recent innovations in *traje* styles in Tecpán involve not only new mo-
tifs but also the adoption of patterns from other towns and the resurrection of older styles. One example of this is the revival of the *xilon* style
*po't*. *Xilon po'ts*, distinguished by their pattern of dark stripes against a
white background, were popular in Tecpán in the 1930s, 1940s, 1950s,
and possibly before. The style was gradually abandoned over the next
three decades until it experienced a revival in the early 1980s. Carol
Hendrickson (1995:189–190) states that in

> the reappearance of the xilon blouse . . . different themes arising both
> within the indigenous experience and within the national arena are
> brought together in a powerful clothing statement. . . . Taken in the
> context of the 1980s, the xilon-style huipiles [*po't*s], though "mere
> cloth" and incapable of any direct, referential statement, brought into
> sharp focus Tecpanecos' pride in their Maya heritage and the active
> role of traje in community life.

In Tecpán, 24.5 percent of Indian women in our sample wore *traje* from
other towns. The greater adoption of foreign *traje* styles in Tecpán reflects, in part, that town's greater integration into national systems. The
use of *traje* from other towns is most often explained by women as part
of a new aesthetic convention: "I wear *traje* from other places because

FIGURE 8.4. Patzún *huipil* with embroidered Maya day names. Author photo.

it looks pretty." Regardless of the motivation, the use of other communities' *traje,* along with local innovations such as the *xilon po't,* emphasize precisely the view of pan-Maya pride and unity promoted by national Maya activists. Again, this is a case of local actions converging with national pan-Mayanist agendas, and it is due to the overlapping symbolic role of *traje* in Maya cognitive models and the similarly perceived structural circumstances in which identity is represented in the Guatemalan context.

### Emblems and Weapons

Individual intentions, local forms of resistance and proactive innovation, and the particular subjectively perceived historical context of a given group are all important determinants of the rate and direction of cultural change. Such a focus on agency and intentionality marks a line of thought that builds on Marxist theory to examine the subtleties of resistance (Scott 1985, 1990), the counterhegemonic strategies of subaltern populations (Hobsbawm 1964; Willis 1977), and the nexus of global expansion and local development (Wolf 1982; Roseberry 1983, 1989; Mintz 1985). Beauty pageants, language usage, *traje* styles, and pedagogical innovations all serve as important vehicles for the politically marginalized Maya populations of Tecpán and Patzún to resist neocolonial imposition and to promote ethnic awareness and pride. To borrow Nelson's (1999) terminology, they are tools that local Maya activists use to "fix" the system before the system fixes them (cf. Watanabe 1995).

In being locally particular, such forms of resistance are especially effective in subverting state policies directed at incorporating Maya peoples into a singular (ladino) nation-state (Smith 1990). This same quality, however, carries the potential to factionalize the Maya *pueblo.* Warren (1998:203) writes that

> there are ongoing tensions and debates in the political process of authenticating Maya culture rather than an easy emergence of standardized forms through the movement. Mayanists stand on both sides of these divides with locally anchored intellectuals not infrequently at odds with transcommunity activists on issues of language and dialect loyalty, though both groups agree on other issues. Norms of community consultation and consensus decision-making have brought the two halves of the movement together at critical junctures, such as in the

commission meetings designed to make policy recommendations about [1996 peace] accord implementation.

Cultural issues have been particularly effective at bringing together Maya peoples in pursuit of a common cause. As I argue in Chapter 10, locally developed forms of ethnic resistance such as those found in Tecpán and Patzún are largely convergent with the national pan-Mayanist agenda, a fact related to both common socioeconomic circumstances and shared cultural logics expressed through salient and dynamic cognitive models.

# 9 *Economic Change and Cultural Continuity*

**I bought my land, and I am going to buy another house . . . it is much better now.**

A MAYA DAY-KEEPER AND ENTREPRENEUR IN TECPÁN

Focusing on economic production, this chapter links the cognitive bases of local Maya identity to broader contexts of political economic change. I begin by looking at the traditional, and still predominant, economic base of Maya culture in Tecpán and Patzún, milpa agriculture, and its associations with cultural paradigms. I then turn to nontraditional export agriculture (particularly broccoli, cauliflower, and snow pea production), which has, over the last ten years, significantly altered local economic relations in the two towns. I relate the rise of nontraditional production to postdependency changes in the postmodern world system and show how local and national forms of Maya identity politics interact with shifting structures of the global political economy.

I thus end this section of the book where Marx would have begun, with the material bases of the ideological superstructure of Maya identities. This is not to diminish the importance of political economy or the material bases of society, but rather to emphasize, as Marx himself did in his more anthropologically sensitive writings, the mutually constitutive nature of cultural forms and material conditions. Material circumstances may often be more intractable than cognitive dispositions, yet it is the indexical conjuncture of the two, with neither singularly determinant, that produces the phenomenon of culture.

What, then, are the material bases of Maya culture? Hunt (1977) and Watanabe (1983) relate Maya cosmological continuity to meta-phorical and metonymic modeling of natural processes. In her analysis of mythical symbolism, Hunt argues that the eternal cycles of agricultural production, and their material imperatives, are the empirical basis for both ancient and modern Maya worldviews. She concludes that the Tzotzil Maya cosmology of Zinacantán is governed by a "root paradigm of ecology, agrarian schedules and invariant astronomical events" (1977:249; see also Gossen 1974). In his study of the Mam town Santiago Chimaltenango, Watanabe shows that space, time, and motion concepts based on solar cycles are "conceptual expressions [related] to those aspects of the physical environment that simultaneously motivate and are ordered by the concepts" (1983:726). Echoing this view, Carlsen and Prechtel (1991) hypothesize that the key Tz'utujil concept of *jaloj-k'exoj* derives from a "conceptualization of observed processes and patterns in the natural environment," metaphorically modeling social change on the empirical observation of agricultural change (ibid.:49).

As these authors suggest, the agrarian roots of Maya culture (based on household subsistence production) are historically related to important contemporary cultural concerns and conceptions. This cultural heritage has conditioned the high value placed on ownership of land and control over one's means of production by most Maya in Tecpán, Patzún, and other communities throughout the highlands. This valuation is, in turn, a key organizational principle of Maya cultural economies and has had a significant impact on changing modes of production.

Baudrillard (1998) posits that in the postmodern world, individuals have come to define themselves through what they consume rather than what they produce, a process brought about by the culmination of alienating workers from the means of production and the concomitant fetishism of commodities. In this sense, then, most Maya today would be decidedly modern or premodern—maintaining strong affective ties to the means of production—while simultaneously integrated into post-modern economies of symbolic consumption and creation. To be an effective economic strategy, controlling one's means of production must also be tied to market access, an issue ever more relevant in these days of post-industrialization in core countries. Controlling one's means of production in a strictly domestic mode is itself sufficient, for a captive market is built into the system. Controlling one's means of production in a system based on specialization and market exchange, however, requires a concomitant access to adequately sized markets to be successful.

## *Traditional Agriculture*

It is not surprising that agriculture, particularly traditional subsistence milpa agriculture, plays an important symbolic role in the cultural dynamics of Tecpán and Patzún. The economies of both Tecpán and Patzún, like that of the country as a whole, are largely dependent on agriculture, although this dependence is more pronounced in Patzún than in Tecpán. My 1994 survey data show that farming was the primary occupation of 49.7 percent of Tecpaneco heads-of-households, 15 percent of whom were involved in nontraditional agricultural export production. (Traditional production is here considered to be maize and beans, wheat, and cattle; the last two were introduced through Spanish contact but are considered traditional because of their almost five hundred years of integration into local economies and ecologies.) An additional 22.7 percent of sampled males were self-employed as commodity producers, merchants, tradesmen, or *transportistas*, and the remaining 25.5 percent reported wage labor as their primary source of income. In Patzún, 68.9 percent of male household heads surveyed in 1994 were farmers, 27 percent of whom were growing nontraditional crops. A lesser percentage of those surveyed (20.4 percent) were self-employed (primarily as itinerant merchants), and only 9.6 percent were primarily employed as wage laborers (see Figure 9.1).

These data reflect the two towns' very different patterns of articulation with national and international markets. From the earliest days of Spanish contact, Tecpán has more closely integrated into the national economy. During the colonial period, it was an important source of wood, lime, and labor for the construction of Guatemala's successive capitals (see Lutz 1994). To this day, it is home to an important regional market where goods produced around the country are traded at both the retail and wholesale level. Thousands of buyers and sellers come together in Tecpán's town center each Thursday, taking over a 15-square-block area centered on the municipal market building. Close proximity to the Pan-American Highway makes Tecpán an excellent location for such an intermediary regional market, which serves as an important point of articulation between local producers and national markets. The market also creates strong demand for labor. As a result, capitalist relations of production (marked by the presence of a large group of people who lack control over the means of production needed to reproduce themselves and are thus forced to sell their labor to capi-

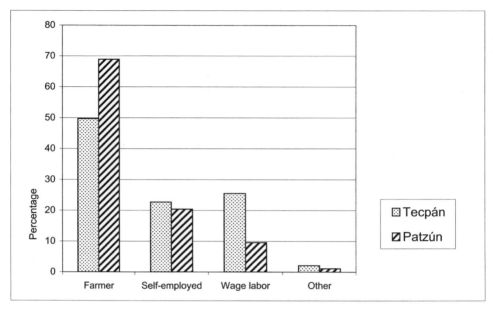

FIGURE 9.1. Primary economic activity of male heads of household in Tecpán and Patzún, 1994. Illustration by the author.

talists) have more profoundly penetrated Tecpán than has been the case in Patzún. There are also between seventy-five and one hundred small sweater factories that employ between one and twenty workers, and the town's two thread factories each employ over fifty individuals. Restaurants located on the Pan-American Highway, lumberyards, and export-oriented meatpacking and cut-carnation operations are also large local employers. In Patzún, subsistence agriculture has provided the basis to expand into nontraditional export crops, sustaining a tradition in which control over the means of production is maintained by households and individuals. A number of forward and backward economic linkages have developed as a result, such as the establishment of several cooperatives and numerous private transport companies.

Both Tecpán and Patzún have long been integrated into regional markets for goods and labor. Throughout the colonial period both towns fell within the 20-league radius of the Spanish capital and were thus subject to labor tribute for large construction projects, although colonial records indicate there was regular resistance to such demands due to tight local labor markets. Ethnographies from the early part of this century also illustrate the importance of regional markets and subregional specialization in agricultural products and artisanal commodities (Wagley 1941; McBryde 1947; Tax 1953; Brintnall 1979; cf. Nash 1958 on industrial capitalism). Particularly notable is the work of Sol Tax, who studied the economy of the Kaqchikel town Panajachel in the late 1930s and early 1940s. Tax shows that although Indians made up a small minority of coffee growers in the area (coffee production being highly capital intensive), they effectively controlled regional trade in onions and other truck crops and were quick to adopt market innovations. Such innovation introduced by regional markets continues to serve as an important avenue for indigenous upward mobility, and many Indians have been able to use their market expertise to expand into nontraditional production. The manner in which labor demands and returns combine with local social obligations has remained largely intact since Tax's study, but now local producers of nontraditional crops have ready and direct access to international markets and buyers, thus reducing resource extraction by intermediaries and improving efficiency.

The amount of land required for a family's subsistence needs depends on a number of variables, of course, including soils and climatic conditions, size of the family, and fertilizer inputs. Generally speaking, however, the average family of six needs six to nine cuerdas[1] of fertilized milpa to supply themselves with maize and beans for a year; as many as fifteen cuerdas of unirrigated, little-fertilized land may be required. The latest data on land-use patterns in the area around Tecpán and Patzún come from the 1979 Censo Nacional Agropecuario (INE 1983). Of the 2,653 farms recorded in Tecpán in 1979, 27.1 percent were less than nine cuerdas; in Patzún, 39.4 percent of the 2,850 farms were less than nine cuerdas.

In and around Tecpán and Patzún, the planting of the milpa (primarily with maize and beans, with squash, mirlitons, peas, chile peppers, and other plants interspersed) takes place at the end of April and the beginning of May. (These dates are generally applicable to the area, but exact times vary slightly as a function of soil conditions, altitude, and exposure to sunlight.) For the planting, for which seeds have been taken out of last year's crop or are bought on the open market, the old overgrown milpa is cut down, cleared, and plowed. Some people plant the beans first, in early April, and then plant the maize in late April so as to have the plantings spread out, but to do this, one uses *cuarentena* seed, which grows faster and is a little more expensive (a little over four quetzales a pound in 1994, or about $0.70). Most individuals use regular maize seed, priced at three quetzales a pound in 1994.

After planting, productive inputs to the milpa are divided into three parts. The first (the *primer trabajo de la milpa,* or "first milpa task") takes place in early June, when the maize stems reach about one inch high. At this time the milpa is weeded, the soil is turned around the base of the stalks, and fertilizer is applied. For growing large ears of maize, the preferred fertilizer is a 15-15-15 or 20-20-0 mix of nitrogen, phosphate, and potash. One quintal (a weight of 100 pounds) of fertilizer (which cost 78 quetzales in 1994, or about $13.50) should ideally be applied to each *cuerda* of land, although for financial reasons many farmers use only half that much. Application of the fertilizer is normally done by hand, and one large handful is placed around every stem. The *segundo trabajo* (second task) takes place when the maize is about one meter high, at the end of August. Again fertilizer is applied, and the land is weeded, with the weeds being placed around the base of the stem as compost to keep the base and roots warm. Then the paths between the rows of maize are dug out, making rows of raised dirt around the stems to protect them from wind and to keep the fertilizer and weeds from washing away. The *tercer trabajo* (third task) takes place when the flower of the maize blooms, about the middle of September. Once again fertilizer is applied, and the field is weeded. Rows are dug out perpendicular to the rows formed during the *segundo trabajo,* resulting in small mounds surrounding the maize stalks that protect them against the winds and contain the fertilizer (see Figure 9.2).

In all, about 100 to 175 man-days of labor per year per three to five hectares of land is required for growing milpa. Time invested may be reduced by omitting one of the three tasks, but it is said that if any of the three tasks is neglected, there will be a poor harvest. Locally grown ears of fresh maize appear in the market around the end of October. The bulk of the maize will be left to dry on the stalks through the first months of the dry season (which lasts from November to April). Harvest of the dried maize takes place in December, preferably before Christmas, although some wait until January.

In Tecpán and Patzún in 1994, milpa land close to town rented for about 200 quetzales (about $34.50) per *cuerda* per year, and land farther out in the *aldeas* was worth proportionally less, based on distance from the town, with some lands renting for as little as 100 quetzales ($17.25) per *cuerda* per year. Many families in the *cabeceras* of Tecpán and Patzún who are engaged full-time in other economic activities maintain ownership of milpa lands to supply their families with maize and beans for the year, employing hired labor or sharecroppers to work the fields.

FIGURE 9.2. Milpa after the *tercer trabajo*. Author photo.

Many, perhaps even most, families maintain two plots of land due to the nature of the bilateral descent system. Formerly, it is reported that inheritance was based on a rule of primogeniture, in which the eldest son inherited the family lands. Today, however, family property is most often divided between all of a man's sons and daughters. In such a system, land is subdivided in each generation, with plot sizes decreasing relatively. As plots become more divided, they soon become too small to support a family. The response of Maya families in Tecpán has been to encourage only some children to pursue milpa agriculture, while their siblings opt for wage labor at an early age or pursue their studies and later enter the labor market. Those who continue to farm try to buy their siblings' adjacent plots and try to consolidate their holdings through land transactions with neighbors. However, since land is much more expensive the closer to the center of town it is, two separate landholdings often result: one close to town and one farther away.

Some farmers switch back and forth between traditional milpa crops and wheat because it is said that the maize and beans are very hard on the land and that wheat gives back nutrients. Wheat has long been an important crop in and around Tecpán. Colonial historians inevitably mention Tecpán's production of wheat, and for years Tecpán has been an important supplier of the country's wheat and wheat flour. Writing about his journeys from 1768 to 1770, Cortés y Larraz (1958) mentions having to cross the Río Molino on arriving in Tecpán, suggesting that at least one mill was already in operation along the river that skirts the modern town. In 1994 there were two operating mills along the river.

Wheat is planted around the same time as the maize. It is initially harvested at the end of September. At this time, it is cut by hand with a sickle, and when a handful is cut, it is tied off with one of the wheat stems. Eight to ten of these handfuls are then tied into a larger bundle to be carried to the storage place on the site. It is then stored there to dry until January, at which time it is threshed. Threshing is accomplished by a machine that travels from plot to plot; it is either owned by a cooperative, which then takes the wheat to sell, or by a private individual. In the latter case, the wheat is then transported to one of the two mills in town and sold there. Wheat in 1994 sold for 50 quetzales ($8.62) per quintal, and one can expect to harvest from four to six quintales per *cuerda*, although, in at least one case in Patzún when a hybrid wheat variety was used, ten quintales were harvested from one *cuerda*.

In 1994, I followed the harvesting of wheat on a friend's land outside of Tecpán. He hired seven men (at 10 quetzales a day, or less than $2), and it took them ten days to harvest ten *cuerdas*. Wages vary somewhat in town, although all are low for agricultural and domestic labor. The state-mandated minimum wage for agricultural labor was 12.5 quetzales ($2.16) per day in 1994. In certain areas around Tecpán and Patzún, a boom in agro-exports has pushed wages higher (up to 15 quetzales, or $2.59, per day); in more remote hamlets, where poverty and limited opportunities make it a buyer's market, a man can often charge only 10 quetzales for a day's labor. And, of course, women's labor is cheaper still.

### *Local Production and Larger Systems*

As dependency theorists have long maintained, the world system is enmeshed in processes largely out of the control of peripheral actors. De Janvry (1981) relates the dependency of local systems on global ones to the disarticulated nature of undeveloped economies. In a disarticulated economy, production is not closely related to patterns of local consumption, meaning that products are largely produced for export and consumption abroad. This results in little or no pressure to increase wages—because products are exported, increased wages do not translate into increased demand—and thus minimal local market power to shape the allocation of productive resources. This pattern is pronounced in the Guatemalan case, where national markets and economic policy are largely oriented toward exportation and household production supplies a parallel economy of subsistence needs.

Studies from other parts of the Maya region have focused explicitly on the linkages between local producers and global markets. Collier (1975, 1990) and Collier, Mountjoy, and Nigh (1994) argue that Maya peasants in Chiapas have been quick to adapt to changing global contexts, strategically employing variable balances between reliance on wage labor and subsistence production, given certain structural constraints exerted by global commodity markets. Working in the same region, Cancian (1979, 1992) shows that changes in macrolevel systems (state politics as well as the global economy) since the 1960s have led to decentralized political and social relations in Maya hamlets, eroding the traditional bases of a strong community identity. Collier and Cancian both represent local conditions as inextricably tied to extralocal contexts while not denying the importance of culturally conditioned agency and intentionality (cf. Wasserstrom 1983).

Smith's work in western Guatemala similarly documents the interplay between local and global processes, but with a focus on how "local-level processes actively shape the larger picture" (1984b:195; 1975, 1978). Drawing on her research in Totonicapán, she shows that local residents have adapted a long tradition of artisanal workshops to pursue petty commodity production as an alternative to seasonal wage labor, thus thwarting the intended course of expansion in the region dictated by capitalist logic (namely, alienation from means of production and the formation of a free-labor market). Petty commodity production has allowed a large class of Maya to retain control over their means of production and has stimulated the development of a local labor market; that this local labor market is not "free" in terms of kinship, social, and political relations between buyers and sellers makes it all the more appealing to local Maya and results in wages higher than economically rational market-clearing rates (Smith 1989).

Smith further reveals that ethnically charged political-economic relations distort regional market structures in western Guatemala. Indian agricultural produce and petty commodities circulate within a structure of low-level rural market centers; regional bulking centers in some twenty Indian towns provide points of articulation between rural Indian producers and non-Indian (ladino)–controlled urban markets. Ladino market towns, the largest of which are also state administrative centers, funnel goods up from lower levels and feed them into the state-level market system (Smith 1975, 1976; cf. Plattner 1975, 1985). This system is marked by the unidirectional flow of goods to higher levels, to urban-based markets from rural Indian markets (a "disarticulated system," in de Janvry's [1981] terms). Thus although producers have pursued self-interested and to a large degree self-defined strategies of production, the marketing of products perpetuates an inequitable core-periphery distinction. Smith writes that "peripheral areas are essentially disenfranchised both politically and economically" (1975:19) and that the profits from nondomestic production "flow to urban-based owners and middlemen, either in the central area or outside of the western region" (ibid.:31). Smith's data reveal the monopolistic role of the commercial elite of major ladino market towns in discouraging competition and thus perpetuating inefficiency in the market. Below I discuss ways in which certain forms of nontraditional agricultural export production are able to largely bypass the distorted regional marketing network Smith documents and sell their production directly to transnational buyers.

## *Postdependency Patterns*

Global economic relations have undergone a dramatic restructuring since Smith's fieldwork, a trend accelerated in the late 1990s by post–Cold War political realignments in the world system. This phase of late capitalism operates under fundamentally changed, (neo)liberalized rules, rules that—to believe politicians and more than a few academic economists espousing their views in the 1990s—permit almost unlimited economic growth, unfettered by previous constraints such as the need to balance unemployment, interest rates, and inflation. In this situation, where capital is highly mobile and most peripheral countries have adopted neoliberal trade policies under pressure from the World Bank and other creditors, low unemployment need not drive up wages and inflation in core economies because production can be quickly moved abroad. Stimulated by tariff-reduction agreements (including the Uruguay round of the Global Agreement on Tariffs and Trade and the Caribbean Basin Initiative), decreasing communication and transportation costs, and the opening of new markets (especially in Eastern Europe), the total volume of world trade more than doubled from 1990 to 2000. In contrast, during this same period, production in the world's most developed economies increased at an annual rate of only 3 percent, and greater than one-third of the increase in the U.S. gross national product came from foreign trade (*The Economist* 1998). This makes clear that the increase in global trade is closely associated with the trend in postindustrial economies to shift agricultural and industrial production to lesser-developed countries, "exporting jobs," as its political opponents are wont to emphasize. Influenced by management theorists who advocate reducing labor and capital costs to return more profit in terms of market value to stockholders (e.g., Dunlop 1997), U.S. corporations have turned to outsourcing production and infrastructural services, eschewing vertical integration to concentrate on core strengths that increasingly take the form of "fictive" (i.e., nonproductive) capital and include intangibles such as marketing savvy and image maintenance. The increasing investment in fictive capital (from artwork to trademarks) underwrites, financially and ideologically, the postmodern (or late modern) condition (Lash and Urry 1987, 1994; Giddens 1990; Jameson 1991; Beck, Giddens, and Lash 1994; Friedman 1994; Kearney 1996).

These changes in global structures demand a rethinking not only of local agency but of the contours of the world system itself. As core areas focus investment in the service and information sectors, industrial and agricultural production are being shifted to peripheral regions such as Guatemala. Consistent with the corporate strategy of downsizing and outsourcing, much of this production is contracted to small local concerns with relatively low overhead expenses. Contracting out off-shore production allows transnational corporations access to cheap labor while hedging the considerable risk of direct capital investment in the politically unstable areas of the world where wages are low-est. Hedging this risk, however, involves a decentralization of capital-accumulation patterns at the global level, and potentially at the regional and local levels as well. Transnationalism encourages direct articula-tion between peripheral economic producers and global markets, unme-diated by state-level, elite-dominated market structures geopolitically encoded on the landscape in metropole/periphery distinctions. This in-creases efficiency, as resources that were formerly allocated toward di-rectly unproductive profit seeking (maintaining the legal distortions in market structures that act to funnel capital flows to the core) are in-vested in production (cf. Bhagwati 1982). In a classic study of artisanal production in northern Italy, Sabel (1982) shows how the breakdown of Fordist mass production led to an expansion of decentralized pro-duction, empowering local workers-cum-producers in ways not dic-tated by the larger system. A similar situation has emerged in parts of highland Guatemala, though here based not on the breakdown of in-dustrial production but on an expansion of traditional agricultural mod-els of production.

### Export Agriculture

Realignments in the global political economy over the last twenty years of the twentieth century created conditions favorable to the emergence of nontraditional agricultural export production in Guatemala. Under pressure from the World Bank, the International Monetary Fund, and the U.S. government, and responding to internal pressure exerted by economically liberal entrepreneurs, Guatemala has adopted a number of neoliberal economic reforms (reducing state regulations, lowering tariff barriers, and liberalizing markets) that have benefited nontradi-tional producers (Seale 1992; Weeks 1995). The United States has en-couraged these policy shifts through bilateral trade liberalization pro-grams, particularly the Generalized System of Preferences and the Caribbean Basin Initiative. Under these regulations, virtually all nontraditional agricultural imports from Guatemala may enter the United States duty-free. Capitalizing on this competitive advantage, farms and packing plants for nontraditional crops have been established in the highland region around Tecpán and Patzún. Located on a fertile and temperate plain straddling the Pan-American Highway and only 75 kilometers from Guatemala City's international airport, the area is ideally suited for the year-round export production of nontraditional vegetables and berries.

Alimentos Congelados Monte Bello, S.A. (ALCOSA) was established in 1972 with funding from the U.S. Agency for International Development and the Latin American Agribusiness Development Corporation to introduce nontraditional export crops in the Kaqchikel region and pack them for export. Initially, nontraditional production was conducted on company-owned lands and contracted out to large plantations. The large commercial farms (mostly owned by absentee landlords) to which ALCOSA had contracted production were unable to meet stringent quality controls at a competitive price due to the high labor and supervisory costs required in growing the fragile hybrids, giving the mostly indigenous small-scale farmers with ALCOSA contracts a clear competitive advantage. Not surprisingly then, ALCOSA "shifted contracts toward the indigenous peasantry until, by 1980, 2,000 such smallholders produced 95 percent of the cole crops [for the processing plants]" (de Janvry et al. 1989:136). Furthermore, with this shift came a dramatic increase in efficiency, quality, and production capacity (Kusterer, Bartres, and Cuxil 1981; de Janvry et al. 1989; von Braun, Hotchkiss, and Immink 1989). Based on ALCOSA's early success, the production of nontraditional exports began to increase dramatically in the early 1980s, and this growth has been sustained into the new millennium. In 1975, when it was purchased by U.S.-based Hanover Brands, ALCOSA was the only company specializing in nontraditional agricultural exports in highland Guatemala; by 1987 there were twelve corporations engaged in such export production, and that number had increased to forty-seven by 1998. The variety of crops produced now includes broccoli, cauliflower, snow peas, miniature vegetables, and various berries, all of which are shipped both fresh and frozen. By the early 1990s, Guatemala had become one of the top suppliers of exotic fruits and vegetables for the U.S. market (Hamm 1992; McCracken 1992). Nontraditional agricultural exports have been the most dynamic sector of the Guatemalan economy in recent years, with annual foreign-exchange earnings topping $300 million in 1996

(AGEXPRONT 1997; EIU 1997); in 1996 nontraditional agricultural products accounted for 12.39 percent of all Guatemalan exports, with earnings surpassing those of both bananas and sugar (cf. Feinberg and Bagley 1986).

Cauliflower was the first nontraditional crop grown in Patzún and Tecpán, introduced during the reconstruction efforts following a 1976 earthquake that destroyed both towns. In subsequent years, only a few farmers adopted the new crops and with variable success as they experimented with new pesticide and fertilizer regimes. During the tense war years in Guatemala, locally remembered as lasting from 1981 to 1984, few farmers were willing to take on the additional risks involved in nontraditional production. It was only by the late 1980s, after military activity subsided, that nontraditional production began its current phase of massive expansion in the area. Nontraditional production has since grown at a rate averaging 30 percent annually; an astonishing 27 million kilograms of cut broccoli were exported from Guatemala in 1997 (an increase of over 1000 percent since 1990), mostly grown by smallholding Maya farmers in the region under study. For packing plants (most of which are subsidiaries of transnational corporations or work under contract for foreign companies), contracting production to smallholders takes advantage of local agricultural expertise (resulting in a higher quality product than can be produced on plantations) and of the marginal cost of household labor (which is absorbed by the producer). Further, this model is a logical extension of corporate profit-maximizing strategies that cut overhead expenses, reduce capital investment, and leverage marginal labor values by outsourcing production (for comparative data from other countries, see Glover 1984; Feder, Just, and Zimmerman 1985; Teubal 1987; and Clark 1997). For farmers, nontraditional production complements traditional subsistence production and is seen as a preferable alternative to seasonal wage labor. In selling their production directly to transnational corporations, rural Maya farmers bypass distorted regional markets (in which information costs are high and terms of trade are unfavorable).

The growth of nontraditional agricultural exports is based on the model pioneered by ALCOSA: contracting out production to smallholders. In 1989, the largest food-processing plant in Central America, INAPSA, was constructed in El Tejar, about 40 kilometers away from Patzún; the plant is able to process more than 50 million pounds of vegetables per year. Again funded by USAID, INAPSH concentrated production on broccoli, cauliflower, brussels sprouts, and snow peas.

INAPSA, having learned its lesson from ALCOSA's experience, contracts most of its production to individual smallholders and cooperatives. In Patzún, there are several agricultural cooperatives with ties to INAPSA; there are none in Tecpán, although a number of individual Tecpaneco smallholders have contracts with the company. In Patzún, this new market has allowed small farmers to gain maximum profit from export crops, while still being able to supply most of their subsistence needs through milpa agriculture.

The ecological mandates of the crops introduced led to the unique pattern of smallholder production found in the Kaqchikel region (cf. Moberg 1992; Stonich 1993). The high labor input required by these exotic crops results in an inverse relationship between plot size and productivity; smallholders are able to subsidize labor inputs with parallel subsistence production, leveraging the marginal costs of household labor (Hirschman 1977; Berry and Cline 1979; Deere and de Janvry 1979; Netting 1993). Recent data from Guatemala show that 63 percent of broccoli production comes from farms of less than 17 acres, and 50 percent from farms of less than 3.4 acres (Barham et al. 1992), and my own research confirms the findings of von Braun, Hotchkiss, and Immink (1989) that nontraditional production is positively correlated with increased production of subsistence crops.

Production of nontraditional agricultural exports is not unlike *maquiladora* (offshore assembly) production: hybrid seeds and seedlings, pesticides, fertilizers, and even packaging are largely imported from the United States; value is added through land use and local labor; and the products are exported, either fresh or frozen, benefiting from liberal U.S. tariff provisions. A crucial difference, and one that is highly valued in Maya culture, is that nontraditional producers retain control over their means of production (see Watanabe 1990b, 1992; Wilk 1997). Thus, nontraditional agricultural production is highly convergent with established local cultural and economic relations, unlike seasonal wage labor.

### Comparative Data

The introduction of new crops as part of nontraditional export schemes is often accompanied by a rapid redistribution of productive resources at local and regional levels and the concentration of capital in the hands of a small class of producers. Access to larger (often global) commodity markets offers new opportunities to small producers, but these same markets increase direct competition that often favors the consolidation of holdings leading to class differentiation. Cocoa production in Western Africa provides a classic example of this process. In both southern Ghana (Hill 1963, 1970) and western Nigeria (Berry 1975, 1985, 1993), cocoa production has led to a highly unequal distribution of wealth, with a small group of successful producers controlling local supplies of capital. As in the case of nontraditional agriculture in Guatemala, barriers to market entry are relatively low and multinational concerns have directly entered local markets. Nonetheless, cocoa farming benefits greatly from economies of scale, thus favoring those producers with access to the capital needed to fund up-front labor costs and farm expansion. Hill (1970) shows that local capital markets throughout the region are highly imperfect; Berry (1975, 1993) goes on to argue that local capital markets develop through preexisting social networks, thus reinforcing certain social hierarchies.

We find a similar situation with citrus export agriculture in Belize (Moberg 1992) and shrimp and melon production in southern Honduras (Stonich 1993). In both cases, pronounced market and ecological factors favor large-scale plantation production, although here it is high market-entry costs that act to increase economic inequality and magnify existing class relations and local factionalism (Moberg 1992:167–169; Stonich 1993:78–87; cf. Raynolds 1997; Sick 1999). In contrast, the labor-intensive production of exotic fruits and vegetables in highland Guatemala is conditioned by ecological and market pressures that favor small- and medium-sized farms over larger ones. In the case of highland Guatemala nontraditional production, the ecological and market pressures for farms to stay below a variable threshold of diminishing returns results in a more equitable pattern of capital accumulation.

The most significant research on nontraditional agricultural production in highland Guatemala is reported in the work of von Braun, Hotchkiss, and Immink (1989); Goldin (1996); and Carletto, de Janvry, and Sadoulet (1999). In 1983 and 1985, von Braun and his team conducted surveys ($n = 399$) of traditional and nontraditional producers in several Kaqchikel communities. Focusing on the relationship between nontraditional production and nutrition, the von Braun study presents persuasive evidence for the efficiency of nontraditional crops (although, concerning environmental risks, see Hoppin 1989; Murray and Hoppin 1990; AVANCSO/PACCA 1992; and Netting 1993). These data support a number of macroeconomic studies that argue that nontraditional agricultural export production makes efficient use of surplus labor (Karp 1988; de Janvry et al. 1989), provides a viable private alternative to government policies favoring import-substitution industrialization (cf. Grindle 1986; Williams 1986), and facilitates the free mobility of capital and labor that makes global markets more efficient (Balassa et al. 1986; Lindenberg 1988; Sardi 1989). These analyses generally adopt a neoclassical approach to economic rationality that fails to fully account for cultural and ethnic variables.

In contrast, Goldin (1996) looks at nontraditional production in the local context of San Pedro Almolonga, a town that is 99 percent K'iche' Maya. Showing a close link between upward mobility and the adoption of nontraditional crops, Goldin argues that nontraditional production accelerates class differentiation (cf. Chayanov 1966). Other studies, noting that the benefits of nontraditional production are normally concentrated in a small class of male landholders, support Goldin's thesis with the view that nontraditional production destroys subsistence bases and increases socioeconomic inequality (Goldin and Sáenz 1993; Lee 1993; AVANCSO 1994; Carletto 1996) while perpetuating gender inequalities in intrahousehold resource allocation (Nieves 1987; Katz 1994; cf. Bossen 1984 and Ehlers 1990).

Nonetheless, as Netting (1993) points out, class differentiation of peasants into capitalist landlords and proletariat agricultural workers is not the inevitable result of capitalist expansion in peripheral areas; local conditions can result in the maintenance of traditional modes of production, although these, too, contain internal structures of inequality that may be exacerbated by an influx of capital resources. In a study of cooperative-member households in the Kaqchikel region, Carletto, de Janvry, and Sadoulet (1999) find a significant relationship between farm size and adoption of nontraditional crops, but they argue that this relationship does not exist at the time of adoption of nontraditional crops and that "it is adoption that created large farms and not large farms that induced adoption" (ibid.:354).

Undeniably, the effects of nontraditional agricultural production have included a dramatic redistribution of land and wealth, but in Tecpán and Patzún, lands have largely been transferred from the demographic minority (but economically more powerful) non-Indian population to Indians. Unsuitable for production on large farms, the fragile hybrid crops were first adopted by smallholding Maya farmers as a profitable supplement to subsistence milpa agriculture. Maya have retained dominance in nontraditional production, and their expansion has been to the detriment of ladino-owned large plantations in terms of land area, labor availability, and profit. Nontraditional production also neatly complements the traditional structure of Maya household economies and the widespread desire of farmers to retain control over their means of production (cf. Watanabe 1992; Raxche' 1996; Wilk 1997; Fischer 1999). At the same time, nontraditional agriculture has created a greater local demand for wage labor, but it is unclear if this has contributed to an increased reliance of landless and land-poor families on wage labor. There has long been an active market for seasonal migrant labor from the region, and laborers usually prefer to work for local employers (even for lower wages) in order to avoid the financial, emotional, and health costs associated with traveling away from their home communities (cf. Collier 1975: 121–123). Individuals who work for Indian nontraditional export growers are often tied to their employer not merely through a labor contract but through kinship and community ties as well, and these employees feel that they are better treated and better paid because of these extra-economic bonds. Labor issues notwithstanding, nontraditional agriculture remains one of the few dynamic sectors of the economy in which Indians have established and maintained a dominant presence. Though some class differentiation has occurred within the Indian population based on nontraditional export earnings, the distribution of resources along ethnic lines has become more equitable in the Kaqchikel communities under study.

### Nontraditional Agriculture: A Case Study

After moving to Tecpán, we soon made friends with Chepe and Eugenia, whom we met first in the market where Eugenia sells fruit and later at social functions in town. Chepe helps Eugenia in her business by buying and hauling fruit from the bulk markets in Guatemala City. Like a growing number of people in Tecpán and Patzún, however, his primary economic activity is export-oriented agricultural production. Chepe's land, located in the *aldea* Cruz de Santiago on the border between Tecpán and Patzún, is mostly family land, where he grew up. In all, there are about 25 *cuerdas* that Chepe, his brothers, and his father farm jointly. Like many who produce export products, Chepe's family keeps a separate plot of milpa land in another *aldea* that supplies the family with maize, beans, and other primary products throughout the year. Chepe's part of the land is about seven *cuerdas*, and he is renting another *cuerda* from a neighbor. In 1994, land in this area, which has fertile soil and is a center for cash-cropping, rented for 350 quetzales (about $60) per *cuerda* per year, although it was rare to find land for rent. Chepe estimated that the land here was worth about 4,000 quetzales (or slightly more than $700) a *cuerda*. In contrast, land in distant *aldeas* where the soil is not as good would sell for a fraction of that price.

Chepe grows snow peas, cabbage, brussels sprouts, carrots, broccoli, beets, radishes, and some black beans and maize. He has been planting export crops, starting with broccoli, since 1979. He uses both organic and chemical fertilizers as well as chemical pesticides. The chemical fertilizers make for a good harvest, but they quickly exhaust the soil; organic fertilizer is used to replenish the nutrients. He also rotates the crops to replenish the soil. There is a twenty-four-hour waiting period after fumigation before crops can be harvested. The chemicals are very strong, and he uses gloves, boots, and a face mask when mixing and applying them; he says that neighbors have sometimes been careless and have become poisoned from applying chemicals. He has attended a number of courses (both free and paid for) sponsored by chemical, seed, and export companies.

Snow peas mature rapidly and are normally ready for harvest sixty days after planting. They are planted and harvested in stages in order to spread out the labor-intensive work required periodically. Production averages one quintal per *cuerda* per cutting. The price for snow peas, like other export crops, is set in dollars, and snow peas range from five cents to two dollars per pound; in 1994 the price was low reportedly because Mexico had increased production for the U.S. market.

Broccoli matures in about three months. Chepe planted broccoli (using plants that he bought as seedlings) on April 18 in 1994 and began harvesting on July 9. Like snow peas, broccoli planting is staggered, and the harvest is spread over two weeks. Broccoli is virtually all sold by contract before planting even begins. Indeed, it is almost impossible to buy broccoli seeds. Companies advance seeds and fertilizer to farmers when they sign a contract to sell their produce to the company. Some companies even advance farmers a portion of the projected proceeds from the future sale. In 1994 broccoli prices were 54 quetzales (just more than $9) for a quintal. Between 35 and 50 quintales of broccoli are produced per *cuerda*, depending on the use of fertilizers, the stage in the crop rotation the field is at, and the weather. Broccoli earns farmers between 2,500 and 3,000 quetzales ($430–$517) per *cuerda* planted, with expenses of 600 to 1,000 quetzales (between $100 and $175) for pesticide, seeds, fertilizer, and rent. Profits can thus be as high

FIGURE 9.3. Fields of nontraditional crops around Tecpán. Author photo.

as 2,400 quetzales ($413) per *cuerda*, though all can be lost if there is an unexpected frost.

Brussels sprouts earn about 150 quetzales (slightly more than $25) for each quintal, and one can harvest about 50–70 quintales per *cuerda*. Cabbage sells for about 125 to 150 quetzales ($20–$25) per quintal for the internal market (in the capital); when it is contracted out, it sells for a lower price. The harvest is about 35–40 quintales to the *cuerda*; contracting to sell the whole *cuerda* earns about 3,000 to 3,500 quetzales (approximately $500–$600). As it is too hot in El Salvador to grow cabbage, convoys of Salvadoreños come to buy cabbage crops by the *cuerda*, bringing their own laborers to do the harvesting. Cauliflower yields about 70 quintales per *cuerda*, and its price is close to that of broccoli.

## *Other Forms of Production*

The rise of nontraditional agricultural production in the Kaqchikel area is directly related to trends in global political economics, particularly the postindustrial trend toward production outsourcing discussed above.

Such outsourcing necessarily involves a degree of decentralization of economic power as more capital accumulates in peripheral areas. Such capital accumulation can and does take many different forms.

One model is exemplified by the carnation plantation outside of Tecpán. A large Colombian-owned operation, the plantation employs more than five hundred workers and ships more than 50,000 cut flowers daily, six days a week, to wholesale florists based in Miami. Marta, who works on the carnation farm, is a ladina woman from the capital who married a Kaqchikel man from Tecpán and moved there with him. In 1989 her husband died of a severe case of diabetes, and she feels socially very isolated living in Tecpán, her in-laws having shunned her for being ladina and her own family resentful of her marriage to an Indian. She makes about 300 quetzales ($51.75) a month, a pay based on her production levels, making her a virtual contract employee. Despite the relatively low pay, she speaks positively of the job and appreciates the freedom that goes with the contract model of production. She has twenty-five flower beds for which she is exclusively responsible. She says the flowers are like children to her, and she misses them when she takes vacation. At work she says that there is very little direct supervision, and she is free to tend and cut the flowers in her greenhouse as she sees fit. For her, the minimal supervision in her job mimics forms of production in which one owns the means of production and is thus appealing.

Patzún has no large employers such as Tecpán's carnation plantation, but a large number of Patzuneros, mainly young unmarried women, make the daily 20–30-kilometer journey down to one of the *maquiladoras* (offshore assembly plants) that stretch along the Pan-American Highway. Many of the *maquiladoras* are owned by Korean corporations, and they have often been cited for labor-abuse violations. The *maquiladora* plants are located in drab gray cinder-block buildings surrounded by tall barbed-wire fences and imposing guardhouses. Among the reports of labor abuses is the claim that workers are chained to their work station and are refused breaks, even to go to the bathroom, until certain quotas are met. *Maquiladora* production is, like that of cut flowers, based on a model of outsourcing and contract production. Yet here there is no illusion of controlling the means of production, and employment in a *maquiladora* is viewed as an alternative of last resort, and even then only as a temporary necessity.

Finally, petty commodity production is an important strategy for many Tecpanecos and Patzuneros. For some artisans, this takes the form of production oriented toward distribution through regional market systems. For others, the artisanal model has been adapted to meet demand for export products as well. Tecpán, for example, is a major producer of woven sweaters, some of which are destined for sale in U.S. department stores, including Sears and Wal-Mart. The sweaters are designed in the United States by clothing companies that obtain contracts for them with large retailers. The U.S. company then contracts production out to a Guatemalan company, small middlemen operations mostly based in Guatemala City. The Guatemalan contractor then subcontracts actual production to a few individual producers in Tecpán, mostly Indian men. The Tecpán subcontractors, normally based out of their homes, own a number of weaving machines and employ several young men (paid on a per-piece basis) to weave the sweaters based on the required design. The quality of sweaters produced varies, ranging from inexpensive 100 percent nylon cardigans with basic designs to expensive 100 percent wool ones woven with elaborate patterns. These Tecpán subcontractors/producers usually do not have the capacity to complete orders in-house and must further subcontract out part of their production to other, smaller weavers in town. For weavers, there is little capital investment required beyond a weaving machine (and inexpensive used machines are readily available), making market-entry costs low. Many weavers start off working for a producer with multiple machines, saving money to buy machines of their own. They then can take over some of the surplus production of their former employer. Most sweaters are woven on manual machines, with weavers producing designs by changing yarn colors by hand. Producing elaborate designs is a skill honed over many years of apprenticeship and practice. The skills needed for weaving, however, are changing. In recent years there has been an influx of computer-controlled weaving machines in Tecpán, the surplus of last-generation technology from the United States and Europe. With these new machines, the pattern is entered via a keyboard and the machine mechanically reproduces it. Skilled older hand weavers are thus less in demand these days than technologically savvy young men. In response to this growing demand, two computer schools have opened in Tecpán.

## Nontraditional Production and Identity Politics

The rise of nontraditional production has dramatically altered the social as well as the economic landscape of the Kaqchikel region. Decentralized economic production at the global level has created new economic opportunities, and dramatic decreases in transportation and communication costs have made economically feasible certain types of export production that would not have been possible just several years ago. Further, the economic ideology of core economies in the global system has come to value lean production as a means of enhancing shareholder values, and outsourcing and offshore production are central elements of this new model.

Tecpanecos and Patzuneros alike are actively engaged in production contracted out by large multinational corporations. Such contract production has been much criticized from a romanticist perspective for eroding the material bases of traditional culture and for coercing Maya peasants into accepting risks they do not fully comprehend. Local perceptions, however, overwhelmingly view such shifts in a positive light for offering new economic alternatives for self and community advancement. Significantly, given the opportunity, Tecpanecos and Patzuneros most often choose to pursue strategies that allow them to maintain some degree of control over lands that produce at least part of their subsistence needs and that allow them to approximate the flexibility of labor inputs built into the agricultural cycle. In this sense, they reflect a widespread pattern of economic adaptation and co-option found throughout the Guatemalan highlands.

Carol Smith (1976, 1978, 1984b) has shown that, in Totonicapán and similar communities, petty commodity production has provided the economic basis for local resistance to incorporation into the "free" capitalist labor market (cf. Cook 1982; Cook and Binford 1990). As Marx pointed out, and as Totonicapanecos acknowledge in their actions, this market is anything but free, in that it alienates individuals from the means of production and erodes the social relations of labor. John Watanabe notes a similar pattern in the economic strategies of Chimaltecos (from the Mam town of Santiago Chimaltenango). Long engaged in the seasonal labor market of coastal plantations, Chimaltecos nonetheless rely primarily on milpa production for their subsistence. He observes that "migrants rationalize such wage labor as an extension of their own interests rather than as a complete alienation from the local subsistence economy" (1990a:188).

The economies of Totonicapán and Santiago Chimaltenango represent two different patterns of articulation with capitalist systems, patterns not simply dictated by global or statal hegemony, but rather unique structures of conjuncture crystallized in practice through the

interaction of locally convergent, self-interested intentions and the demands of capitalist expansion. Tecpán and Patzún offer alternative patterns of articulation with capitalist labor and commodity markets. Patzún's economy shares a number of basic features with that of Santiago
Chimaltenango—a long history of exporting seasonal plantation labor,
primary reliance on local subsistence production, and an incipient local
wage-labor market—although more and more it has turned toward export agricultural production. Tecpán in many ways more closely resembles Totonicapán's strategy—petty commodity production, a developed
local wage-labor market, and declining economic (but not cultural) importance of subsistence agriculture. We might be tempted to draw a
Redfieldian continuum of the towns' integration into the capitalist system. What such a continuum would overlook, however, is its most significant aspect: that all of these towns are pursuing strategies of self-
interested resistance to larger systems. Their strategies are different,
predicated as they are on the confluence of material and social factors
in the place of community (as noted by John Watanabe), and their differences may intentionally or de facto provide an effective resistance
to the homogeneity of state hegemony (as Carol Smith argues). In addition to their classification as a form of resistance, all of these economic strategies share a concern with control over means of production, which is not only resistance to capitalist incorporation per se (most
Maya I know are not ideologically opposed to capitalism) but maintenance of particular culturally valued relations of production. The above
discussions suggest that nontraditional production is actually fortifying
the material bases of Maya culture by allowing a more decentralized
pattern of capital accumulation among Maya agriculturalists and petty
commodity producers. Interpreted through the framework of cultural
logics, these agricultural innovations are perfectly consistent with the
dynamic construction of Maya-ness.

Friedman (1994) relates the flight of productive capital out of core
economies and into peripheral ones with the emergence of fluid postmodern identity spaces. With job security much reduced in the West,
and flexibility highly valued, an important historical basis of identity
has been eroded. The grounding of identity in the material relations of
production no longer holds the importance that it once did in the West,
a situation exacerbated by postmodern desires to accumulate fictive
rather than productive capital. The material bases of postmodernity in
the West have, in many ways, accelerated modernist development in the
rest of the world. Productive capital is being invested in developing

areas at an unprecedented rate, resulting in the decentralization of post-dependency relations. Unlike the dependency model of exporting raw materials to core countries, postdependency global relations of production (specifically the outsourcing of manufacturing, assembly, and packing to low-wage peripheral formations) are less effective in concentrating capital accumulation in core countries. Productive transnational capital, or at least part of it, invested in peripheral regions comes under the control of previously marginalized producers through contractual arrangements. At the national level in Guatemala, this decentralization has produced a class of economically liberal and newly wealthy entrepreneurs who have become unlikely allies of pan-Mayanists in pressing for government reform and deregulation.

Equally important in terms of the pan-Maya movement has been the trickle-down effect of subcontracted production that has allowed a significant number of rural Maya to retain control over their means of production while actively engaging in the global economy. This process has materially underwritten the resurgence in Maya identity politics at the local level, producing a *class* of Maya farmers and entrepreneurs with the available resources to pursue long-term socioeconomic gains through directed cultural change (cf. Kearney 1996; Warren 1998). New modes of direct articulation with transnational markets have also placed rural Maya in contact with foreigners who hold Maya culture in esteem. No matter what misguided or romantic notions this valuation may stem from, it has provided crucial external validation of the importance of cultural heritage in the face of long-standing ladino derision.

### Change and Continuity

Despite the many economic changes in Tecpán and Patzún over the last twenty years, agriculture has remained at the heart of symbolic and material existence for most Indians. Whether traditional or nontraditional, agricultural cycles continue to regulate (or be regulated by) a calendar round of annual events. As I have argued, the Maya of Tecpán and Patzún place a high cultural value on controlling one's means of production. Given the agricultural bias of local economies, it is not surprising, then, that land purchases are by far the preferred form of capital investment, even when returns fall below those of available alternatives such as bank savings. This valuation of control over means of production is part of a foundational cognitive schema in the Maya cultural logic of economic production (Fischer 1999).

For most Indians, the seasonal cycle of agricultural rejuvenation is intimately tied to implicit notions of cosmic and social balance, the covenantal relationship discussed in Chapter 6. In practical terms, this involves balancing the needs and abilities of individuals against those of the community as well as balancing the needs of the present against those of the future. The "welfare ethic" so lamented in the United States and Europe is all but absent in Tecpán and Patzún: one must work to live, one must give to receive. Working the land is simultaneously a material imperative and a spiritual obligation. Labor is only partially commodified because it is intimately tied to one's metaphysical soul, and thus working is both a spiritual and a physical exercise. The product of family and hearth-group labor is pooled and redistributed based on need, balancing inequalities in effort and ability. Likewise, the needs of the present must be weighed against the needs of the future, and a delicate balance reached between consumption and savings.

PART
IV

*Conclusion*

# 10 Convergent Strategies and Cultural Logics

This is not racism. Guatemala is a hand that needs all of its fingers, and if one is missing we all feel the loss. If Maya culture dies, Guatemala will be worse off because of it.

A LOCAL MAYA ACTIVIST IN TECPÁN

While benefiting from an anti-essentialist valuation of subaltern agency, Maya scholars and peasants alike continue to assert the legitimacy of an essentialist cultural paradigm, arguing that there is a quality to Maya-ness that transcends the minutia of opportunistic construction. I began my fieldwork prepared to document the constructed nature of Maya identity, and to show how this construction is influenced by contemporary political and economic conditions. At first, I thought that my Maya interlocutors' assertions of the essential nature of their identity were naive, misplaced, or ill-informed. Certainly, many Maya folk models can be challenged from a scientific perspective, such as the belief that proficiency in a Mayan language is genetically inherited or that maize tortillas are the only effective nourishment for the Maya body. And yet these beliefs also carry the value of socially sanctioned truth, and thus significantly affect real-world actions. It was this realization that led me to question the tenets of strong constructivist positions that view Maya identity as nothing more than the product of counter-hegemonic resistance (Martínez Peláez 1971; Hawkins 1984; Flores Alvarado 1993) or the romantic musings of anthropologists (Castañeda 1996).

Conversations with both pan-Maya leaders and Kaqchikel Maya living in Tecpán and Patzún repeatedly directed my attention to the ways that cultural logics are deployed in novel circumstances, maintaining an important sense of continuity in the face of changing circumstances. Domingo, a forty-five-year-old Kaqchikel religious specialist, eloquently explained the essence of such continuity through change to me one July day in 1994 during an interview at his home in Tecpán. Although he is an *aj q'ij* (maintaining the count of the sacred 260-day calendar and acting as a spiritual intermediary for individuals during ceremonies), Domingo does not conform to stereotypes of Maya traditionalists. He owns two trucks and makes his living primarily by hauling produce for farmers, an income meagerly augmented by the donations he accepts for performing ceremonies. His business is expanding, his success is palpable, and we meet for our interview in the formal living room of his new two-story whitewashed cinder-block home just off Tecpán's central plaza. Don Domingo explained the importance of ritual and sacrificial giving in the maintenance of the covenant between humans and a divine world force. This covenant, widespread in Mesoamerican ideologies and prominent in origin myths, mandates that humans make sacrifices to propitiate the god(s) in order to ensure agricultural and reproductive fertility. Just as sacrifices must be made to continue the covenant, the covenant must continue to perpetuate the grand cycle of cosmic and terrestrial existence. As Don Domingo warned me, "one should not play with God." As an *aj q'ij*, Domingo often diagnoses and treats illnesses attributable to metaphysical causes, a process that he describes as "looking in the souls of patients and cleaning them out," bringing them into harmony with the forces of the cosmos and thus making them content and "normal." In discussing the resurgence in Maya culture after the violence of the early 1980s, Domingo explains how this, too, is part of a larger cosmological cycle:

> Let's consider all that has happened with the people here in [19]81 and [19]80. How many thousands of people died? Thousands, not hundreds, died. They were buried just anywhere as if they were animals. The blood of these people went to the earth and was consummated before God, right? This blood is their spirit, right? Thus our people have now won — and we remember how it was before. We already paid and gave alms. I bought my land, and I am going to buy another house . . . it is much better now.

Listening to these words, I remember looking down to make sure my tape recorder was on, capturing one of those all-too-rare instances in ethnographic fieldwork when an interlocutor eloquently sums up a salient cultural concept that hitherto has remained implicit. Don Domingo's remarks reference the Mesoamerican cosmological paradigm of cyclic continuation as part of a sacred covenant, as discussed in Chapter 6. The structuring properties of this "foundational idea" (Gossen 1986) result in its potential to *react* to the contingencies imposed by macrostructural dynamics as well as to *enact* novel forms of interpretation and action based on the reconciliation of "mythistory" (Tedlock 1993) and available sociomaterial resources through referential practice. For Don Domingo, the paradigm of cyclic regeneration provides not only a framework for situating the almost unthinkable atrocities of the violence but also acts as a justification and a mandate for future action (cf. Warren 1993). In justifying present or future action, cosmological paradigms are particularly open to idiosyncratic interpretations that may, because of shared structural conditions or communicative power, become normative in the sense of self-fulfilling prophecies (cf. Fox 1985; Kapferer 1988; Ortner 1989). Such internally logical paradigms underwrite Maya cultural creativity and have given rise to the particular form of indigenous identity politics found in Guatemala.

### Maya Culture and Global Processes

Friedman (1994) and Jameson (1991), among others, note that postmodern capitalism has produced a significant crisis of identity, both collective and individual, in the West. With the modernist project in disrepute, the firm ideological grounding of societal progress has been eroded—a questioning of metanarratives, in Lyotard's (1984) words. This has in turn resulted in an almost frantic search for roots. Ethnicity and cultural authenticity speak to this need for solid grounding, and both have become powerful symbolic commodities in the postmodern world. Examples range from heated academic debates over native heritage (e.g., Haley and Wilcoxon 1997; Field 1999) to pop culture (e.g., the popularity of ethnic art and clothing, the New Age quest for indigenous spiritual knowledge) to the staid institutional corridors of international political economy (the United Nations, the World Bank, USAID, and the European Union, among others, have all begun to enact policies specifically targeted at indigenous groups).

In terms of political economy, the rise in concern over indigenous issues has been coterminous with the ascendance of neoliberal approaches to development. Using the leverage of huge debts acquired during the 1970s and 1980s, international institutions based in the West have been able to impose neoliberal economic reforms on debtor countries, seen primarily in the opening of markets and the privatization of state industries. For critics, these reforms carry the stench of social Darwinism, an irrational belief in the equilibrating power of the market to reward productivity. And yet, such reforms are responsible for opening new political and economic spaces to previously marginalized peoples such as the Maya. Maya leaders have strategically co-opted aspects of the discourse and philosophy of the new, neoliberal world order and integrated them into a program consistent not only with external conditions but also with the internal logics of Maya culture.

In the pan-Mayanist project, authenticity is conveyed through claims of ethnic continuity as well as by the constraints of grassroots interpretations and acceptance of innovations. This is an authenticity based not on the etymologies of specific symbols but rather on the structural continuities of a dynamic and culturally logical framework of cognition. In this book, I have argued for the existence of certain cognitively based models that are dynamically generated through cultural logics. Culture is not reducible to some sense of timeless essence, nor is it deconstructable to ad hoc idiosyncratic change. It is based on meaningful relations internalized by individuals but with sufficient overlap in idiosyncratic variation to produce delimited fields of ethical (in the sense of sharing an ethos) discourse. It is untenable to divorce the cognitive from the political economic in accounting for the influence of macrosystems in microcontexts. Nor should one grant, a priori, a position of analytic privilege to forces of either change or continuity in ethnographic analyses. I have argued that the complexity of identity politics is best understood in terms of culturally logical constructions of self-identity (based on changing inter-subjective consensuses of appropriateness) deployed in the context of local, national, and global systems of political economy. Neither global structure nor individual agency alone can explain the form of identity politics; these forces are mediated by the logics of culture, and from this mediation emerge the changes and continuity that characterize the pan-Maya movement and other forms of identity politics around the world.

The pan-Maya movement provides us with an example of self-directed change in Maya culture (albeit in the context of external political-economic contingencies). As I have argued, the underlying goal of pan-Maya cultural activism is nothing less than the creation of a culturally salient and accepted category of pan-Maya identity to encompass and perhaps ultimately replace the long-standing community-based allegiances characteristic of Maya groups. Pan-Mayanists often characterize their work as "raising the consciousness" of the masses, implying that they are simply creating cognitive and social space to allow a latent cultural characteristic to come to the fore. To what extent a concept of pan-Maya unity existed in precolumbian times is unknown, although competition between expansive city-states in the Classic and Postclassic Periods suggests that community-based allegiances have a long history in the area. Regardless, even were an authentic and autochthonous Maya pattern from the past knowable and known, it could not be transposed *in toto* on present circumstances. Pan-Mayanists are not blind to this fact, but freely acknowledge that they have to construct cultural alternatives that are both true to their conceptions of their past and viable in the context of contemporary Guatemalan society.

Promoting a pan-Maya identity involves fundamentally restructuring the way millions of individuals view the world and their position therein. Maya activists began their task through linguistic innovations, encouraging, for example, use of the term "Maya" as the primary signifier of Indian self-identity. Surprisingly, given the entrenched cultural paradigm that equates community with identity, pan-Mayanists have had notable success in gaining acceptance for their restructuration of inter-subjectively conceived ethnic relations. Identifying oneself as Maya, rather than as a person from town X or a speaker of language Y, no longer raises eyebrows in Tecpán and Patzún, and the towns' ladino registrars have recently relented to allow children to be legally given a Maya name. More significantly, an increasing number of Maya people are unself-consciously using the new vocabulary of pan-Mayanism — and the subtle shifts in cultural logics that it implies — to situate themselves in their social and material worlds. Yet, far from marking a sharp break with the past, such new cultural paradigms are effective precisely because they adapt to changing circumstances by building on received constructions.

This is not the purely instrumental constructivism of cloaking new types of oppression in the time-honored guise of history. Rather, it is the conscious and unconscious dialectic reconciliation of received cultural logics and changing real-world circumstances that both reproduces and alters cultural patterns. The cumulative result of such cognitive modeling is the apparent irony of "authentic" cultural continuity being actively constructed by intentional, self-interested individuals in contexts not entirely of their own making. But we must not lose sight of the fact that this is not an ironic endeavor for the subjects of our analysis, nor do their self-interests correspond to some universal concept of utility. If culture is like a game, then it is as much Scrabble as Battleship, with actors building words and meanings not by tearing down the existing structure but by adding to it, and changing it indelibly.

## *Local Agendas*

The strength of nativistic or revitalization movements such as the pan-Maya movement is, at least in part, a function of the severity of subjugation that a population has suffered (Wallace 1956; Edmonson 1960). Patzún, because of its geographic isolation and cultural insulation, has experienced much less direct and intense contact with national systems (and a concomitant lesser degree of subordination) than has Tecpán. Patzuneros have been able to maintain (though, of course, with innovations) the agricultural orientation of their economy; they use local-style *traje* predominately; and they have had shorter, less intense contact with state organs such as the military. Of course, Patzún's culture does not exist in a vacuum. They increasingly sell their agricultural products to multinational companies; they have received large amounts of aid from Norway; and most Patzuneros have relatives living in the capital or abroad. Nonetheless, Patzuneros have been able to maintain a strategic isolationism not found in Tecpán. Tecpán's diversified economy is closely tied to national markets; women in Tecpán are much more likely to wear *traje* from other communities; and the Pan-American Highway and the extensive bus system have allowed greater mobility for Tecpanecos. As a result, more Tecpanecos have attended university, and more have then gone on to leadership roles within the pan-Maya movement. In Patzún, leaders are more likely to stay at home and work within the community for change at the local, not the national, level.

Local cultural activists in Tecpán and Patzún, even those who take pains to distance themselves from the perceived elitism of the pan-Maya movement, advocate a philosophy remarkably consistent with the pan-Maya agenda. Below I quote from notes I made during the speech of a local activist in Tecpán, a man highly critical of the opportunism of pan-Maya activists.

FIELDNOTES — JANUARY 23, 1994, TECPÁN

At the meeting tonight called to discuss the possible formation of a Maya school in Tecpán, Don Jacinto stood up and gave a few words. He recounted how in the 1970s there was a strong current of cultural activities in Tecpán, something that has been lost, due in part to the effects of the violence, the disappearances, migration, and so on, and that the youth are not continuing. He spoke passionately of language being the heart of the culture, noting that something essential is lost when one speaks in a second language: "Language is the life spirit of a culture. When does life begin? At birth. When the baby emerges and cries, the midwife says that it is a healthy baby, but when the baby emerges and does not cry out, it is dead. So it is with culture: when it speaks in its own tongue, it is alive, but when it loses its linguistic ability, it is dead." He also talked about the influence of Western countries, particularly "el norte," and the negative impact it has here: often people adopt a technology simply because it comes from there, and thus abandon their own heritage: "We must always ask ourselves, is this really advancement? Foreign technology may be useful for our people, but it should not be blindly adopted." He also talked about Guatemala's different cultures, that now the constitution recognizes the country as multicultural and multilingual: "Now we have the right to organize and exercise our cultural rights, as before we didn't, we were persecuted for speaking a dialect, but no more." He said that Guatemala must play on its multiculturalism to form a true Guatemala-ness: "This is not racism. Guatemala is a hand that needs all of its fingers, and if one is missing, we all feel the loss. If Maya culture dies, Guatemala will be worse off because of it." He ended by telling a story of a Guatemalan ladino who went to Europe for a United Nations meeting: "All the participants stood and clapped for this representative of Maya culture, and he didn't know the first thing about the Maya! And then the same man went to India and was presented to an old man, a historian, seated cross-legged with his knees sticking up in Indian fashion. When the elderly historian learned his guest was from Guatemala, he got up with great effort and hugged the Guatemalan, saying that it was an honor to meet a Maya, a descendent of the great Maya civilization who invented the zero before we did. Upon his return, the ladino dedicated himself to learn more about the Maya culture that is so venerated in the rest of the world."

Don Jacinto's speech could have easily come from the lips of a pan-Mayanist intellectual, so convergent are its ideological presuppositions as well as its specific examples.

### Convergent Strategies

In both Tecpán and Patzún there is a movement to revitalize traditionalist Maya religion. Maya ceremonies are reportedly better attended than they have been for over two decades, and a number of young people have taken up apprenticeships with *aj q'ijab*. The reason for this trend is difficult to discern. At least in part, it is due to the reduced level of violence in the area. Simply put, it is once again safe to visit altars and attend ceremonies in the mountains. It is further related to a global revalorization of all things Maya that has been spearheaded by the national pan-Maya movement. Local Maya religious specialists have taken advantage of materials produced by pan-Mayanist research, and most now employ hieroglyphic symbols to represent day names, Long Count dates, and other elements of Classic Maya culture. Regardless of the origin of this trend, it is undeniable that these local Maya religious revitalization efforts are consistent with the agenda of national pan-Maya organizations. Traditional Maya religion and its models of balance and equilibrium strongly influence pan-Mayanist activities, as seen in their attempts at consensus building.

For pan-Mayanists, Guatemala's political and economic systems are structurally inequitable. To achieve their goal of political-economic equality, Maya leaders must balance a multitude of competing intentions. The most problematic of these is the perceived disjuncture between the movement's urban-based leadership and its largely rural constituency divided by community allegiances. Some have predicted that the persistence of community-based allegiances will one day be the downfall of the pan-Maya movement. Yet the data I have presented suggest a more optimistic alternative: that community-based allegiances share underlying features that transcend geographic parochialism. The constructivism of both local and national Maya cultural activists is not merely instrumental nor is it simply self-interested deployment of "weapons of the weak" and "hidden transcripts" (to use James Scott's phrases). Its acceptability (and thus power) also derives from its articulation with salient cultural logics. As I have shown, the symbols deployed in expressions of identity politics are not chosen out of thin air nor are they magically divorced from their historic cultural context — even in their novel, circumstantial application they perpetuate dynamics of cultural logics. In short, a common cultural heritage encoded in a dynamic yet enduring cultural logics and exercised in broadly similar structural conditions has resulted in a significant convergence of Maya identity politics as practiced at the local and national levels.

There are important disagreements of interest between local and national activists, and community animosities persist. Yet, local Maya culture and the presentation of cultural distinctiveness to reaffirm locally defined ethnic boundaries has a pronounced constructed quality, not unrelated to the overt constructivism practiced within the pan-Maya movement: the unified alphabet has gained limited acceptance, pan-Mayanist educational institutions operate in both towns, and Maya shamans have adopted a number of symbols promoted by Maya scholars. More significant than these direct points of articulation, however, is the broad convergence of local activities with national pan-Mayanist goals. The practice of teaching within the public school system, the resurgence of interest in the native religion, and the innovative patterns of *traje* use in Tecpán and Patzún are all grassroots efforts that, although independently developed, support the national pan-Mayanist ideology.

Although such local projects are best characterized as latent pan-Mayanism, they are nonetheless crucial for the national movement's future. Having obtained a degree of success within the national political system, the pan-Maya movement must now turn to the Indian masses to solidify their base of support. If it can continue to build on these points of ideological convergence and cultural commonality, the pan-Maya movement promises to fundamentally redefine the role of Maya culture in Guatemalan society.

# *Notes*

## *Chapter 1. Maya Culture and Identity Politics*

1. Throughout this book I use pseudonyms and sometimes change personal details to protect the privacy of individuals in these still politically uncertain times. Exceptions are made in certain cases for public comments made by pan-Mayanist leaders.

2. See Bunzl 1996 for a sensitive history of the intellectual and moral heritage of the culture concept in the Boasian tradition.

3. Gilroy's provocative argument merits further mention. The effectiveness of his critical stance stems from both his incisive writing and his structural position within the global political economy of Western academia. A successful scholar of African descent, Gilroy symbolically represents those who have been denied voice through the essentializing maneuvers of the academy; that his words are widely read (and presented under the imprint of prestigious university presses) may be seen as representative of a fundamental, if not yet complete, shake-up in traditional structures of academic power, structures built upon the containment of subaltern views through modernist essentialism (cf. Bourdieu 1988, Jameson 1991, Kearney 1996). But Gilroy refuses to toe the ideological line of subaltern subversion of the culture concept, showing how cultural forms developed through the black diaspora on both sides of the Atlantic have a common substrate (though not an unchanging one, perhaps conceived best as a thematic tempo rather than as a rigid structure) firmly rooted in West African tradition. Gilroy effectively refutes vulgar essentialism of the sort that would state "the black man thinks . . ." while reaffirming the importance of continuity in the face of dramatic change.

4. This approach is closely related to a revaluation of subaltern agency in early Maya history. See, for example, Farriss 1984 and Jones 1989.

5. Of course, natives are also subject to critiques from foreign scholars. Perhaps the most dramatic example is David Stoll's (1998) critique of Nobel laureate Rigoberta Menchú's life history (Menchú 1984). Stoll accuses Menchú of consciously or unconsciously altering her autobiography to better fit her revolutionary political agenda, and he marshals convincing evidence to show that certain events in her

story are not corroborated by other witnesses. The story was quickly picked up by the popular press, and the *Wall Street Journal*'s editorial on the subject proclaimed "A Nobel Prize for Lying." Rigoberta's opponents in Guatemala see in these revelations proof of the nefarious and calculating character underlying the image she presents to the world as an oppressed Indian woman cloaked in her traditional dress (see Nelson 1999). The controversy has brought to the fore issues of truth and authority in Guatemalan studies, with many lamenting the political fallout from this desecration of the country's most prominent Indian icon and others arguing that we should not promote an anthropological double standard by patronizingly protecting "our subjects" from such critiques (see Fischer 2001).

6. I have benefited greatly from interactions with other foreign scholars both studying and participating in Maya cultural activism. In particular, the work of Kay Warren (1998) and Diane Nelson (1999) on pan-Mayanism in Guatemala has influenced my approach, as has the work of Gary Gossen (1999) with the Zapatistas in Chiapas, Mexico. Nora England and Judie Maxwell have served as role models in the praxis of anthropology and social justice.

### Chapter 2. Tecpán and Patzún

1. Thanks to Carol Hendrickson for revising these figures and for checking points of fact throughout this book.

2. The document is housed in the Archivo General de Centro América in Guatemala City under the call number A5 3957 6062.

3. Charles Hale and Carol Hendrickson generously shared with me their notes on the chronology of Patzún and Tecpán alcaldes.

### Chapter 4. The Rise of Pan-Maya Activism

1. Comparative ethnic-based movements have also emerged in other parts of Mesoamerica. See Campbell 1994, Nash 1995, and Gossen 1999.

2. I should also note that, conversely, some Protestants and Catholics alike find the pan-Mayanist philosophy distasteful, and some even see Kaqchikel language instruction as leading down a path that ends in pagan rituals.

3. Non-Kaqchikel or K'iche' leaders exert their influence most effectively with organizations such as the ALMG, which are structured in a way that gives proportional representation to each of Guatemala's twenty-one Mayan language groups. Even here, however, K'iche's and Kaqchikeles have a long history of dominating the groups.

4. Don José died in 1998 at his home in Tecpán; I learned of his death by reading Enrique Sam Colop's online newspaper column (www.prensalibre.com).

### Chapter 5. Constructing a Pan-Maya Identity in a Postmodern World

1. These examples come from data collected by Judith Maxwell, who served as a consultant to the neologism project of the Comunidad Lingüística Kaqchikel. For more detail on Kaqchikel neologisms, see Fischer and Maxwell 1999.

2. In its original context, this passage describes how the creator god Heart of

Sky (Uk'ux Kaj) met with the Plumed Serpent deity (Q'ukumatz) to plan and execute the creation of the world. By transposing the context, however, the producers of *Mayab' Winäq* present the reading as a politically suggestive call to contemporary Maya unity. Thanks to Gary Gossen for offering an English translation that captures the feel of the poetic Spanish version used by *Mayab' Winäq*.

3. *Jotaytzij* publishes articles in Spanish and Mayan languages, and native authors are encouraged to write in their maternal tongue. Each month one Mayan language is highlighted, and major stories are translated into that language. The editors would like to rotate the language of *Jotaytzij* among all of the country's Mayan linguistic groups, but at present they must rely on translators and journalists who come overwhelmingly from the most politically active groups such as the K'iche' and the Kaqchikel.

### Chapter 6. Souls, Socialization, and the Kaqchikel Self

1. In the cycle of generational rejuvenation, grandparents and grandchildren hold structurally equivalent positions. In Kaqchikel, the kinship term for "grandfather" is the same term used for a man's grandchildren (*mam*), and female children are often named for one of their grandmothers. In this way, the inter-generational rejuvenation of the family mirrors the grand cosmic cycles of rejuvenation and accumulation (cf. Carlsen and Prechtel 1991).

2. Virtually all ethnographers and linguists recognize the value of key words in translating other cultural realities; we implicitly acknowledge as much in our liberal peppering of ethnography with words in the language of the people under study. Edmund Leach, among others, anticipated Wierzbicka's argument in his 1954 *Political Systems of Highland Burma*, which presented an understanding of Shan and Kachin cultures based on a thick description of the terms *gumsa* and *gumlao* and the meaningful relations they signified. Leach found no useful English translation of the terms *gumsa* and *gumlao*, for they indexed highly unique cultural ideas, and they have since become part of the anthropological canon. Likewise, very few ethnographies written about the Maya lack a glossary to define the many indigenous terms the author has found necessary to include in the English text. (A notable exception would be Dennis Tedlock's [1993] strategy of poetically translating even highly unique cultural concepts into English. Nonetheless, he too marks these words as culturally significant by translating them with unusual English constructions.)

3. It should be noted here that both *anima* and *k'u'x* are normally possessed, but are used here in unpossessed form.

4. Interestingly, power is associated with heat, and weakness with cold. From a Freudian perspective, the womb is the primal metonymy of power: within the womb the child is, or at least feels, omnipotent, the master of his or her tiny universe. The primary narcissism of life in the womb results in postnatal crises as children enter the social world, precisely the crises of weakness and vulnerability entailed in the Maya notion of metaphysical coldness.

5. Traditionally the *tuj* is built out of adobe with a low conical roof; the structures are often described as "little volcanoes," an appropriate metaphor, given their shape and the profusion of smoke that billows forth as the fire gets started. Volcanoes and mountains are considered sacred places in Kaqchikel cosmology and are

endowed with powerful *k'u'x* forces. Caves and indentations in mountains and volcanoes are often chosen as places of ritual, for they allow supplicants to get physically closer to the *k'u'x* of the earth. Entering a *tuj*, one must crawl through the doorway on hands and knees, much as if entering a small cave opening. Certain rituals, especially those related to pregnancy and childbirth, take place within the *tuj*. Thus, the *tuj* acts as a personal and convenient symbolic representation of a sacred cave and the *k'u'x* forces it contains.

6. My wife became pregnant with our son Johannes during our 1994 fieldwork in Tecpán. I am grateful to both her and her midwife for sharing with me some of the rituals and treatments associated with pregnancy to which I would not otherwise have been privy.

7. During the ninth-day postnatal ceremony, the newborn child is bathed by an elder sibling in the *tuj*, after which the older child is given a bowl of soup containing the meat of a whole chicken that he or she has to eat in its entirety. This part of the ceremony acts to symbolically mitigate potential sibling rivalry, showing the elder sibling that his or her future subsistence (based on the continual regeneration of the agricultural cycle) will not be threatened by the complementary act of corporeal reproduction. Thanks to Carol Hendrickson for suggestions on this section.

8. Heightening the irony, his rejection of his heritage is also viewed skeptically by the town's affluent non-Indians, placing him, from the view of an observer, in an interminable liminal state vis-à-vis identity.

9. In a Maya creation myth, three hearthstones are placed on the back of a turtle, from which grows the world tree, a maize plant. I am grateful to William Harrison for explaining to me this and countless other Maya stories derived from iconographic studies.

10. The metaphor of sighing used here is significant, as breath (*uxla'*) was perceived to be closely related to the soul in colonial Kaqchikel ethnopsychology (Hill and Fischer 1999).

### Chapter 7. Hearth, Kin, and Communities

1. Nelson's (1999) *A Finger in the Wound* provides a more provocative analysis of body metaphors in the context of Guatemalan ethnic relations, building on Foucault's notion of orthopedic change in the body politic.

2. The average age of respondents to my survey was 38.5 years, with a range of 12 to 88 years. The majority of respondents were female (84 percent in Patzún, 81 percent in Tecpán), but data were collected on all household members, and the average level of education was just over 3 years (3.5 years in Patzún, 3.3 years in Tecpán).

3. Ladinos are often viewed by Indians as prone to cheating Indians in financial transactions (although honest ladino shopkeepers are recognized and patronized) and to initiating graft when in public office (although, again, dishonest Indian politicians are acknowledged and shunned for falling prey to the lure of ill-gotten gains). Such views lead to a preference among Indians to deal with other Indians, where feasible, in their economic and political transactions.

## Chapter 8. Local Forms of Ethnic Resistance

1. Hendrickson 1995, McAllister 1996, and Nelson 1999 offer insightful inter-pretations of the image of the Indian in Guatemalan beauty pageants.

2. Hendrickson notes that in the 1980 elections only one ladina was crowned queen (the Reina Franciscana), with another ladina crowned Madrina de Deporte (the Godmother of Sport); the Indian winners were crowned Princesa Iximche' and Princesa Ixmukane. In the 1983 elections, there were likewise four winners: the Reina Franciscana, the Madrina de Deporte, the Princesa Iximche' (the indigenous fair queen), and the Princesa Ixmukane, who also carried the title of Reina del Agricultor (Queen of the Farmers; see Hendrickson 1995:81–83). In the 1994 elec-tions, the title Princesa Ixmukane had been taken over by the candidate of a lo-cal weaving cooperative, and elections were held for only two positions, the ladina Reina Franciscana and the Indian Princesa Iximche'.

## Chapter 9. Economic Change and Cultural Continuity

1. In both Tecpán and Patzún, land is most often measured in *cuerdas*. A *cuerda* is a regionally variable unit of measurement that in Tecpán and Patzún generally equals 40 *varas*, with a *vara* measuring roughly 1 meter. There are approximately 8.6 *cuerdas* of this size to a hectare.

# *Glossary*

*aj itz*   A religious specialist associated with malevolent sorcery.

*aj q'ij*   Day-keeper; a normally benevolent religious specialist.

**alcalde**   Mayor; also sometimes used to denote the highest office in a *cofradía.*

*aldea*   Village; an administrative and rural territorial unit that is part of a *municipio.*

*anima*   From the Spanish *ánima* (spirit); a vitalistic force unique to humans located in the heart.

*b'anob'al*   Behavior, action (as opposed to thought).

*cabecera municipal*   Town center, the seat of municipal government.

*caserío*   Hamlet; an administrative and rural territorial unit that is part of a *municipio,* smaller than an *aldea.*

*ch'ip*   The last child; literally, "womb closer."

*cofradía*   Catholic religious brotherhood introduced by the Spaniards but today considered characteristically Maya.

*corte*   Spanish term for *uq.* See *uq.*

*costumbre*   Customs, commonly used to denote more traditional elements of Maya culture.

*cuerda*   A measurement of land that varies between communities in Guatemala; around Tecpán and Patzún there are approximately 8.6 *cuerdas* to a hectare.

*evangélico*   A member of a Protestant sect, most of whom practice "evangelical" Christianity.

*finca*   A large farm, often including a number of household compounds and owned by an absentee landlord.

*huipil*   Spanish term for *po't.* See *po't.*

*indigenismo*   A modernist social and political philosophy that emerged in Latin America in the late nineteenth century and promoted the cultural assimilation of Indians.

*kaxlan*   Non-Maya or foreign, from Maya derivations of "Spanish."

*k'u'x*   Variously translated as "heart," "soul," "center," or "essence."

**ladino**   A non-Indian Guatemalan, generally considered to be of mixed-blood descent and socialized in Spanish language and Western-based culture; most ladinos in Guatemala do not use the term to describe themselves, although it is frequently employed by scholars and Maya.

*milpa* Plot of land primarily sown with maize and beans, usually interplanted with various types of squash; considered to be the traditional basis of Maya subsistence.

*municipio* Township; an important administrative unit below the level of regional departments in Guatemala; often considered to be the primary referent of Indian self-identity.

*pila* An outdoor sink with deep holding tanks where clothes and dishes are washed and water is stored; *pilas* are found in many households in Tecpán and Patzún, and the towns also maintain a number of communal *pilas*.

*po't* A blouse woven in a traditional Maya style with designs associated with particular Maya communities; *huipil* in Spanish.

*pueblo* Translated as either "people" or "town," depending on the context; in pan-Mayanist discourse it has come to be associated with more inclusive notions of community.

quetzal The Guatemalan unit of currency; in 1993–1994 the value fluctuated between 5.3 and 6.1 quetzales to the U.S. dollar.

quintal A weight of 100 pounds.

*rodillera* An apron-like piece of apparel woven from wool and worn as part of the traditional Kaqchikel male dress.

*tuj* A traditional Maya sweat bath used for both bathing and ritual purposes.

*traje* Traditional Maya dress; for women it consists of a *po't* and an *uq*; considered to be a primary emblem of ethnic identity for Maya women.

*troje* A room or small separate building in household compounds where dried maize is stored.

*uq* A wrap-around skirt worn as part of traditional Maya women's *traje*; *corte* in Spanish.

*(la) violencia* The period of violence from the late 1970s through the mid-1980s in Guatemala.

*winäq* A Maya person; also "twenty."

# Bibliography

Abu-Lughod, Lila. 1986. *Veiled sentiments: Honor and poetry in a Bedouin society*. Berkeley: University of California Press.

———. 1991. Writing against culture. In *Recapturing anthropology: Working in the present*, ed. Richard G. Fox, pp. 137–162. Santa Fe: School of American Research Press.

Adams, Richard N. 1990. Ethnic images and strategies in 1944. In *Guatemalan Indians and the state: 1542–1988*, ed. Carol Smith, pp. 141–162. Austin: University of Texas Press.

———. 1991. Strategies of ethnic survival in Central America. In *Nation-states and Indians in Latin America*, ed. Greg Urban and Joel Sherzer, pp. 181–206. Austin: University of Texas Press.

———, ed. 1957. *Political changes in rural Guatemalan communities: A symposium*. Middle American Research Institute Publication No. 4. New Orleans: Tulane University.

AGEXPRONT (Asociación Guatemalteca de Exportadoras de Productos No-Tradicionales). 1997. *Agricultural statistics*. http://www.quetzalnet.com/agexpront.

Allen, Arthur. 1992. Unriddling the glyphs: A new generation of Mayanists lets the Maya in on their secrets. *Lingua Franca* 3(1): 52–58.

Alvarado, Pedro de. 1972. *An account of the conquest of Guatemala in 1524*. Edited and translated by Sedley J. Mackie. Boston: Milford House.

Anderson, Benedict. 1983. *Imagined communities: Reflections on the origin and spread of nationalism*. London: Verso.

Annis, Sheldon. 1987. *God and production in a Guatemalan town*. Austin: University of Texas Press.

Appadurai, Arjun. 1996. *Modernity at large: Cultural dimensions of globalization*. Minneapolis: University of Minnesota Press.

———, ed. 1988. *The social life of things: Commodities in cultural perspective*. Cambridge: Cambridge University Press.

Arias, Arturo. 1990. Changing Indian identity: Guatemala's violent transition to modernity. In *Guatemalan Indians and the state, 1542–1988*, ed. Carol Smith, pp. 230–257. Austin: University of Texas Press.

AVANCSO (Asociación para el Avance de las Ciencias Sociales en Guatemala). 1988. *La política de desarrollo del Estado guatemalteco 1986–1987.* Cuadernos de Investigación No.2. Guatemala City: AVANSCO.

———. 1992. *Donde está el futuro? Procesos de reintegración en comunidades de retornados.* Cuadernos de Investigación No.8. Guatemala City: AVANSCO.

———. 1994. *Apostando al futuro con los cultivos no-tradicionales de exportación: Riesgos y oportunidades en la producción de hortalizas en Patzún, Chimaltenango.* Guatemala City: AVANCSO.

AVANCSO/PACCA (Policy Alternatives for the Caribbean and Central America). 1992. *Growing dilemmas: Guatemala, the environment, and the global economy.* Austin: Documentation Exchange.

B'alam, Pakal (José Obispo Rodríguez Guaján). 1994. *Kojtz'ib'an pa Kaqchi'.* Guatemala City: Cholsamaj.

Balassa, Bela, Gerardo M. Bueno, Pedro-Pablo Kuczynski, and Mario Henrique Simonsen. 1986. *Toward renewed economic growth in Latin America.* Washington, D.C.: Institute for International Economics.

Baran, Paul. 1957. *The political economy of growth.* New York: Monthly Review Press.

Barham, Bradford, Mary Clark, Elizabeth Katz, and Rachel Schurman. 1992. Nontraditional agriculture exports in Latin America. *Latin American Research Review* 27(2): 43–82.

Barre, Marie Chantal. 1982. Políticas indigenistas y revindicaciones indias en América Latina, 1940–1980. In *América Latina: Etnodesarrollo y etnocidio,* ed. Guillermo Bonfil, pp. 39–82. San José, Costa Rica: Facultad Latinoamericana de Ciencias Sociales.

Barry, Tom. 1992. *Inside Guatemala.* Albuquerque, N.M.: The Inter-Hemispheric Education Resource Center.

Barth, Fredrik. 1969. Introduction. In *Ethnic groups and boundaries: The social organization of cultural difference,* ed. Fredrik Barth, pp. 9–38. London: George Allen & Unwin.

Bastos, Santiago, and Manuela Camus. 1993. *Quebrando el silencio: Organizaciones del pueblo maya y sus demandas (1986–1992).* Guatemala City: Facultad Latinoamericano de Ciencias Sociales.

———. 1995. *Abriendo caminos: Las organizaciones mayas desde el Nobel hasta el Acuerdo de derechos indígenas.* Guatemala City: Facultad Latinoamericano de Ciencias Sociales.

Baudrillard, Jean. 1998. *The consumer society: Myths and structures.* London: Sage.

Beck, Ulrich, Anthony Giddens, and Scott Lash. 1994. *Reflexive modernization: Politics, tradition, and aesthetics in the modern social order.* Cambridge: Polity Press.

Berlin, Heinrich. 1950. La historia de los Xpantzay. *Antropología e Historia de Guatemala* 2(2): 40–53.

Berry, R. Albert, and William R. Cline. 1979. *Agrarian structure and productivity in developing countries.* Baltimore: Johns Hopkins University Press.

Berry, Sara. 1975. *Cocoa, custom, and socio-economic change in rural western Nigeria.* Oxford: Clarendon Press.

———. 1985. *Fathers work for their sons.* Berkeley: University of California Press.

————. 1993. *No condition is permanent: The social dynamics of agrarian change in sub-Saharan Africa.* Madison: University of Wisconsin Press.

Berryman, Phillip. 1984. *The religious roots of rebellion: Christians in Central American revolutions.* Maryknoll, N.Y.: Orbis Books.

Bhabha, Homi K. 1994. *The location of culture.* London: Routledge.

————, ed. 1990. *Nation and narration.* London: Routledge.

Bhagwati, Jagdish. 1982. Directly unproductive profit-seeking activities. *Journal of Political Economy* 90(5): 988–1002.

Bloch, Maurice. 1985. From cognition to ideology. In *Power and knowledge: Anthropological and sociological approaches,* ed. Richard Fardon, pp. 21–48. Edinburgh: Scottish Academic Press.

Boas, Franz. 1938. *The mind of primitive man.* New York: Macmillan.

Bonfil Batalla, Guillermo. 1981. Utopía y revolución: El pensamiento político contemporáneo de los indios en América Latina. In *Utopía y revolución: El pensamiento político contemporáneo de los indios en América Latina,* ed. Guillermo Bonfil Batalla, pp. 11–53. Mexico City: Editorial Nueva Imagen.

Boremanse, Didier. 1993. The faith of the real people: The Lacandon of the Chiapas rain forest. In *South and Meso-American native spirituality: From the cult of the feathered serpent to the theology of liberation,* ed. Gary H. Gossen, pp. 324–351. New York: Crossroad Publishing.

————. 1998. *Hach Winik: The Lacandon Maya of Chiapas, Southern Mexico.* Albany: Institute for Mesoamerican Studies, State University of New York at Albany.

Bossen, Laurel H. 1984. *The redivision of labor: Women and economic choice in four Guatemalan communities.* Albany: State University of New York Press.

Bourdieu, Pierre. 1977. *Outline of the theory of practice.* Cambridge: Cambridge University Press.

————. 1988. *Homo academicus.* Stanford: Stanford University Press.

Bricker, Victoria R. 1973. *Ritual humor in highland Chiapas.* Austin: University of Texas Press.

————. 1981. *The Indian Christ, the Indian King: The historical substrate of Maya myth and ritual.* Austin: University of Texas Press.

Brintnall, Douglas E. 1979. *Revolt against the dead: The modernization of a Mayan community in the highlands of Guatemala.* New York: Gordon and Breach.

Brinton, Daniel. 1969. *The annals of the Cakchiquels: The original with a translation, notes, and introduction.* New York: AMS Press.

Brown, R. McKenna. 1991. Language maintenance and shift in four Kaqchikel towns. Ph.D. diss., Center for Latin American Studies, Tulane University.

Brown, R. McKenna, Edward F. Fischer, and Raxche'. 1998. Mayan visions for a multilingual society: The Guatemalan Peace Accords on Indigenous Identity and Languages. *Fourth World Bulletin on Indigenous Law and Politics* 6: 28–33.

Browning, John. 1996. Un obstáculo imprescindible: El indígena en los siglos XVIII y XIX. In *Memoria del Segundo Encuentro Nacional de Historiadores.* Guatemala City: Universidad del Valle.

Brumann, Christoph. 1999. Writing for culture: Why a successful concept should not be discarded. *Current Anthropology* 40 (supplement): S1–S27.

Bulmer-Thomas, Victor. 1987. *The political economy of Central America since 1920.* Cambridge: Cambridge University Press.

Bunzl, Matti. 1996. Franz Boas and the Humboltian tradition: From *Volksgeist* and *Nationalcharakter* to an anthropological concept of culture. In *Volksgeist as method and ethic: Essays on Boasian ethnography and the German anthropological tradition*, ed. George W. Stocking, pp. 17–78. Madison: University of Wisconsin Press.

Calder, Bruce J. 1970. *Crecimiento y cambio de la iglesia católica guatemalteca, 1944–1966*. Seminario de Integración Social Guatemalteca Estudio No.6. Guatemala City: Editorial José de Pineda Ibarra.

Cambranes, J. C. 1985. *Coffee and peasants: The origins of the modern plantation economy in Guatemala, 1853–1897*. Antigua, Guatemala: Centro de Investigaciones Regionales de Mesoamérica.

Campbell, Howard. 1994. *Zapotec renaissance: Ethnic politics and cultural revivalism in southern Mexico*. Albuquerque: University of New Mexico Press.

Cancian, Frank. 1979. *The innovator's situation: Upper-middle-class conservatism in agricultural communities*. Stanford: Stanford University Press.

———. 1992. *The decline of community in Zinacantán: Economy, public life, and social stratification, 1960–1987*. Stanford: Stanford University Press.

Cardoso, Fernando H., and Enzo Faletto. 1979 [1967]. *Dependency and development in Latin America*. Translated by Marjory Mattingly Urquidi. Berkeley: University of California Press.

Carey, David. n.d. Kina'oj ri Kaqchikela' richin ri ojer k'an xb'anantaj: The Kaqchikel historical perspective. Manuscript.

Carletto, Calogero. 1996. Non-traditional agro-exports among smallholders in Guatemala. Ph.D. diss., University of California, Berkeley.

Carletto, Calogero, Alain de Janvry, and Elisabeth Sadoulet. 1999. Sustainability in the diffusion of innovations: Smallholder nontraditional agro-exports in Guatemala. *Economic Development and Cultural Change* 47(2): 345–369.

Carlsen, Robert S. 1997. *The war for the heart and soul of a highland Maya town*. Austin: University of Texas Press.

Carlsen, Robert S., and Martin Prechtel. 1991. The flowering of the dead: An interpretation of highland Maya culture. *Man* 26: 23–42.

Carmack, Robert M. 1973. *Quichean civilization: The ethnohistoric, ethnographic, and archaeological sources*. Berkeley: University of California Press.

———. 1988. The story of Santa Cruz Quiché. In *Harvest of violence: The Maya Indians and the Guatemalan crisis*, ed. Robert M. Carmack, pp. 39–69. Norman: University of Oklahoma Press.

Castañeda, Quetzil. 1996. *In the museum of Maya culture: Touring Chichén Itzá*. Minneapolis: University of Minnesota Press.

Chatterjee, Partha. 1993. *The nation and its fragments: Colonial and postcolonial histories*. Princeton: Princeton University Press.

Chavero, Alfredo, ed. 1979. *El lienzo de Tlaxcala*. Mexico City: Editorial Innovación.

Chávez, Adrián Inés. 1961. *El idioma Quí-chè y su grafía*. Quetzaltenango, Guatemala: Author. Mimeograph.

———. 1967. *Kí-chè Tib: Escritura Kí-chè y otras temas*. Quetzaltenango, Guatemala: Author.

Chayanov, A. V. 1966. *The theory of peasant economy*. Homewood, Ill.: American Economic Association.

Clark, Mary A. 1997. Transnational alliances and development policy in Latin

America: Nontraditional export production in Costa Rica. *Latin American Research Review* 32(2): 71–97.

Clifford, James. 1988. *The predicament of culture: Twentieth-century ethnography, literature, and art.* Cambridge: Harvard University Press.

COCADI (Coordinadora Cakchiquel de Desarrollo Integral). 1985. *El idioma, centro de nuestra cultura.* Chimaltenango: COCADI.

Cojtí Cuxil, Demetrio. 1984. Problemas de la identidad nacional guatemalteca. *Revista Cultura de Guatemala* 5(1): 17–21.

———. 1990. Lingüística e idiomas mayas en Guatemala. In *Lecturas sobre la lingüística maya,* ed. Nora England and Stephen R. Elliot, pp. 1–25. Antigua, Guatemala: Centro de Investigaciones Regionales de Mesoamérica.

———. 1991. *Configuración del pensamiento político del pueblo maya.* Quetzaltenango, Guatemala: Asociación de Escritores Mayances de Guatemala.

———. 1994. *Políticas para la reivindicación de los mayas de hoy (fundamento de los derechos específicos del pueblo maya).* Guatemala City: Cholsamaj.

———. 1997. *Ri maya' moloj pa Iximulew; El movimiento maya (en guatemala).* Guatemala City: Editorial Cholsamaj.

Cojtí Macario, Narciso. 1984. Principios ortográficos del Dr. Kaufman y PLFM. In *Ponencia No.4 del Segundo Congreso Lingüístico Nacional: Simbologías de los alfabetos mayas,* pp. 21–25. Guatemala City: Instituto Indigenista Nacional.

Colby, Benjamin N. 1967. Psychological orientations. In *Handbook of Middle American Indians, Vol. 6: Social Anthropology,* ed. Manning Nash; gen. ed., Robert Wauchope. Austin: University of Texas Press.

Colby, Benjamin N., and Lore M. Colby. 1981. *The daykeeper: The life and discourse of an Ixil diviner.* Cambridge: Harvard University Press.

Collier, George A. 1975. *Fields of the Tzotzil.* Austin: University of Texas Press.

———. 1990. Seeking food and seeking money: Changing productive relations in a highland Mexican community. *United Nations Research Institute for Social Development Discussion Paper,* No. 11. Geneva, Switzerland: United Nations Research Institute for Social Development.

Collier, George A., Daniel C. Mountjoy, and Ronald B. Nigh. 1994. Peasant agriculture and global change: A Maya response to energy development in southeastern Mexico. *BioScience* 44(6): 398–407.

Collier, Jane Fishburne. 1997. *From duty to desire: Remaking families in a Spanish village.* Princeton: Princeton University Press.

COMG (Consejo de Organizaciones Mayas de Guatemala). 1991. *Rujunamil ri mayab' amaq': Derechos específicos del pueblo maya.* Guatemala City: COMG.

Conklin, Beth A. 1997. Body paint, feathers, and VCRs: Aesthetics and authenticity in Amazonian activism. *American Ethnologist* 24(4): 711–737.

Conklin, Beth A. and Laura R. Graham. 1995. The shifting middle ground: Amazonian Indians and eco-politics. *American Anthropologist* 97(4): 695–710.

Cook, Scott. 1982. *Zapotec stoneworkers: The dynamics of rural simple commodity production in modern Mexican capitalism.* Austin: University of Texas Press.

Cook, Scott, and Leigh Binford. 1990. *Obliging need: Rural petty industry in Mexican capitalism.* Austin: University of Texas Press.

Cortés y Larraz, Pedro. 1958. *Descripción geográfico-moral de la diócesis de Guatemala.* Guatemala City: Tipografía Nacional.

Crapanzano, Vincent. 1980. *Tuhami: Portrait of a Moroccan.* Chicago: University of Chicago Press.

D'Andrade, Roy G. 1995. *The development of cognitive anthropology.* Cambridge: Cambridge University Press.

Danforth, Loring M. 1995. *The Macedonian conflict: Ethnic nationalism in a transnational world.* Princeton: Princeton University Press.

Davis, Shelton H. 1988. Introduction: Sowing the seeds of violence. In *Harvest of violence: The Maya Indians and the Guatemalan crisis,* ed. Robert M. Carmack, pp. 3–38. Norman: University of Oklahoma Press.

Dawkins, Richard. 1976. *The selfish gene.* Oxford: Oxford University Press.

Deere, Carman Diana, and Alain de Janvry. 1979. A conceptual framework for the empirical analysis of peasants. *American Journal of Agricultural Economics* 69: 601–611.

de Janvry, Alain. 1981. *The agrarian question and reformism in Latin America.* Baltimore: Johns Hopkins University Press.

de Janvry, Alain, Robin Marsh, David Runsten, Elizabeth Sadoulet, and Carol Zabin. 1989. Rural development in Latin America: An evaluation and a proposal. *Inter-American Institute for Cooperation on Agriculture Program Paper Series,* No. 12. San José, Costa Rica: IICA.

de Paz, Marco Antonio. 1993. *Maya' amaaq' xuq junamilaal; Pueblo Maya y democracia.* Seminario Permanente de Estudios Mayas, Cuaderna No. 3. Guatemala City: Editorial Cholsamaj.

de Soto, Hernando. 1986. *El otro sendero: La revolución informal.* Lima: Editorial El Barranco.

Diskin, Martin. 1995. Anthropological fieldwork in Mesoamerica: Focus on the field. *Latin American Research Review* 30(1): 163–175.

Dunlop, Albert J. 1997. *Mean business: How I save bad companies and make good companies great.* New York: Simon and Schuster.

Ebel, Roland H. 1988. When Indians take power: Conflict and consensus in San Juan Ostuncalco. In *Harvest of violence: The Maya Indians and the Guatemalan crisis,* ed. Robert M. Carmack, pp. 174–191. Norman: University of Oklahoma Press.

*The Economist.* World trade, fifty years on. May 16, 1998: 21–23.

Edmonson, Munro S. 1960. Nativism, syncretism, and anthropological science. In *Nativism and syncretism,* ed. Munro S. Edmonson, pp. 181–204. New Orleans: Middle American Research Institute, Tulane University.

———. 1971. *The book of counsel: The Popol Vuh of the Quiche Maya of Guatemala.* New Orleans: Middle American Research Institute, Tulane University.

———. 1993. The Mayan faith. In *South and Meso-American native spirituality: From the cult of the feathered serpent to the theology of liberation,* ed. Gary H. Gossen, pp. 65–85. New York: Crossroad Publishing.

Ehlers, Tracy Bachrach. 1990. *Silent looms: Women and production in a Guatemalan town.* Boulder: Westview Press.

EIU (Economist Intelligence Unit). 1997. *Country report: Guatemala, El Salvador.* London: The Economist Intelligence Unit.

Eliade, Mircea. 1954. *The myth of the eternal return, or cosmos and history.* Princeton: Princeton University Press.

England, Nora. 1996. The role of language standardization in revitalization. In

*Maya cultural activism in Guatemala,* ed. Edward F. Fischer and R. McKenna Brown, pp. 178–194. Austin: University of Texas Press.

Ewald, Robert H. 1967. Directed change. In *Handbook of Middle American Indians. Volume 6: Ethnology,* ed. Manning Nash; gen. ed., Robert Wauchope, pp. 490–511. Austin: University of Texas Press.

Fabian, Johannes. 1991. *Time and the work of anthropology: Critical essays, 1971–1991.* Chur, Switzerland: Harwood Academic Publishers.

Falla, Ricardo. 1978a. *Quiché rebelde: Estudio de un movimiento de conversión religiosa, rebelde a las creencias tradicionales, en San Antonio Ilotenango, Quiché (1948–70).* Guatemala City: Editorial Universitaria.

———. 1978b. El movimiento indígena. *Estudios Centroamericanos* 33(356–357): 437–461.

———. 1988. Struggle for survival in the mountains: Hunger and other privations inflicted on internal refugees from the Central Highlands. In *Harvest of violence: The Maya Indians and the Guatemalan crisis,* ed. Robert M. Carmack, pp. 235–255. Norman: University of Oklahoma Press.

———. 1994. *Massacre in the jungle.* Boulder: Westview Press.

Farriss, Nancy M. 1984. *Maya society under colonial rule: The collective enterprise of survival.* Princeton: Princeton University Press.

Feder, Gershon, Richard Just, and David Zimmerman. 1985. Adoption of agriculture innovations in developing countries: A survey. *Economic Development and Culture Change* 33: 255–298.

Feinberg, Richard E., and Bruce M. Bagley. 1986. *Development postponed: The political economy of Central America in the 1980s.* Boulder: Westview Press.

Field, Les W. 1994. Who are the Indians? Reconceptualizing indigenous identity, resistance, and the role of social sciences in Latin America. *Latin American Research Review* 29(3): 237–248.

———. 1999. Complicities and collaborations: Anthropologists and the "unacknowledged tribes" of California. *Current Anthropology* 40(2): 193–210.

Fischer, Edward F. 1993. The West in the future: Cultural hegemony and the politics of identity. *American Anthropologist* 95(4): 1000–1002.

———. 1996. Induced culture change as a strategy for socioeconomic development: The pan-Maya movement in Guatemala. In *Maya cultural activism in Guatemala,* ed. Edward F. Fischer and R. McKenna Brown, pp. 51–73. Austin: University of Texas Press.

———. 1999. Cultural logic and Maya identity: Rethinking constructivism and essentialism. *Current Anthropology* 43(4): 473–499.

———. 2001. Derechos humanos y relativismo cultural: La ética antropológica en el area maya. In *Representaciones de los derechos humanos en el area maya,* ed. Julián López García and Pedro Pitarch. Madrid: Sociedad Española de Estudios Mayas.

Fischer, Edward F., and R. McKenna Brown, eds. 1996. *Maya cultural activism in Guatemala.* Austin: University of Texas Press.

Fischer, Edward F., and Judith M. Maxwell. 1999. Political linguistics and Maya worldview: The creation of neologisms in Kaqchikel Mayan. *Texas Linguistic Forum* 42: 64–73.

Flores Alvarado, Humberto. 1993. *Movimiento indígena en Guatemala: Diagnóstico y expresiones de unidad.* Guatemala City: Instituto de Investigación y Autoformación Política and Fundación Friedrich Ebert.

Foster, George. 1965. Peasant society and the image of the limited good. *American Anthropologist* 67(2): 293–315.

Fox, Richard G. 1985. *Lions of the Punjab: Culture in the making.* Berkeley: University of California Press.

—. 1997. Passage from India. In *Between resistance and revolution: Cultural politics and social protest,* ed. Richard G. Fox and Orin Starn, pp. 65–82. New Brunswick, N.J.: Rutgers University Press.

Frank, Andre Gunder. 1967. *Capitalism and underdevelopment in Latin America: Historical studies of Chile and Brazil.* New York: Monthly Review Press.

Freidel, David A., Linda Schele, and Joy Parker. 1993. *Maya cosmos: Three thousand years on the shaman's path.* New York: William Morrow.

Friedman, Jonathan. 1994. *Cultural identity and global process.* London: Sage Publications.

Fuentes y Guzmán, Francisco Antonio de. 1933. *Recordación florida: Discurso historial y demonstración natural, material, militar y política del Reyno de Guatemala.* Guatemala City: Sociedad de Geografía e Historia.

Gall, Francis. 1983. *Diccionario geográfico de Guatemala.* Guatemala City: Instituto Geográfico Nacional.

Gall, Henry. 1993. *Henry's hint$ on Guatemala.* Guatemala City: Zotz Press.

Gálvez Borrell, Víctor, and Alberto Esquit Choy. 1997. *The Mayan movement today: Issues of indigenous culture and development in Guatemala.* Guatemala City: FLACSO.

García Canclini, Néstor. 1993. *Transforming modernity: Popular culture in Mexico.* Translated by Lidia Lozano. Austin: University of Texas Press.

—. 1995. *Hybrid cultures: Strategies for entering and leaving modernity.* Translated by Christopher L. Chiappari and Silvia L. López. Minneapolis: University of Minnesota Press.

García Hernández, Abraham. 1986. Breve historia de la Asociación de Escritores Mayences de Guatemala. *Winak Boletín Intercultural* 2(3): 138–160.

Garrard-Burnett, Virginia. 1998. *Protestantism in Guatemala: Living in the New Jerusalem.* Austin: University of Texas Press.

Geertz, Clifford. 1973. *The interpretation of cultures; Selected essays.* New York: Basic Books.

Gentner, Dedre, and Albert L. Stevens, eds. 1983. *Mental models.* Hillsdale, N.J.: Erlbaum.

Giddens, Anthony. 1984. *The constitution of society: Outline of the theory of structuration.* Berkeley: University of California Press.

—. 1990. *The consequences of modernity.* Stanford: Stanford University Press.

—. 1999. *The third way: The renewal of social democracy.* Cambridge, England: Polity Press.

Gillin, John. 1952. Ethos and cultural aspects of personality. In *Heritage of conquest: The ethnology of Middle America,* ed. Sol Tax, pp. 193–222. Glencoe, Ill.: The Free Press.

Gilroy, Paul. 1993. *The black Atlantic: Modernity and double consciousness.* Cambridge: Harvard University Press.

Glover, David. 1984. Contract farming and smallholder outgrower schemes in less-developed countries. *World Development* 12(11–12): 1143–1157.

Godelier, Maurice. 1972. *Rationality and irrationality in economics.* Translated by Brian Pearce. New York: Monthly Review Press.

Goldin, Liliana R. 1996. Economic mobility strategies among Guatemalan peasants: Prospects and limits of nontraditional vegetable cash crops. *Human Organization* 55(1): 99–107.

Goldin, Liliana R., and Eugenia Sáenz de Tejada. 1993. Uneven development in western Guatemala. *Ethnology* 32(3): 237–251.

Gossen, Gary H. 1974. *Chamulas in the world of the sun: Time and space in a Maya oral tradition.* Cambridge: Harvard University Press.

———. 1986. Mesoamerican ideas as a foundation for regional synthesis. In *Symbol and meaning beyond the closed community: Essays in Mesoamerican ideas,* ed. Gary H. Gossen, pp. 1–8. Albany: Institute for Mesoamerican Studies, State University of New York.

———. 1999. *Telling Maya tales: Tzotzil identities in modern Mexico.* New York: Routledge.

*El Gráfico.* 1976. Tezahuic: "El partido que nos proponemos crear suprimirá la discriminación racial." *El Gráfico* 14(4443): 8.

Grindle, Marilou. 1986. *State and countryside: Development policy and agrarian politics in Latin America.* Baltimore: Johns Hopkins University Press.

Gudeman, Stephen, and Alberto Rivera. 1990. *Conversations in Colombia: The domestic economy in life and text.* Cambridge: Cambridge University Press.

Guillemin, George F. 1977. Urbanism and hierarchy at Iximché. In *Social process in Maya prehistory: Studies in honour of Sir Eric Thompson,* ed. Norman Hammond, pp. 227–264. New York: Academic Press.

Gumperz, John J., and Stephen C. Levinson, eds. 1996. *Rethinking linguistic relativity.* Cambridge: Cambridge University Press.

Gupta, Akhil, and James Ferguson. 1992. Beyond "culture": Space, identity, and the politics of difference. *Cultural Anthropology* 7: 6–23.

———, eds. 1997. *Culture, power, place: Explorations in critical anthropology.* Durham, N.C.: Duke University Press.

Habermas, Jürgen. 1990. *Moral consciousness and communicative action.* Translated by Christian Lenhardt and Shierry Weber Nicholsen. Cambridge: MIT Press.

Haley, Brian, and Larry R. Wilcoxon. 1997. Anthropology and the making of Chumash tradition. *Current Anthropology* 38(5): 761–794.

Hamm, Shannon Reid. 1992. The U.S. supply of vegetables. In *Vegetable markets in the Western Hemisphere,* ed. Rigoberta A. López and Leo C. Polopolus, pp. 3–19. Ames: Iowa State University Press.

Handler, Richard. 1988. *Nationalism and the politics of culture in Quebec.* Madison: University of Wisconsin Press.

Handy, Jim. 1984. *Gift of the devil: A history of Guatemala.* Toronto: Between the Lines Press.

Hannerz, Ulf. 1992. When culture is everywhere: Reflections on a favorite concept. *Ethnos* 57: 95–111.

———. 1996. *Transnational connections: Culture, people, places.* New York: Routledge.

Hastrup, Kirsten. 1995. *A passage to anthropology: Between experience and theory.* London: Routledge.

Hawkins, John. 1984. *Inverse images: The meaning of culture, ethnicity and family in postcolonial Guatemala.* Albuquerque: University of New Mexico Press.

Hendrickson, Carol. 1991. Images of the Indian in Guatemala: The role of indigenous dress in Indian and Ladino constructions. In *Nation-states and Indians in Latin America*, ed. Greg Urban and Joel Sherzer, pp. 287–306. Austin: University of Texas Press.

———. 1995. *Weaving identities: Construction of dress and self in a highland Guatemala town*. Austin: University of Texas Press.

———. 1996. Women, weaving, and education in Maya revitalization. In *Maya cultural activism in Guatemala*, ed. Edward F. Fischer and R. McKenna Brown, pp. 156–164. Austin: University of Texas Press.

Herrera, Guillermina. 1990. Las lenguas indígenas de Guatemala: Situación actual y futuro. In *Lecturas sobre la lingüística maya*, ed. Nora C. England and Stephen R. Elliot, pp. 27–50. Guatemala City: CIRMA.

Hervik, Peter. 1992. Mayan culture: Beyond boundaries. *Ethnos* 57(3/4): 183–199.

———. 1994. Shared reasoning in the field: Reflexivity beyond the author. In *Social experience and anthropological knowledge*, ed. Kirsten Hastrup and Peter Hervik, pp. 78–100. London: Routledge.

———. 1999. *Mayan people within and beyond boundaries: Social categories and lived identity in Yucatán*. Amsterdam: Harwood Academic Publishers.

Herzfeld, Michael. 1997. *Cultural intimacy: Social poetics in the nation-state*. Chicago: University of Chicago Press.

———. 1998. Factual fissures: Claims and contexts. *Annals of the American Academy of Political and Social Science* 560: 69–82.

Hill, Polly. 1963. *Migrant cocoa farmers of southern Ghana*. Cambridge: Cambridge University Press.

———. 1970. *Studies in rural capitalism in west Africa*. Cambridge: Cambridge University Press.

Hill, Robert M. 1989. Social organization by decree in colonial highland Guatemala. *Ethnohistory* 36(2): 170–198.

———. 1992. *Colonial Cakchiquels: Highland Maya adaptation to Spanish rule, 1600–1700*. Fort Worth: Harcourt Brace Jovanovich.

Hill, Robert M., and Edward F. Fischer. 1999. States of heart: An ethnohistorical approach to Kaqchikel-Maya ethnopsychology. *Ancient Mesoamerica* 10: 317–332.

Hill, Robert M., and John Monaghan. 1987. *Continuities in highland Maya social organization: Ethnohistory in Sacapulas, Guatemala*. Philadelphia: University of Pennsylvania Press.

Hirschman, Albert O. 1977. A generalized linkage approach to development, with special reference to staples. In *Essays on Economic Development and Cultural Change*, ed. Manning Nash, pp. 67–98. Chicago: University of Chicago Press.

Hobsbawm, Eric J. 1964. *Labouring men: Studies in the history of labour*. London: Weidenfeld and Nicolson.

———. 1983. Introduction: Inventing traditions. In *The invention of tradition*, ed. Eric Hobsbawm and Terence Ranger, pp. 1–14. Cambridge: Cambridge University Press.

Hoppin, Polly. 1989. *Pesticide use in four nontraditional crops in Guatemala: Implications for residues*. Baltimore: Center for International Crop Protection.

Hunt, Eva. 1977. *The transformation of the hummingbird: Cultural roots of a Zinacantecan mythical poem*. Ithaca: Cornell University Press.

INE (Instituto Nacional de Estadística). 1983. *Censo nacional agropecuario 1979.* Guatemala City: INE.

———. 1991. *Censo nacional.* Guatemala City: INE.

———. 1996. *X Censo nacional de población y V de habitación.* Guatemala City: INE.

Jameson, Fredric. 1991. *Postmodernism, or the cultural logic of late capitalism.* Durham, N.C.: Duke University Press.

Johnson, Mark. 1987. *The body in the mind: The bodily basis of meaning, imagination, and reason.* Chicago: University of Chicago Press.

Jones, Grant D. 1989. *Maya resistance to Spanish rule: Time and history on a colonial frontier.* Albuquerque: University of New Mexico Press.

Kapferer, Bruce. 1988. *Legends of people, legends of state: Violence, intolerance, and political culture in Sri Lanka and Australia.* Washington, D.C.: Smithsonian Institution Press.

Karp, Philip E. 1988. Guatemala. In *Struggle against dependence: Nontraditional export growth in Central America and the Caribbean,* ed. Eva Paus, pp. 65–84. Boulder: Westview Press.

Katz, Elizabeth. 1994. The impact of non-traditional export agriculture on income and food availability in Guatemala: An intra-household perspective. *Food and Nutrition Bulletin* 15(4): 23–26.

Kaufman, Terrence S. 1976. *Proyecto de alfabetos y ortografías para escribir las lenguas mayances.* Guatemala City: Editorial José de Pineda Ibarra.

Kearney, Michael. 1995. The local and the global: The anthropology of globalization and transnationalization. *Annual Review of Anthropology* 24: 547–565.

———. 1996. *Reconceptualizing the peasantry: Anthropology in global perspective.* Boulder: Westview Press.

Kirchoff, Paul. 1943. Mesoamérica: Sus límites geográficos, composición étnica y caracteres culturales. *Acta Americana* 1: 92–107.

Klor De Alva, J. Jorge. 1993. Aztec spirituality and Nahuatized Christianity. In *South and Meso-American native spirituality: From the cult of the feathered serpent to the theology of liberation,* ed. Gary H. Gossen, pp. 173–197. New York: Crossroad Publishing.

Knauft, Bruce M. 1996. *Genealogies for the present in cultural anthropology.* New York: Routledge.

Knorr-Cetina, Karin D. 1981. The micro-sociological challenge of macro-sociology: Towards a reconstruction of social theory and methodology. In *Advances in social theory and method: Toward an integration of micro- and macro-sociologies,* ed. Karin Knorr-Cetina and Aaron V. Cicourel, pp. 1–47. Boston: Routledge & Kegan Paul.

Krueger, Chris, and Kjell Enge. 1985. *Security and development conditions in the Guatemalan highlands.* Washington, D.C.: Washington Office on Latin America.

Kusterer, Kenneth, Maria R. Estrada de Bartres, and Josefina X. Cuxil. 1981. *USAID Evaluation Special Study No. 4.* Washington, D.C.: USAID.

Lacan, Jacques. 1981 [1956]. *Speech and language in psychoanalysis.* Translated by Anthony Wilden. Baltimore: Johns Hopkins Press.

Laclau, Ernesto. 1977. *Politics and ideology in Marxist theory.* London: Verso.

Lakoff, George. 1987. *Women, fire, and dangerous things.* Chicago: University of Chicago Press.

Lakoff, George, and Mark Johnson. 1980. *Metaphors we live by*. Chicago: University of Chicago Press.

Lash, Scott, and John Urry. 1987. *The end of organized capitalism*. Cambridge, England: Polity.

———. 1994. *Economies of signs and space*. London: Sage.

Leach, Edmund R. 1954. *Political systems of highland Burma: A study of Kachin social structure*. Cambridge: Harvard University Press.

Lee, Kathryn Anne. 1993. Illusion of autonomy: The impacts of nontraditional export agriculture on small farmers in Guatemala. Master's thesis, University of California, Berkeley.

Lévy-Bruhl, Lucien. 1926. *How natives think*. Translated by Lilian A. Clare. London: G. Allen and Unwin.

Lévi-Strauss, Claude. 1966. *The savage mind*. Chicago: University of Chicago Press.

———. 1995. *The story of lynx*. Translated by Catherine Tihanyi. Chicago: University of Chicago Press.

Lindenberg, Marc. 1988. Central America's elusive economic recovery. *World Development* (16)2: 237–254.

Linnekin, Jocelyn. 1983. Defining tradition: Variations on the Hawaiian identity. *American Ethnologist* 10: 241–252.

———. 1991. Cultural invention and the dilemma of authenticity. *American Anthropologist* 93(2): 446–449.

Lolmay (Pedro García). 1999. Lengua e identidad. Paper read at the 3rd Congreso de Estudios Mayas, Universidad Rafael Landívar, Guatemala City, 4–6 August.

López Austin, Alfredo. 1988. *The human body and ideology: Concepts of the ancient Nahuas*. Salt Lake City: University of Utah Press.

López Raquec, Margarita. 1989. *Acerca de los alfabetos para escribir los idiomas mayas de Guatemala*. Guatemala City: Ministerio de Cultura y Deportes.

Lovell, W. George, and Christopher H. Lutz. 1995. *Demography and empire: A guide to the population history of Spanish Central America, 1500–1821*. Boulder: Westview Press.

Lucy, John A. 1992a. *Grammatical categories and cognition: A case study of the linguistic relativity hypothesis*. Cambridge: Cambridge University Press.

———. 1992b. *Language diversity and thought: A reformulation of the linguistic relativity hypothesis*. Cambridge: Cambridge University Press.

Lutz, Christopher H. 1994. *Santiago de Guatemala, 1541–1773: City, caste, and the colonial experience*. Norman: University of Oklahoma Press.

Lutz, Christopher H., and W. George Lovell. 1990. Core and periphery in Colonial Guatemala. In *Guatemalan Indians and the State, 1540 to 1988*, ed. Carol A. Smith, pp. 35–51. Austin: University of Texas Press.

Luxemburg, Rosa. 1913. *Die Akkumulation des Kapitals*. Berlin: Jugendinternationale.

Lyotard, Jean François. 1984. *The postmodern condition: A report on knowledge*. Translated by Geoff Bennington and Brian Massumi. Minneapolis: University of Minnesota Press.

Marcus, George E., and Michael M. J. Fischer. 1986. *Anthropology as cultural critique: An experimental moment in the human sciences*. Chicago: University of Chicago Press.

Martínez Peláez, Severo. 1971. *La patria del criollo*. Guatemala City: Editorial Universitaria.

Marx, Karl. 1963 [1852]. *The Eighteenth Brumaire of Louis Bonaparte.* New York: International Publishers.

McAllister, Carlota. 1996. Authenticity and Guatemala's Maya queen. In *Beauty queens on the global stage: Gender, contests, and power,* ed. Colleen Ballerino Cohen, Richard Wilk, and Beverly Stoeltje, pp. 105–124. New York: Routledge.

McBryde, Webster. 1947. *Cultural and historical geography of south-western Guatemala.* Institute of Social Anthropology Pub. 4. Washington, D.C.: The Smithsonian Institute.

McCracken, Vicki A. 1992. The U.S. demand for vegetables. In *Vegetable markets in the Western Hemisphere,* ed. Rigoberta A. López and Leo C. Polopolus, pp.20–43. Ames: Iowa State University Press.

McCreery, David. 1994. *Rural Guatemala, 1760–1940.* Stanford: Stanford University Press.

Meillassoux, Claude. 1981. *Maidens, meal, and money: Capitalism and the domestic community.* Translated by Felicity Edholm. Cambridge: Cambridge University Press.

Menchú, Rigoberta. 1984. *I, Rigoberta Menchú: An Indian woman in Guatemala,* ed. Elisabeth Burgos-Debray; trans. Ann Wright. London: Verso.

Miller, Hubert J. 1990. Catholic leaders and spiritual socialism during the Arévalo administration in Guatemala, 1945–1951. In *Central America: Historical perspectives on the contemporary crisis,* ed. Ralph Lee Woodward, pp. 85–105. New York: Greenwood Press.

Mintz, Sidney. 1985. *Sweetness and power: The place of sugar in modern history.* New York: Penguin Books.

Moberg, Mark. 1992. *Citrus, strategy, and class: The politics of development in southern Belize.* Iowa City: University of Iowa Press.

Molina Mejía, Raúl. 1984. Toward understanding the political situation. In *Guatemala: Tyranny on trial, testimony of the Permanent People's Tribunal,* ed. Susanne Jonas, Ed McCaughan, and Elizabeth Sutherland Martínez, pp. 37–40. San Francisco: Synthesis Publications.

Monaghan, John. 1995. *The covenants with earth and rain: Exchange, sacrifice, and revelation in Mixtec sociality.* Norman: University of Oklahoma Press.

———. 2000. Theology and history in the study of Mesoamerican religions. In *Supplement to the Handbook of Middle American Indians, Vol. 6: Ethnology,* ed. John Monaghan; gen. ed., Victoria R. Bricker, pp. 24–49. Austin: University of Texas Press.

Montejo, Victor. 1991. In the name of the pot, the sun, the broken spear, the rock, the stick, the idol, ad infinitum and ad nauseam: An expose of Anglo anthropologist's obsessions with and invention of Mayan gods. Paper presented at the 1991 Annual Meeting of the American Anthropological Association, San Francisco.

———. 1999. *Voices from Exile: Violence and Survival in Modern Maya History.* Norman: University of Oklahoma Press.

Morales, Mario Roberto. 1997. No me defiendas compadre. *Siglo XXI,* May 9, 1997.

Murray, Douglas, and Polly Hoppin. 1990. *Pesticides and nontraditional agriculture: A coming crisis for U.S. development policy in Latin America.* Austin: Institute of Latin American Studies, University of Texas.

Nash, June C. 1970. *In the eyes of the ancestors: Belief and behavior in a Maya community.* New Haven: Yale University Press.

————. 1995. The reassertion of indigenous identity: Mayan responses to state intervention in Chiapas. *Latin American Research Review* 30(3): 7–41.

Nash, Manning. 1958. *Machine age Maya: The industrialization of a Guatemalan community.* American Anthropological Association Memoir No. 87. Menasha, Wis.: American Anthropological Association.

Nelson, Diane M. 1991. The reconstruction of Mayan identity. *Report on Guatemala* 12(2): 6–7, 14.

————. 1999. *A finger in the wound: Body politics in Quincentennial Guatemala.* Berkeley: University of California Press.

Netting, Robert McC. 1993. *Smallholders, householders: Farm families and the ecology of intensive, sustainable agriculture.* Stanford: Stanford University Press.

Nieves, Isabel. 1987. *Exploratory study of intrahousehold resource allocation in a cash-cropping scheme in highland Guatemala.* Washington, D.C.: International Research Center on Women.

Obeyesekere, Gananath. 1981. *Medusa's hair: An essay on personal symbols and religious experience.* Chicago: University of Chicago Press.

————. 1997. Comments on Robert Borofsky's "Cook, Lono, Obeyesekere, and Sahlins." *Current Anthropology* 38(2): 267–272.

Ortner, Sherry B. 1984. Theory in anthropology since the sixties. *Comparative Studies in Society and History* 26(1): 126–166.

————. 1989. *High religion: A cultural and political history of Sherpa Buddhism.* Princeton: Princeton University Press.

Otzoy, Irma. 1988. Identity and higher education among Mayan women. Master's thesis, Dept. of Anthropology, University of Iowa.

————. 1996. Maya clothing and identity. In *Maya cultural activism in Guatemala,* ed. Edward F. Fischer and R. McKenna Brown, pp. 189–206. Austin: University of Texas Press.

Oxlajuuj Keej Maya' Ajtz'iib' (Ixkem, Ajpub', Lolmay, Nik'te', Pakal, Saqijix, Waykan). 1992. Anales de los Kaqchikeles. Unpublished manuscript.

————. 1993. *Maya' Chii': Los idiomas mayas de Guatemala.* Guatemala City: Cholsamaj.

Paul, Benjamin D., and William J. Demarest. 1988. The operation of a death squad in San Pedro La Laguna. In *Harvest of violence: The Maya Indians and the Guatemalan crisis,* ed. Robert M. Carmack, pp. 119–154. Norman: University of Oklahoma Press.

Payeras, Mario. 1983. *Days of the jungle: The testimony of a Guatemalan guerrillero, 1972–1976.* New York: Monthly Review Press.

Plattner, Stuart. 1975. The economics of peddling. In *Formal methods in economic anthropology,* ed. Stuart Plattner, pp. 55–76. Washington, D.C.: American Anthropological Association.

————. 1985. Equilibrating market relationships. In *Markets and marketing,* ed. Stuart Plattner, pp. 133–152. Lanham, Md.: University Press of America.

Quemé, Rigoberto, Guillermo Rodríguez Guaján, Ricardo Mejía, and Otilia Lux de Cojtí. 1990. Estrategias para la consolidación de la Academia de las Lenguas Mayas de Guatemala. In *Reporte del II Seminario: Situación actual y futuro de la Academia de las Lenguas Mayas de Guatemala,* pp. 68–74. Guatemala City: Academia de las Lenguas Mayas de Guatemala.

Raxche' (Demetrio Rodríguez Guaján). 1992. Introduction. In *Cultura maya y políticas de desarrollo.* 2d ed. Chimaltenango, Guatemala: COCADI.

————. 1996. Maya culture and the politics of development. In *Maya cultural activism in Guatemala,* ed. Edward F. Fischer and R. McKenna Brown, pp. 74–88. Austin: University of Texas Press.

Raynolds, Laura. 1997. Restructuring national agriculture, agro-food trade, and agrarian livelihoods in the Caribbean. In *Globalizing food: Agrarian questions and global restructuring,* ed. David Goodman and Michael J. Watts, pp. 119–132. London and New York: Routledge.

Recinos, Adrián, trans. 1984. *Crónicas indígenas de Guatemala.* Guatemala City: Academia de Geografía e Historia de Guatemala.

Recinos, Adrián, and Delia Goetz, trans. 1953. *The annals of the Cakchiquels: Title of the lords of Totonicapan.* Norman: University of Oklahoma Press.

Reddy, William M. 1997. Against constructionism: The historical ethnography of emotions. *Current Anthropology* 38(3): 327–351.

Redfield, Robert. 1941. *The folk culture of Yucatan.* Chicago: University of Chicago Press.

————. 1956. *Peasant society and culture.* Chicago: University of Chicago Press.

Restall, Matthew. 1997. *The Maya world: Yucatec culture and society, 1550–1850.* Stanford: Stanford University Press.

Richards, Michael. 1985. Cosmopolitan world-view and counterinsurgency in Guatemala. *Anthropological Quarterly* 3: 90–107.

Richards, Michael, and Julia Becker Richards. 1996. Maya education: A historical and contemporary analysis of Mayan language education policy. In *Maya cultural activism in Guatemala,* ed. Edward F. Fischer and R. McKenna Brown. Austin: University of Texas Press.

Rodseth, Lars. 1998. Distributive models of culture: A Sapirian alternative to essentialism. *American Anthropologist* 100(1): 55–69.

Rogoff, Barbara. 1990. *Apprenticeship in thinking: Cognitive development in social context.* New York: Oxford University Press.

Roseberry, William. 1983. *Coffee and capitalism in the Venezuelan Andes.* Austin: University of Texas Press.

————. 1989. *Anthropologies and histories: Essays in culture, history, and political economy.* New Brunswick, N.J.: Rutgers University Press.

Rude, George. 1980. *Ideology and popular protest.* New York: Pantheon Books.

Sabel, Charles. 1982. *Work and politics: The division of labor in industry.* Cambridge: Cambridge University Press.

Sahlins, Marshall. 1976. *Culture and practical reason.* Chicago: University of Chicago Press.

————. 1985. *Islands of history.* Chicago: University of Chicago Press.

Said, Edward. 1978. *Orientalism.* New York: Pantheon Books.

Sam Colop, Enrique. 1991. *Jub'aqtun omay kuchum kaslemal: Cinco siglos de encubrimiento.* Seminario Permanente de Estudios Mayas, Cuaderna No. 1. Guatemala City: Editorial Cholsamaj.

————. 1996. The discourse of concealment and 1992. In *Maya cultural activism in Guatemala,* ed. Edward F. Fischer and R. McKenna Brown, pp. 146–156. Austin: University of Texas Press.

————. 1997. Par de gringos despistados. *Prensa Libre.*

Sandstrom, Alan. 1991. *Corn is our blood: Culture and ethnic identity in a contemporary Aztec Indian village.* Norman: University of Oklahoma Press.

Sardi, Jorge Ospina. 1989. Trade policy in Latin America. In *Lessons in development: A comparative study of Asia and Latin America,* ed. Seiji Naya, Miguel Urrutia, Shelley Mark, and Alfredo Fuentes, pp. 77–92. San Francisco: Institute of Contemporary Studies.

Schele, Linda, and Nikolai Grube. 1996. The workshops for Maya on hieroglyphic writing. In *Maya cultural activism in Guatemala,* ed. Edward F. Fischer and R. McKenna Brown, pp. 131–140. Austin: University of Texas Press.

Schlesinger, Stephen, and Stephen Kinser. 1982. *Bitter fruit: The untold story of the American coup in Guatemala.* Garden City, N.Y.: Doubleday.

Scott, James C. 1985. *Weapons of the weak: Everyday forms of peasant resistance.* New Haven: Yale University Press.

———. 1990. *Domination and the arts of resistance: Hidden transcripts.* New Haven: Yale University Press.

Seale, James L. 1992. Vegetable trade and the Caribbean Basin Initiative. In *Vegetable markets in the western hemisphere,* ed. Rigoberta A. López and Leo C. Polopolus, pp. 201–216. Ames: Iowa State University Press.

Sewell, William H. 1992. A theory of structure: Duality, agency, and transformation. *American Journal of Sociology* 98(1): 1–29.

Sexton, James. 1978. Protestantism and modernization in two Guatemalan towns. *American Ethnologist* 5: 280–302.

Shore, Bradd. 1996. *Culture in mind: Cognition, culture, and the problem of meaning.* Oxford: Oxford University Press.

Sick, Deborah. 1999. *Farmers of the golden bean: Costa Rican households and the global coffee economy.* DeKalb: Northern Illinois University Press.

Smith, Carol A. 1975. Production in western Guatemala: A test of von Thünen and Boserup. In *Formal methods in economic anthropology,* ed. Stuart Plattner, pp. 5–37. Washington, D.C.: American Anthropological Association.

———. 1976. Exchange systems and the spatial distribution of elites: The organization of stratification in agrarian societies. In *Regional Analysis, Vol. 2: Social Systems,* ed. Carol A. Smith, pp. 309–374. New York: Academic Press.

———. 1978. Beyond dependency theory: National and regional patterns of underdevelopment in Guatemala. *American Ethnologist* 5: 574–617.

———. 1984a. Labor and international capital in the making of a peripheral social formation: Economic transformations of Guatemala, 1850–1980. *Wilson Center Working Paper No. 138.* Washington, D.C.: The Wilson Center.

———. 1984b. Local history in global context: Social and economic transformations in Western Guatemala. *Comparative Studies in Society and History* 26(22): 193–228.

———. 1988. Destruction of the material bases for Indian culture: Economic changes in Totonicapán. In *Harvest of violence: The Maya Indians and the Guatemalan crisis,* ed. Robert M. Carmack, pp. 206–231. Norman: University of Oklahoma Press.

———. 1989. Survival strategies among petty commodity producers. *International Labor Review* 128: 791–813.

———. 1990. Introduction: Social relations in Guatemala over time and space. In *Guatemalan Indians and the state, 1542 to 1988,* ed. Carol A. Smith, pp. 1–30. Austin: University of Texas Press.

———. 1991. Maya nationalism. *NACLA Report on the Americas* 23(3): 29–33.

Smith, Waldemar. 1977. *The fiesta system and economic change.* New York: Columbia University Press.

Spivak, Gayatri. 1987. *In other worlds: Essays in cultural politics.* New York: Methuen.

———. 1994. Can the subaltern speak? In *Colonial discourse and post-colonial theory: A reader,* ed. Patrick Williams and Laura Chrisman, pp. 66–111. New York: Columbia University Press.

Stephens, John L. 1949. *Incidents of travel in Central America, Chiapas, and Yucatan.* New Brunswick, N.J.: Rutgers University Press.

Stoll, David. 1982. *Fishers of men or founders of empire? The Wycliffe Bible Translators in Latin America.* London: Zed Press.

———. 1988. Evangelicals, guerrillas, and the army: The Ixil Triangle under Ríos Montt. In *Harvest of violence: The Maya Indians and the Guatemalan crisis,* ed. Robert M. Carmack, pp. 90–116. Norman: University of Oklahoma Press.

———. 1993. *Between two armies in the Ixil towns of Guatemala.* New York: Columbia University Press.

———. 1998. *Rigoberta Menchú and the story of all poor Guatemalans.* Boulder: Westview Press.

Stonich, Susan. 1993. *"I am destroying the land!": The political ecology of poverty and environmental destruction in Honduras.* Boulder: Westview Press.

Strauss, Claudia, and Naomi Quinn. 1997. *A cognitive theory of cultural meaning.* Cambridge: Cambridge University Press.

Sturm, Circe. 1996. Old writing and new messages: The role of hieroglyphic literacy in Maya cultural activism. In *Maya cultural activism in Guatemala,* ed. Edward F. Fischer and R. McKenna Brown, pp. 114–130. Austin: University of Texas Press.

Tax, Sol. 1937. The municipios of the midwestern highlands of Guatemala. *American Anthropologist* 39(3): 423–444.

———. 1941. World view and social relations in Guatemala. *American Anthropologist* 43(1): 27–42.

———. 1953. *Penny capitalism: A Guatemalan Indian economy.* Smithsonian Institution Institute of Social Anthropology Publication No. 16. Washington, D.C.: Smithsonian Institution.

Tedlock, Barbara. 1982. *Time and the highland Maya.* Albuquerque: University of New Mexico Press.

Tedlock, Dennis. 1993. *Breath on the mirror: Mythic voices and visions of the living Maya.* San Francisco: HarperCollins.

Tedlock, Dennis, trans. and ed. 1985. *Popol Vuh: The definitive edition of the Mayan book of the dawn of life and the glories of gods and kings.* New York: Simon and Schuster.

Terray, Emmanuel. 1972. *Marxism and "primitive" societies: Two studies.* Translated by Mary Klopper. New York: Monthly Review Press.

Teubal, Miguel. 1987. Internationalization of capital and agroindustrial complexes: Their impact on Latin American agriculture. *Latin American Perspectives* (14)3: 316–364.

Thompson, E. P. 1966. *The making of the English working class.* New York: Vintage Books.

Thompson, J. Eric S. 1970. *Maya history and religion.* Norman: University of Oklahoma Press.

Torres-Rivas, Edelberto. 1984. Presentation by the prosecutor. In *Guatemala: Tyranny on trial, testimony of the Permanent People's Tribunal*, ed. Susanne Jonas, Ed McCaughan and Elizabeth Sutherland Martínez, pp. 7–23. San Francisco: Synthesis Publications.

Turner, Terence. 1991. Representing, resisting, rethinking: Historical transformations of Kayapo culture and anthropological consciousness. In *Colonial situations: Essays on the contextualization of ethnographic knowledge*, ed. George W. Stocking, pp. 285–313. Madison: University of Wisconsin Press.

Tyler, Stephen A. 1978. *The said and the unsaid: Mind, meaning, and culture.* New York: Academic Press.

UNDP (United Nations Development Programme). 1999. *Human Development Report 1999.* Oxford: Oxford University Press.

van den Berghe, Pierre L. 1981. *The ethnic phenomenon.* New York: Elsevier.

Vázquez, Francisco. 1937. *Crónica de la Provincia del Santísimo Nombre de Jesús de Guatemala de la Orden de N. Seráfico Padre San Francisco en el Reino de la Nueva España.* Guatemala City: Tipografía Nacional.

Vogt, Evon Z. 1976. *Tortillas for the gods: A symbolic analysis of Zinacanteco rituals.* Cambridge: Harvard University Press.

Von Braun, Joachim, David Hotchkiss, and Maarten Immink. 1989. *Nontraditional export crops in Guatemala: Effects on production, income, and nutrition.* Washington, D.C.: International Food Policy Research Institute.

Wagley, Charles. 1941. *Economics of the Guatemalan village.* Memoirs of the American Anthropological Association No. 58. Menasha, Wis.: American Anthropological Association.

Wallace, Anthony F. C. 1956. Revitalization movements. *American Anthropologist* 58: 264–281.

———. 1961. *Culture and personality.* New York: Random House.

Wallerstein, Immanuel. 1974. *The modern world system: Capitalist agriculture and the origins of the European world economy in the sixteenth century.* New York: Academic Press.

———. 1979. *The capitalist world-economy.* Cambridge: Cambridge University Press.

Warren, Kay B. 1978. *The symbolism of subordination: Indian identity in a Guatemalan town.* Austin: University of Texas Press.

———. 1992. Transforming memories and histories: The meaning of ethnic resurgence for Mayan Indians. In *Americas: New interpretive essays*, ed. Alfred Stepan, pp. 189–219. New York: Oxford University Press.

———. 1993. Interpreting *la violencia* in Guatemala: Shapes of Kaqchikel silence and resistance in the 1970s and 1980s. In *The violence within: Cultural and political opposition in divided nations*, ed. Kay B. Warren, pp. 25–56. Boulder: Westview Press.

———. 1996. Reading history as resistance: Maya public intellectuals in Guatemala. In *Maya cultural activism in Guatemala*, ed. Edward F. Fischer and R. McKenna Brown, pp. 121–145. Austin: University of Texas Press.

———. 1998. *Indigenous movements and their critics: Pan-Maya activism in Guatemala.* Princeton: Princeton University Press.

Wasserstrom, Robert. 1983. *Class and society in central Chiapas.* Berkeley: University of California Press.

Watanabe, John M. 1983. In the world of the sun: A cognitive model of Mayan cosmology. *Man* 18(4): 710–728.

———. 1990a. Enduring yet ineffable community in the western periphery of Guatemala. In *Guatemalan Indians and the state, 1542 to 1988,* ed. Carol A. Smith, pp. 183–204. Austin: University of Texas Press.

———. 1990b. From saints to shibboleths: Image, structure, and identity in Maya religious syncretism. *American Ethnologist* 17(1): 129–148.

———. 1992. *Maya saints and souls in a changing world.* Austin: University of Texas Press.

———. 1995. Unimagining the Maya: Anthropologists, others, and the inescapable hubris of authorship. *Bulletin of Latin American Research* 14(1): 25–45.

Watanabe, John M., and Barbara B. Smuts. 1999. Explaining religion without explaining it away: Trust, truth, and the evolution of cooperation in Roy A. Rappaport's "The obvious aspects of ritual." *American Anthropologist* 101(1): 98–112.

Weeks, John. 1995. Macroeconomic adjustment and Latin American agriculture since 1980. In *Structural adjustment and the agricultural sector in Latin America and the Caribbean,* ed. John Weeks, pp. 61–92. New York and London: St. Martin's Press and the Institute of Latin American Studies, University of London.

Weiner, Tim, and Sam Dillon. 1995. In Guatemala's dark heart, C.I.A. tied to death and aid. *New York Times,* April 2, 1995, A1, A6.

Whatemore, Mark, and Peter Eltringham. 1990. *The real guide to Guatemala and Belize.* London: Rough Guides.

Wierzbicka, Anna. 1997. *Understanding cultures through their key words: English, Russian, Polish, German, and Japanese.* Oxford: Oxford University Press.

Wilk, Richard. 1995. Learning to be local in Belize: Global systems of common difference. In *Worlds apart: Modernity through the prism of the local,* ed. Daniel Miller, pp. 110–133. London: Routledge.

———. 1997. *Household ecology: Economic change and domestic life among the Kekchi Maya in Belize.* DeKalb: Northern Illinois University Press.

Williams, Robert G. 1986. *Export agriculture and the crisis in Central America.* Chapel Hill: University of North Carolina Press.

Willis, Paul E. 1977. *Learning to labour: How working class kids get working class jobs.* London: Saxon House.

Wilson, Richard. 1993. Anchored communities: Identity and history of the Maya-Q'eqchi'. *Man* 28(1): 121–138.

———. 1995. *Maya resurgence in Guatemala: Q'eqchi' experiences.* Norman: University of Oklahoma Press.

Wolf, Eric R. 1957. Closed corporate peasant communities in Mesoamerica and Central Java. *Southwestern Journal of Anthropology* 13(1): 1–18.

———. 1982. *Europe and the people without history.* Berkeley: University of California Press.

———. 1986. The vicissitudes of the closed corporate community. *American Ethnologist* 13: 325–329.

Woodward, Ralph Lee. 1993. *Rafael Carrera and the emergence of the Republic of Guatemala, 1821–1871.* Athens: University of Georgia Press.

Zapeta, Alfonso Efraín. 1993. *Título de los Señores Coyoy.* Guatemala City: Comisión

Interuniversitaria Guatemalteca de Conmemoración de Quinto Centenario del Descubrimiento de America.

Zapeta, Estuardo. 1997. Maya cultural activism in Guatemala. *Siglo XXI,* February 18, 1997.

———. 1999. *Huellas de B'alam: 1994–1996.* Guatemala City: Editorial Cholsamaj.

Žižek, Slavoj. 1997. Multiculturalism, or, the cultural logic of multinational capitalism. *New Left Review* 225: 28–51.

# Index

Abu-Lughod, Lila, 10, 13–14, 19
Academia de la Lengua Maya Kí-chè (ALMK), 89
Academia de las Lenguas Mayas de Guatemala (ALMG), 98–99, 113, 123–124, 204, 209, 254
acculturation, 69–70, 105, 206–207. *See also* modernization
agriculture, 142, 167–168, 171, 217–223. *See also* milpa; nontraditional agricultural exports
*aj itz*, 60
*aj q'ij*, 111, 152, 180, 244; resurgence of, 250; role in community, 179, 187, 193–194. *See also* Maya religious ceremonies
Alimentos Congelados Monte Bello, S.A. (ALCOSA), 227, 228–229
alphabet. *See* orthography
Alvarado, Pedro de, 48, 50
Anderson, Benedict, 10, 19, 127
*anima*, 150, 151–153, 158, 162, 164, 255
Appadurai, Arjun, 10, 17
Arbenz, Jacobo, 74–75, 89
Archivo General de Centro América (AGCA), 52–53, 176, 254
Arévalo, Juan José, 74–75, 87
Arias, Arturo, 93

army. *See* Guatemala, military
Asociación de Escritores Mayences de Guatemala (AEMG), 90–91
authenticity: claims to, 114, 116, 131, 198; constructions of, 116–117, 136, 246–247; critiques of, 10–11, 84–85, 178; and language, 121, 123, 202; representations of, 128, 191–192, 195; and *traje*, 118–119

B'alam, Pakal, 120
balance, 147–148, 165, 199, 240; and reciprocity, 159–160; relation to soul, 151, 153, 155
Baran, Paul, 22
Barrios, Justo Rufino, 68–69
beauty pageants, 191–201, 257
Berryman, Phillip, 91–92
Bhabha, Homi, 10
Bonfil Batalla, Guillermo, 67
Boremanse, Didier, 147, 150, 165
Bourdieu, Pierre, 16, 18, 145, 253. *See also* doxa
Bricker, Victoria R., 14, 59
broccoli, 32, 227, 228, 233–234. *See also* nontraditional agricultural exports
Browning, John, 68
Brumann, Christoph, 11–12, 15

Calder, Bruce, 92
calendars, 127, 147–148, 198, 204
Cambranes, J. C., 70
Campbell, Howard, 178
Cancian, Frank, 223
Canclini, Néstor García, 10, 65
capital: accumulation of, 231, 238; and
    disintermediation, 66–67, 238–239;
    fictive, 67, 225, 238; and Guatema-
    lan economy, 72–74; in world mar-
    kets, 23, 66, 71
capitalism: global, 22–24, 65–67, 225,
    245; and relations of production,
    217–218, 237–238. *See also* means of
    production
Cardoso, Fernando, 22, 23
Carey, David, 50
Caribbean Basin Initiative (CBI), 225,
    226
Carlsen, Robert, 14, 147, 165, 216, 255
Carmack, Robert, 163
Carrera, Rafael, 68
Castañeda, Quetzil, 10, 243
Catholic Action, 91, 104–105, 106
Catholicism, 91–92, 142, 149, 179–
    187; and pan-Mayanism, 101, 112,
    254 n.2; and Protestantism, 90, 193.
    *See also* Catholic Action; Patzún,
    Catholic Church; Tecpán, Catholic
    Church
caves, 154
Central Intelligence Agency (CIA),
    75, 80
Chatterjee, Partha, 10, 17–18, 19
Chávez, Adrián, 87–89, 92, 96, 97, 112
Chayanov, A. V., 144, 171, 231
children, 46–48, 134; and family rela-
    tions, 171–172; souls of, 143–145,
    152. *See also* education; socialization
Chimaltenango, 33–34
Cholsamaj, 128–132, 134–135
Christian Democrats, 54–55, 57, 78, 95
civil patrols, 58
clandestine graves, 59–60
Clifford, James, 10
coffee, 71–73
*cofradías*, 38, 91, 182–187

cognitive models, 20–22, 168, 199, 213;
    change and continuity in, 163–164,
    190, 201, 239, 245–246; construc-
    tion of, 146, 158. *See also anima;*
    *k'u'x*
Cojtí Cuxil, Demetrio, 31, 90, 97, 114,
    120, 131
Colby, Benjamin, 15–16, 142
Cold War, 75–81
Collier, George, 191, 223, 232
*comités cívicos*, 55, 57
community, 17
computers, 120, 135, 208, 236
Congreso Lingüístico Nacional, 89, 96,
    97–98
Consejo de Organizaciones Mayas de
    Guatemala (COMG), 99, 125–127
cooperatives, 39–40, 96
corn. *See* maize
covenant, 142, 157, 240, 244, 245
Crapanzano, Vincent, 19
cultural logics, 15–20, 243–244; defini-
    tion of, 15–16; and economics, 239–
    240; and idiosyncracies, 19–20; and
    *k'u'x*, 141, 161–162, 164–166; and
    pan-Mayanism, 84, 191, 247
culture, 11–14, 19–20, 84–85, 192–
    193; change and continuity, 15,
    190–191; construction of, 115–116,
    163. *See also* essentialism; identity;
    cultural logics
Cúmez, Pedro, 94
cyclicity. *See* calendars; time

Danforth, Loring, 86
day-keeper. *See aj q'ij*
De Janvry, Alain, 72, 223, 224, 227,
    229, 231
Democracia Cristiana (DC). *See* Chris-
    tian Democrats
Diskin, Martin, 25
doxa, 16–17, 107, 146, 201

earth lords, 38–39
earthquake (1976), 36–38
Edmonson, Munro, 48, 149, 150, 248
education, 102, 205–209; of pan-

Mayanist leaders, 105–106, 108–
109. *See also* Patzún, schools; Tecpán, schools
England, Nora, 111, 119, 254
Esquit, Alberto, 86, 103, 192
essentialism, 8–9, 84, 116; critiques of,
25–26, 190, 243, 253 n.3; and government policy, 67–70; strategic, by
Maya leaders, 11, 84
ethnicity, 116–117, 168, 190–191,
246–247
export production, 70–73, 226–229.
*See also* nontraditional agricultural
exports

Fabian, Johannes, 191
Falla, Ricardo, 91, 92, 94
Ferguson, James, 10, 17, 167
fertilizer, 219, 233
Field, Les, 25
Fordism, 66–67. *See also* post-Fordism
foreign aid. *See* Guatemala, foreign aid
Fox, Richard, 23–24, 83
Frank, Andre Gunter, 22
Friedman, Jonathan, 66, 67, 75, 81, 85,
135, 145, 225, 238, 245
Fuentes y Guzmán, Francisco, 48–49,
51, 174

games, 46–48, 145
Garrard-Burnett, Virginia, 89
Geertz, Clifford, 7
gender, 118–119, 191, 231
Giddens, Anthony, 14, 18–19, 81–82,
225
Global Agreement on Tariffs and Trade
(GATT), 225
globalization: cultural aspects of, 50–
51, 86; economic aspects of, 20, 23,
66–67, 229–230; and neoliberal
reforms, 81–82, 225
Goldin, Liliana, 230, 231
Gossen, Gary, 14, 59, 148, 216, 245,
254, 255
Gross National Product (GNP), 70,
225
Guatemala: constitution, 98, 210;

demography, 5–6, 128–131; economy, 70–74, 79–82; foreign aid,
37–38, 79–82; history, 52–53, 67–
70, 74–82; military, 57–61, 75–81,
162–164, 196–198, 200; policies
toward Indians, 67–70, 77, 95, 163–
164, 205–206, 213–214
guerrilla movements, 75–78, 92, 96,
127–128. *See also la violencia*
Gupta, Akhil, 10, 17, 167

Habermas, Jürgen, 22
Handler, Richard, 10, 85
Handy, Jim, 74–75
Hannerz, Ulf, 12, 17
Hawkins, John, 117, 243
heart. *See k'u'x*
hearth, 160, 172–174, 240; in Maya
cosmology, 147, 159, 256 n.9. *See
also* stoves
hegemony, 10–11, 191; critiques of,
103, 115–116, 144; expansion and
contraction of, 67, 79, 86–87; and
the Guatemalan state, 75, 81–82,
127, 238
Hendrickson, Carol, 28, 59, 111, 152,
254 nn.1, 3, 256 n.7; on beauty
pageants, 196, 257 n.1; on Indian
identity in Tecpán, 12, 16, 33, 35; on
*traje,* 118–119, 209–210, 211
Hervik, Peter, 10, 17, 26
Herzfeld, Michael, 12, 26, 191
hieroglyphs, 124–127, 135, 198, 210–
212
Hill, Robert, 50, 51, 147, 151, 176, 185,
189, 256
Hobsbawm, Eric, 10, 19, 213
Hunt, Eva, 14, 147, 215–216

identity, 12–13, 243–244, 246–247;
constructions of, 85–86, 116–117,
144–145, 163; politics of, 191, 192–
193, 245; and religion, 188–189
idiosyncracy, 19–20
imagined communities, 10, 19
imports, 72–74, 229
import substitution, 231

*indigenista* policies, 69
inheritance, 169–170, 222
Instituto Indigenista Nacional (IIN), 90
Instituto Lingüístico del Verano (ILV).
    *See* Summer Institute of Linguistics
Instituto Nacional de Estadística
    (INE), 35, 131, 219
international law, 86
invented traditions, 10, 19
Iximche', 103, 104, 174, 175

Jameson, Fredric, 66, 245, 253
Johnson, Mark, 168

Kapferer, Bruce, 1, 15, 24
Kaqchikel history, 48–54, 103–104,
    174–176
Kaqchikel language 87, 120–123, 202–
    205, 254 n.1
Kaufman, Terrence, 92–93, 123
Kearney, Michael, 45, 86, 225, 239, 253
K'iche', 119, 231, 255 n.3; history of,
    48, 87; relations with Kaqchikeles,
    103–104, 254 n.3
kidnappings, 4
kinship, 169–174, 222, 255
Kirchoff, Paul, 9
Knauft, Bruce, 9
*k'u'x*, 141, 150–151, 153–165, 255,
    256

labor, 217–218, 240; and nontraditional
    production, 230–231; plantation,
    45, 69, 73; reciprocal, 155. *See also*
    wages
Lacan, Jacques, 144–145
ladinos, 35, 256 n.3; attitudes of toward
    pan-Mayanism, 97, 103, 117; eco-
    nomic position of, 53, 72; elites and
    Guatemalan society, 6, 7, 69–70, 77,
    95, 128; in Tecpán and Patzún, 38,
    50, 54–56, 180–181, 195–196, 199
Lakoff, George, 168
land: communal, 53–54, 56, 57, 69,
    113; holdings, 227, 229, 231–232;
    inheritance of, 169–170, 222; mea-
    surements of, 257 n.1; reform, 74–

75, 100, 113; rent, 220, 232–233;
    and subsistence requirements, 219
Lash, Scott, 66, 225
liminality, 150–151, 152, 256
linguistics, 87–91, 92–93, 96–98, 120–
    124, 201. *See also* Mayan languages
Linnekin, Jocelyn, 10, 85
literacy, 133, 181
Lolmay, 167
long count. *See* calendars
Lovell, George, 70
Lucas Garcia, Romeo, 54, 77, 95
Lucy, John, 97
Lutz, Christopher, 70, 217
Luxemburg, Rosa, 23

maize: cultural valuation of, 143, 147,
    165, 256 n.9; and subsistence farm-
    ing, 217, 219–221, 232; symbolic
    role in pan-Mayanism, 94, 95, 198
maps, 127–132
maquiladora, 229, 235
marriage, 110, 142, 169, 172, 194–195
Martínez Peláez, Severo, 117, 243
Marx, Karl, 68, 215
Maxutio, 61
Maxwell, Judith, 27, 28, 119, 120–123,
    254
Mayab' Winäq, 115, 133–134
Maya history, 124, 148
Mayan languages, 5; map of, 5; as
    marker of identity, 16, 55, 120–124,
    201–205; promotion of, 87–91, 92–
    93, 96–98. *See also* Kaqchikel lan-
    guage; orthography
Maya religious ceremonies, 155, 187–
    188; revivals of, 101, 249–250. *See
    also aj q'ij*
McAllister, Carlota, 192, 199, 257
McCreery, David, 53, 69
means of production: capital intensive,
    23, 72; control over, 69, 216–218,
    224, 232, 236; in world system, 66–
    67, 70
Menchú, Rigoberta, 253–254 n.5
Mesoamerica, 9
metaphors, 7–8, 16, 120–123, 167, 172

military. *See* Guatemala, military
milpa, 9, 32, 45, 217, 219–222, 237
Moberg, Mark, 72, 230
modernization, 67–70, 87
Monaghan, John, 142, 147, 150, 165, 189
monkeys, 59–61
Montejo, Victor, 10, 180
mountains, 44, 153, 155–156, 250
*municipio*, 177–178

Nash, June, 165, 254
Nelson, Diane, 69–70, 86, 201, 211, 213, 257 n.1; on community identity, 177–178; on fluidarity, 26–27; on Foucault, 205–206, 256 n.1; on post-Fordism, 67, 82; on theoretical fashions, 10, 191, 254 n.5
neoliberalism, 81–82, 225, 245–246
neologisms, 120–123, 202–203, 254
nontraditional agricultural exports (NTAX), 72–73, 224, 226–234

Obeyesekere, Gananath, 9, 19
orthography, 87–89, 90, 96–98, 123–124, 204. *See also* hieroglyphs
Otzoy, Irma, 97, 118
Oxlajuuj Keej Maya' Ajtz'iib' (OKMA), 106, 120, 176

Pan-American Highway, 32, 217, 227
pan-Mayanism, 84–86, 98–100, 116–117, 243–248; and foreign scholars, 25–26; and Guatemalan politics, 93–97; history of, 4–6, 86–98; leaders, 33, 90–91, 100–114; and local communities, 136–137, 199, 201, 248–251; organizational structure, 89, 99–100
Partido Revolucionario (PR), 54, 94
Patrullas de Acción Cívico (PACs). *See* civil patrols
Patzún, 31–36, 42; *aldeas*, 34, 178; *cantones*, 177; Catholic Church in, 180–182; demography, 35, 51–52, 172; employment, 45, 217–218, 235; history, 50–51; map, 177; military presence, 57–58; municipal government, 54–55; name, 49–50; schools, 207, 208–209; *traje* styles and use, 209, 210–212
Peace Accords (1996), 79, 98, 99–100, 136
Peace Corps, 28, 92
petty commodity production, 224, 235–236, 237
pila, 42, 108
plantations. *See* labor, plantation
Plattner, Stuart, 224
political economy, 20, 65–82
Popol Wuj, 87, 134
post-Fordism, 24, 66–67, 225–226, 234–235, 237, 239. *See also* Fordism
poverty, 6, 133
Protestantism, 142, 149, 179–181; and Catholicism, 90, 193; and pan-Mayanism, 101, 188–189, 254 n.2. *See also* Summer Institute of Linguistics
Proyecto Lingüístico Francisco Marroquín (PLFM), 92–93, 97–98, 106, 109, 123
Pulchich, 155–156

Quetzaltenango, 93, 102, 104, 109
Quinn, Naomi, 21

radio, 133–134
Raxche', 100, 119
reciprocity, 142, 145, 149, 155, 158–159
Reddy, William, 10
Redfield, Robert, 9
religion, 101, 179–189
residence, 172–174
Restall, Matthew, 169
Richards, Julia, 209
Richards, Michael, 77, 198, 209
Ríos Montt, Efraín, 77–78
rituals. *See* Maya religious ceremonies
Rodseth, Lars, 12, 15

sacrifice, 142–143, 155
Sahlins, Marshall, 20, 22, 190

Said, Edward, 10
saints, 180, 182–188. *See also* San Francisco; San Bernardino
Sam Colop, Enrique, 25–26, 124, 135
San Bernardino, 182, 185, 196
San Francisco, 182–185, 193, 196
Schele, Linda, 119, 125, 142, 147
Scott, James, 213, 250
Sewell, William, 19
Shore, Bradd, 21, 115
Smith, Carol, 66, 213, 224, 237
socialization, 19–20, 142–146, 168, 172
souls, 149–150
Spivak, Gayatri, 10
state. *See* Guatemala
Stoll, David, 90, 96, 124, 253–254
Stonich, Susan, 230
stoves, 40–41, 160
Strauss, Claudia, 21
subsistence production. *See* milpa
Summer Institute of Linguistics (SIL), 89–91, 92, 102, 105, 106, 123–124, 188
*justo*, 151–152
sweat bath. *See tuj*
sweater factories, 218, 236

Taussig, Michael, 38
Tax, Sol, 84, 177, 219
Tecpán, 31–42; *aldeas*, 33, 178, 207, 232; barrios, 174–176; beauty pageants, 196–201; Catholic Church in, 36–37, 38, 180–182; demography, 35, 51, 172; employment, 217–219, 235–236; government, 54–57; history, 50–54, 174–176; language use, 201–205; map, 175; market, 32, 178, 217; military presence, 58–61; name, 48–49; schools, 205–209; *traje* styles and use, 209–213
Tedlock, Barbara, 147, 148
Tedlock, Dennis, 11, 245, 255
Tezaguic, Fernando, 94–95
time, 147–148, 159
Títulos de los Xpantzay, 52–53, 176
Tlaxcalans, 48–49

*traje*, 207, 209–213; innovations in style, 118–119, 210–213, 248, 251; as marker of identity, 16, 55, 117–118, 178, 198. *See also* Patzún, *traje* styles and usage; Tecpán, *traje* styles and usage
transnationalism, 66, 86, 226
*troje*, 42, 174
*tuj*, 42–44, 153, 194, 255–256

United Fruit Company (UFCO), 75
United Nations, 131, 137, 245
United Nations Development Programme (UNDP), 6
United States: military aid, 79–81, 96; political intervention, 75–76; trade, 73, 227, 229, 235, 236
United States Agency for International Development (USAID), 102, 137, 207, 227, 228, 245
Urry, John, 66, 225

*la violencia*, 75–78, 96, 244; effects of in communities, 57–61, 163–164; justifications of, 76–77, 197–198; and pan-Mayanism, 86, 92
Vogt, Evon, 154, 165

wages, 45, 73, 223, 232, 235, 237
Wallerstein, Immanuel, 22, 23
Warren, Kay, 190; on community, 84, 177, 213–214; on pan-Mayanism, 86, 100, 102, 116, 239, 254n.6; on politics of fieldwork, 25; on religion, 104, 179, 189; work in San Andrés Semetabaj, 61, 245
Wasserstrom, Robert, 223
Watanabe, John, 25, 26, 103, 143; on community, 17, 84, 177, 180; on Maya cosmology, 14, 147, 216; on pan-Mayanism, 11; on production, 232, 237; on socialization, 145, 146; on souls, 141, 157, 164–165
wheat, 222–223
Wierzbicka, Anna, 150, 255
Wilk, Richard, 83, 232
Wilson, Richard, 17, 38, 85, 163, 165

Wolf, Eric, 84, 186, 213
Woodward, Ralph Lee, 68
world system theory, 22–24, 65–67, 223
Wycliffe Bible Translators. *See* Summer Institute of Linguistics

Xel-hú, 93–94
Xpantzay. *See* Título de los Xpantzay

Zapeta, Estuardo, 135–136
Žižek, Slavoj, 11, 83, 117